lonely planet

Cape Town

Jon Murray

Cape Town

2nd edition

Published by
Lonely Planet Publications   ABN 36 005 607 983
90 Maribyrnong St, Footscray Victoria 3011, Australia
Head Office: Locked Bag 1, Footscray, Victoria 3011, Australia
Branches: 150 Linden Street, Oakland CA 94607, USA
            10a Spring Place, London NW5 3BH, UK
            1 rue du Dahomey, 75011 Paris, France

Printed by
The Bookmaker International Ltd
Printed in China

Photographs by
Susan Storm
Gerhard Dreyer
Mike Reed

Front cover: Town Hall with Table Mountain in the background (Dag Sundberg, The Image Bank)

This Edition
March 1998

Although the authors and publisher have tried to make the information as accurate as possible, they accept no responsibility for any loss, injury or inconvenience sustained by any person using this book.

National Library of Australia Cataloguing in Publication Data

Murray, Jon.
Cape Town.

Ed. 2.
Includes index.
ISBN 0 86442 485 X.

1. Cape Town (South Africa) - Guidebooks. I. Title.
(Series: Lonely Planet city guide).

916.873550464

Jon Murray

Jon Murray spent some years alternating between travelling and working with various publishing companies in Melbourne (Australia) before joining Lonely Planet as an editor. He was soon travelling again, this time researching Lonely Planet's guidebooks. He wrote the first edition of this book, and is co-author of Lonely Planet's *South Africa, Lesotho & Swaziland* and author of *New South Wales & the ACT*.

He has updated several other Lonely Planet guides, including *Papua New Guinea* and sections of *Australia* and *Africa on a shoestring*. He spends a lot of time battling blackberries on his bush block near Daylesford, Victoria.

From the Author

Thanks to all my friends in Cape Town, including two new arrivals. Special thanks to the Lonely Planet people for their carrot rather than stick approach to overcoming tardiness.

From the Publisher

This second edition of *Cape Town* was edited at the Lonely Planet office in Melbourne by Russell Kerr. It was proofed by Justin Flynn, who also helped out on the Cape Floral Kingdom section. The Health section was checked by Isabelle Young, and Quentin Frayne went over the Language section with a linguist's eye.

Rachael Scott scaled many a kloof in producing new maps for this edition; she also designed the book and nursed it through layout. Illustrations were drawn by Trudi Canavan and the cover was designed by Margie Jung. Tim Fitzgerald pitched in with some last-second layout assistance.

Thanks to Geoff Stringer and Richard Plunkett for their ever-patient advice – and for Richard's contribution to the Cape Wineries section. Thanks to David Andrew for hatching the Birdlife on the Cape section.

We'd like to thank Susan Storm for her on-the-spot update of the *Blue Train* text; Kurt Ambrose, who kindly provided cricket resources; and Noel and Dudley Gross, who offered timely and helpful information on the Cape's parks and reserves. Also, thanks to Jon Murray for striving to fill a rather long editorial wish list.

Last but not least, special thanks to all the people who found the time and energy to write to us from all over the world with their comments, advice and travellers' tales. The many to whom we are grateful include:

Caroline Bay, M Brown, Helen Bull, R & A Chittleborough, Andrew Florides, MW Friedlander, Aleksandra Golebiowska, Manuela Hanni, Mark Higgitt, Bernd Pfefferkorn, Alex Ross, Marc Tebrugge, Marjolein van Rest, S Zienoger.

Warning & Request

A travel writer's job is never done. Things change – prices go up, schedules change, good places go bad and bad places go bankrupt, hotels are renovated and renamed (or even burn down), telephone numbers get another digit and recommended travel agents close down.

Remember, this book is a guide, not an oracle. If something in Cape Town isn't identical to the way it's described in this book, don't get mad, get out a pen or fire up your PC and write to Lonely Planet. Your letters will be used to help update future editions. Excerpts from correspondence may also appear in our quarterly newsletter, *Planet Talk*, or in the postcards section of our Web site – so please let us know if you don't want your letter published or your name acknowledged.

We greatly appreciate all information that is sent back to us from travellers. Back at Lonely Planet, Julie Young coordinates a small team who read and acknowledge every reader's letter, postcard and email, and ensure that every morsel of information finds its way to the appropriate authors, editors and publishers.

Everyone who writes to us will find their name in the next edition of the appropriate guide and will also receive a free subscription to *Planet Talk*. The best contributions will also be rewarded with a free copy of the next edition, or another Lonely Planet guide if you prefer. We give away lots of books, but unfortunately not every letter or postcard receives one.

Contents

Introduction

Cape Town is one of the most beautiful cities in the world. No matter how long you stay, the image of the mountains and the sea will linger in your mind.

About 40km from the Cape of Good Hope, near the southern tip of the vast African continent, Cape Town is also one of the most geographically isolated of the world's great cities. Dominated by a 1000m flat-topped mountain with virtually sheer cliffs, it's surrounded by superb mountain walks, vineyards and beaches.

You don't have to venture far from the city for more beaches (with whales), and the superb scenery, vineyards and historic towns of the Winelands and the Breede River Valley.

It's tempting to compare Cape Town with great coastal cities such as Rio de Janeiro, Sydney, San Francisco and Vancouver. No doubt some consider these cities more beautiful. None, however, surpasses the drama of Cape Town's site or its 350 years of history. Long before travel writers discovered it, Francis Drake's chronicler described the Cape of Good Hope as 'the most stately thing, and the fairest cape we saw in the whole circumference of the earth'.

Like all South African cities, Cape Town is ambivalent – European but not European, African but not African – a mixture of the third and first worlds. The cafés and bars around the Victoria & Alfred Waterfront could be in any cosmopolitan capital, but the townships on the bleak, windswept plains to the east of the city could only be in Africa.

Despite this, Cape Town has a reputation for being the most open-minded and relaxed city in South Africa, and perhaps the safest city in Africa for visitors.

Cape Town works as a city in a way that few on the African continent do. There is a sense of history, and even in the city centre, historic buildings have been preserved. There are restaurants, cafés and bars, parks and gardens, markets and shops – all the things that make living in a city worthwhile. And then there are a few things that most cities don't have: mountains, magnificent surf beaches and outstanding vineyards.

Facts about Cape Town

HISTORY

Signs of the first humans have been found in several places in South Africa. The most recent sign, 117,000-year-old fossilised footprints near Langebaan Lagoon (north of Cape Town), has prompted one researcher to speculate that 'Eve' (the very first human; the common ancestor of us all) lived here. This is drawing a very long bow, but it is interesting that white South Africans are excited about this theory, when less than a decade ago many insisted that their god had created whites and blacks separately.

Little is known about the early humans in South Africa but there are signs that they conducted funerals, which indicates at least basic culture. Untangling the tales of our ancestors will be an almost impossible task. We don't even know if the earliest historically recorded inhabitants of South Africa – the San peoples – are direct descendants or if they returned to the area after aeons of travel.

San & Khoikhoi

The San (known to Europeans as Bushmen) were nomadic hunters and gatherers, and the Khoikhoi (known as Hottentot) were semi-nomadic hunters and pastoralists. Both groups were closely related, however, so the distinction was by no means hard and fast. Because of this, the term Khoisan is now widely used. Culturally and physically, they developed differently to the negroid peoples of Africa.

The earliest dated San painting is about 28,000 years old. It is believed the Khoikhoi developed from San groups in present day Botswana. Perhaps they came in contact with pastoralist Bantu tribes, as in addition to hunting and gathering food, they became pastoralists, with cattle, oxen and sheep. They migrated south, reaching the Cape of Good Hope about 2000 years ago. For centuries, perhaps even millennia, the San and the Khoikhoi intermarried and coexisted. It was also not uncommon for impoverished Khoikhoi to revert to a hunter-gatherer existence, or for the San to acquire domestic animals.

The migration of the Bantu peoples into southern Africa (by the 3rd century they had settled modern KwaZulu-Natal) resulted in many Khoisan peoples being dislodged or absorbed in other parts of South Africa, but the Bantu did not reach the Cape Town area. Their westward expansion halted around the Great Fish River (in Eastern Cape Province, about 700km east of Cape Town) because they were agricultural people and further west there was not enough rainfall to support their crops.

 You can see extremely detailed models of Khoisan people, made from life casts, in the South African Museum.

Portuguese Visit & Move On

The Portuguese came in search of a sea route to India and that most precious of medieval commodities – spice. Bartholomeu Dias rounded the Cape in 1487, naming it Cabo da Boa Esperanca (Cape of Good Hope), but his eyes were fixed on the trade riches of the east coast of Africa and the Indies.

In 1503 Antonio de Saldanha became the first European to climb Table Mountain. But the Portuguese had no interest in a permanent settlement – the Cape offered little more than fresh water, attempts to trade with the Khoisan often ended in violence, and the coast and its fierce weather posed a terrible threat to their tiny caravels.

Dutch Come to Stay

By the end of the 16th century English and Dutch traders were beginning to challenge the Portuguese, and the Cape became a regular stopover for their scurvy-ridden crews. In 1647 a Dutch East Indiaman was wrecked in Table Bay; its crew built a fort and stayed for a year before they were rescued.

This crystallised the value of a permanent settlement in the minds of the directors of the Dutch East India Company (Vereenigde Oost Indische Compagnie or VOC). They had no intention of colonising the country, but simply of establishing a secure base where ships could shelter and stock up on fresh supplies of meat, fruit and vegetables.

Jan van Riebeeck was the man they chose to lead a small expedition from the flagship *Drommedaris*. His specific charge was to build a fort, barter with the Khoisan for meat and plant a garden. He reached Table Bay on 6 April 1652, built a mud-walled fort not far from the site of the surviving stone castle and planted gardens that have now become the Company's Gardens (also known as the Botanical Gardens).

In 1660, in a gesture that takes on an awful symbolism, van Riebeeck planted a bitter-almond hedge to separate the Khoisan and the Europeans. It ran around the western foot of Table Mountain down to Table Bay. The hedge may have protected the 120 Europeans but, having excluded the Khoisan, the settlement suffered a chronic labour shortage. In another wonderfully perverse move, van Riebeeck proceeded to import slaves from Madagascar, India, Ceylon, Malaya and Indonesia.

 Magistrates (*landdrost* in Afrikaans) were first appointed while the colony was under Dutch (VOC) rule, and they were essentially governors of their areas. *Drostdys*, the homes and offices of the landdrost, are today some of the earliest and most impressive buildings in the country. The Drostdy Museum at Swellendam is one of the earliest and best drostdys.

 Sections of van Riebeeck's hedge can still be seen in the Kirstenbosch Botanic Gardens.

The Settlement Grows

The European men of the community were largely employees of the VOC and over-whelmingly Dutch – a tiny official elite and a majority of ill-educated soldiers and sailors, many of whom had been pressed into service. In 1685 they were joined by about 200 Huguenots, French Calvinists who had fled from persecution by King Louis XIV.

There was a shortage of women in the colony so the female slaves and Khoisan survivors were exploited both for labour and sex. In time, the slaves intermixed with the Khoisan. The offspring of these unions formed the basis for sections of today's coloured population.

Despite the VOC's almost complete control, Cape Town thrived, providing a comfortable European lifestyle for a growing number of artisans and entrepreneurs servicing ships and crews. Cape Town became known as the Tavern of the Seas, a riotous port used by every navigator, privateer and merchant travelling between Europe and the East (including Australia).

 The Huguenots gave the Cape's wine industry a substantial boost, and in Franschhoek there is a museum devoted to them.

Crime and Punishment Cape Style

The 18th century was not the best of times to fall foul of the law anywhere, but at the Cape it could be particularly unpleasant. Torture was routine but inventive, and executions were common. The preferred method was 'breaking on the wheel'. The victim was tied to a wagon wheel, his limbs were smashed with hammers, the wheel was hoisted onto a pole (to give the populace a better view) and he was left to die. It could take days ...

It wasn't just the manner in which criminals were punished that offends modern sensibilities. The ways in which you could find yourself on the wrong side of the law were also alarming.

In 1773 a ship, the *Jonge Thomas*, foundered in Table Bay. The crew was in imminent danger of drowning as the ship broke up. However, the government ordered that no one should approach the ship, and erected gallows on the foreshore to deal with anyone who tried. If the crew drowned, so be it, but the VOC's cargo must not be pilfered.

A local dairyman named Woltemade ignored this warning and swam his horse to the wreck. He rescued 18 sailors before being drowned himself, so depriving the government hangman of work. ∎

Boers Begin to Trek

The white population did not reach 1000 until 1745, by which time small numbers of free (meaning non-VOC) burghers were drifting away from the close grip of the company into other areas of Africa. These were the first of the *trekboers* (literally trekking farmers – they followed their cattle herds) who developed a unique culture and eventually their own language, based on the argot of their slaves – Afrikaans.

They were fiercely independent and lived lives based on rearing cattle, not all that different from the cultures of the black tribes with whom they come into conflict as they gradually drifted into the interior. The date of their voluntary withdrawal from the outside world is significant. The Boers, many of whom were illiterate and most of whom had no other source of information than the Bible, missed out on the great social, political and philosophical developments of Europe in the 18th century.

The excellent Kleinplassie Farm Museum in Worcester celebrates Afrikaner folk culture.

Khoisan Devastated

The trekboers' inevitable confrontations with the Khoisan were disastrous. The indigenous people were driven from their traditional lands, ravaged by introduced diseases and almost destroyed by superior weapons. The survivors were left with no option but to work for Europeans in a form of bondage little different from slavery.

The British abolished the slave trade in 1808 and the remaining Khoisan were finally given the explicit protection of the law (including the right to own land) in 1828. These moves contributed to Afrikaners' dissatisfaction and the Great Trek (1834-40).

British Take Over

Dutch power was fading by the end of the 18th century and in response to the Napoleonic Wars, the British decided to secure the Cape. In 1806, at Bloubergstrand, 25km north of Cape Town, the British defeated the Dutch and the colony was permanently ceded to the Crown on 13 August 1814.

Cape Town's economy benefited from the British takeover, as the British allowed free trade, denied by the VOC. During the first half of 19th century, before the Suez Canal opened, British officers serving in India would holiday at the Cape.

In 1860 construction of the Alfred Basin in the docks commenced, finally giving Cape Town a stormproof port. However, in 1869 the Suez Canal was opened, dramatically decreasing the amount of shipping that sailed via the Cape.

The discovery and exploitation of diamonds and gold in the centre of South Africa in the 1870s and 80s meant that Cape Town would not remain the dominant city in the country, though as a major port it was a beneficiary of the mineral wealth that laid the foundations for an industrial society.

Simon's Town, the former British naval base, still feels more British than South African.

The Great Trek

Tensions between the Boers (farmers – in this context cattle graziers) and the government had been building for some time, but the reason given by many trekkers for leaving the Cape colony and heading into the uncharted heart of southern Africa was an 1833 act banning slavery. Most Boers grudgingly accepted that slavery might be wrong, but the British seemed to go a step further and proclaim the equality of races.

This resulted, for example, in servants bringing actions against their masters for nonpayment of wages and for assault. For an illiterate farmer who rarely saw a government official, much less ventured to Cape Town, to be summoned to a distant court which used a language he could not speak, all because of a complaint by a coloured servant, was an extreme insult. And it seemed to go against nature. If the law would not distinguish between races, how could a people maintain their culture, their purity?

Reports from early treks told of vast, uninhabited – or at least poorly defended – grazing lands, and from 1836 increasing numbers of Voortrekker ('Fore-trekker', pioneer) families crossed Orange River, beginning a decade of migration known as the Great Trek. The trekkers entered their promised land, where there was space enough for their cattle to graze and for their culture of anti-urban independence to flourish.

Despite outlawing slavery, the British introduced new laws that laid the basis for an exploitive labour system little different from slavery. Thousands of dispossessed blacks sought work in the colony, but it was made a crime to be in the colony without a pass – and without work. It was also a crime to leave your job.

In 1854, a representative parliament was formed in Cape Town, but much to the dismay of the Dutch and English farmers to the north and east, the British government and Cape liberals insisted on a multiracial constituency (albeit with financial qualifications that excluded the vast majority of blacks and coloureds).

Boer War & After
After the Great Trek the Boers established several independent republics, the largest being the Orange Free State (today's Free State Province) and the Transvaal (today's Gauteng, Mpumalanga and Northern provinces). When the world's richest gold reef was found in the Transvaal (a village called Johannesburg sprang up beside it), the British were miffed that the Boers should control such wealth and precipitated war in 1899. The Boers were vastly outnumbered but their tenacity and knowledge of the country resulted in a long and bitter conflict. The British finally defeated them in 1902. Cape Town was not directly involved in any of the fighting but tensions between the British and the Afrikaners ran high.

By 1910 the Union of South Africa was established, creating a single country out of the British colonies and the Boer Republics. Non-whites had few rights, although in the Cape some non-whites could vote (but they could not stand for election). The Afrikaners were economically and socially disadvan-

taged compared to the English-speaking minority, who controlled most of the capital and industry in the new country. This, plus lingering bitterness over the war and distaste at having to compete for low-paying jobs with non-whites led to strident Afrikaner nationalism and the formation of the National Party.

Racism Rules
In 1948 the National Party came to power on a platform of apartheid (literally the state of being apart) and the insane and inhuman apparatus of the apartheid state began to be erected. Mixed marriages were prohibited, interracial sex was made illegal and every individual was classified by race. The Group Areas Act defined where people of each 'race' could live and the Separate Amenities Act created separate public facilities – separate beaches, separate buses, separate toilets, separate schools and separate park benches. Blacks were compelled to carry passes at all times and were prohibited from living in or even visiting towns without specific permission.

The Dutch Reformed Church even gave apartheid a religious justification: the separateness of the races was divinely ordained. The *volk* (literally the people but it means Afrikaners) had a holy mission to preserve the purity of the white race in its promised land.

A system of Homelands (sometimes called Bantustans) was set up, whereby just 13% of South Africa was allocated to blacks, who made up about 75% of the population. The idea was that each black group had a traditional area where it belonged – and must now stay. The government defined 10 such groups, based largely on dubious 19th century scholarship.

Apart from the inequity of the land allocation, not to mention the injustice of making decisions about people who couldn't vote, this plan was crazy, as it ignored the huge numbers of blacks who had never lived in 'their' homeland. Millions of people who had lived for generations in other areas were forcibly removed and dumped in bleak, unproductive areas with no infrastructure. Starvation was a real possibility.

The Homelands were regarded as self-governing states and it was planned that they would become independent countries. Four of the 10 homelands were nominally independent by the time that apartheid was demolished (they were not recognised as independent countries by the UN), and their dictators held power with the help of the South African military.

Of course, the white population depended on cheap black labour to keep the economy booming, so many black 'guest workers' were admitted to South Africa. But unless a black had a job and a pass, they were liable to be jailed and sent back to the homeland.

This caused massive disruption to black communities and families. Not surprisingly, people without jobs gravitated to towns and cities to be near their husbands, wives and parents. Illegal squatter settlements grew up on the outskirts, and although these were regularly bulldozed and the residents carted back to their homelands, they would just as regularly rise again.

Path to Democracy

In the 1980s, amid deepening economic gloom caused by international sanctions and the increasing militancy of the black opposition groups (which had begun with the Soweto students' uprising in 1976), it became obvious that continuing with apartheid would lead to disaster. Unfortunately, such was the siege mentality among white South Africans that many would have preferred their country to go up in flames than to allow majority rule.

Luckily, despite government propaganda reinforcing this view, senior politicians were secretly talking with the African National Congress (ANC). Even luckier, they were dealing with a man of the calibre of Nelson Mandela.

In early 1990, President De Klerk began to repeal discriminatory laws, and the ANC, the Pan African Congress (PAC) and the Communist Party were legalised. On 11 February he released Nelson Mandela, 27 years after Mandela had first been incarcerated.

During 1990 and 91, virtually all the old apartheid regulations were repealed: the

Apartheid & the Townships

After the introduction of apartheid, voting rights for non-whites in the Cape were revoked. Since the coloureds had no Homeland (tiny and unproductive areas the government set aside for blacks), the western half of Cape Province (roughly equivalent to today's Western Cape Province) was declared a 'coloured preference area'. Blacks could not be employed here unless it could be proved there was no suitable coloured person for the job. As no new black housing was built, illegal squatter camps mushroomed on the sandy plains to the east of Cape Town. In response, the government bulldozed the shanties, dragged away the occupants and dumped them in Homelands. Within weeks, the shanties would rise again.

The government tried for decades to eradicate squatter towns such as Crossroads, which were focal points for black resistance to apartheid. In its last attempt, between May and June 1986, an estimated 70,000 people were driven from their homes and hundreds were killed. Even this brutal attack was unsuccessful and the government accepted the inevitable and began to improve conditions. Vast new townships are rapidly growing at Khayelitsha and Mitchell's Plain.

There were also official coloured townships, where people forcibly removed from the 'whites only' central areas were dumped. Because they had better facilities than the neighbouring black settlements, there was tension betweeen the black and coloured communities. This resulted in the formation of gangs in the coloured townships, initially self-protection forces but now the private armies of gangsters and drug lords. ■

The most infamous forced removals were from District Six. The District Six Museum tells the story. One coloured group, the Cape Muslims of the Tana Baru (Bo-Kaap) area, successfully resisted forced removals and their neighbourhood remains in the heart of the city.

Separate Amenities Act, the Group Areas Act and the Population Registration Act (which classified people by race).

In late 1991, the Convention for a Democratic South Africa (CODESA) began negotiations on the formation of a multiracial transitional government and a new constitution extending political rights to all groups. The negotiations did not proceed smoothly but it was apparent that both the National Party and the ANC were determined that free elections of some sort would take place at some time.

However, thrashing out the details was a complex process and the ANC suspected that the government was drawing it out as long as possible. The political violence that was wracking the country could only damage the ANC's vote at the election.

By 1992 the CODESA talks had become a straight negotiation between the National Party and the ANC, excluding the smaller parties. The Zulu-based Inkatha movement (now called the Inkatha Freedom Party – IFP) and some of the Homelands' governments left CODESA, demanding a federal structure for the new constitution. Right-wing whites, who wanted a *volkstaat* (literally people's state – an Afrikaner homeland), joined them in an unlikely alliance.

A compromise between the ANC and the National Party was eventually reached. Both sides accepted that an interim government of national unity would rule after the election for no more than five years, and that the final version of the constitution was to be written within two years by members of the new parliament to be elected on 26 and 27 April 1994.

Across the country at midnight on 26 April 1994, *Die Stem* (the old national anthem) was sung and the old flag was lowered. Then the new rainbow flag was raised and the new anthem, *Nkosi Sikelele Afrika* (God Bless Africa), was sung. People were once jailed for singing this beautiful hymn.

The Election Voting for 'special' voters (mainly the old and disabled) had been held on 26 April under the eyes of thousands of foreign observers and an equally large foreign press corps. Although there had been a couple of serious bombings by far-right militants, it was clear when general voting began the next day that the biggest problems would be poor organisation and a lack of ballot papers.

This proved to be the case, and 27 April was a day of queues several km long, closed polling stations and allegations of irregularities. Surprisingly, though, this didn't result in chaos and people generally took the delays in good spirit. That night the army was called in to help print and airlift nine million additional ballot papers, and on 28 April voting went smoothly. The polls were kept open until everyone who wanted to vote had done so, and there was a further day of voting in remote areas of some former Homelands.

The ANC won 62.7% of the vote, less than the 66.7% which would have enabled it to overrule the interim constitution. However, as the interim constitution was largely the work of the ANC, that wasn't a problem, and the public perception that the ANC cannot ride roughshod over the constitution has been good for stability. As well as deciding the national government, the election decided the provincial governments, and the ANC won in all but two of the provinces.

The National Party won 20.4% of the vote, enough to guarantee it representation in Cabinet. As white voters are only 15% of the electorate this was a very good result for the party. The National Party also won the provincial election in Western Cape (of which Cape Town is the capital) thanks to a scare-mongering campaign directed at the coloured population.

For the full story of the election, read the excellent book *Election '94 South Africa*, edited by Andrew Reynolds (paperback, R40).

You can take a tour of Robben Island, where Mandela and other high-ranking ANC officials were imprisoned.

New South Africa
Despite the scars of the past and the enormous problems ahead, South Africa today is

an immeasurably more optimistic and relaxed country than it was a few years ago. Among whites there is a sort of dazed relief that while their oldest fears (three centuries old) have come true, nothing much has changed. Some are even finding that life without racism is much more enjoyable. Among blacks there is the exhilaration of

Important Dates in Southern Africa

c40,000 BC	San settle Southern Africa
c300 AD	Bantu arrive in KwaZulu area
1487	Bartholomeu Dias sails around the Cape
c1500	Sotho settle in Lesotho
1652	Dutch settlement in Table Bay (Cape Town)
1688	Huguenots arrive at the Cape
c1690	Boers move into hinterland
1780	Dutch fight Xhosa at Great Fish River
1795	British capture Cape Town
1806	British defeat Dutch in battle at Bloubergstrand
1814	Colony at the Cape ceded to the British
1815	Shaka Zulu seizes power – the *difaqane* begins
1820	British settlers arrive in Eastern Cape
1830s	The Voortrekkers undertake the Great Trek
1838	Boers defeat Zulu at the Battle of Blood River
1852	Boer Republic of Transvaal created
1858	British defeat Xhosa
1860	Indians arrive in Natal
1869	Diamonds found near Kimberley
1871	Gold discovered in Eastern Transvaal
1877	British annexe the Boer's Transvaal Republic
1881	Boers defeat British and Transvaal becomes the South African Republic
1886	Gold discovered on the Witwatersrand
1893	Mohandas Gandhi arrives in Natal
1899-1902	Anglo-Boer War
1905	Government Commission recommends separate development for blacks
1910	Union of South Africa created, federating the British colonies and the old Boer republics; blacks denied the vote; Lesotho and Swaziland become British protectorates
1912	South African Native National Council established, the forerunner of the ANC
1913	Natives Land Act restricts black ownership of land to 7.5% of the country
1928	Communist Party begins agitation for full democracy
1948	National Party wins government; the party retains control until 1994; apartheid laws, such as the one making inter-racial sex illegal, begin to be passed
1955	ANC adopts Freedom Charter
1960	Sharpeville massacre; ANC banned
1961	South Africa leaves British Commonwealth and becomes a republic
1963	Nelson Mandela jailed for life
1966	Lesotho gains independence from Britain
1968	Swaziland gains independence from Britain
1975	South Africa invades Angola
1976	Soweto uprisings begin
1977	Steve Biko murdered
1985	State of Emergency declared – official murder and torture rife, black resistance strengthens
1990	Ban lifted on ANC; Nelson Mandela freed
1991	Talks on a new constitution begin; political violence escalates
1992	Whites-only referendum agrees to reform
1994	Democratic elections held and Nelson Mandela sworn in as president; Mandela opens the first post-apartheid parliament in Cape Town
1996	The notorious Robben Island Prison is decommissioned
1997	Cape Town fails in its bid to host the 2004 Olympics; many African members of the IOC apparently felt that this wasn't a bid on behalf of Africa, but a bid on behalf of white businesspeople

freedom gained and optimism for the future. New and old arts and cultures, long denigrated, are flowering. There is a lot of catching up to do and the next few years will be very exciting.

Economic inequality presents a thorny problem. Although the apartheid system is dead, economic apartheid lives on despite affirmative-action programmes. With an economy geared to low wages and a legacy of very poor education for blacks, it will be a generation at least before the majority gain much economic benefit from their freedom.

As a traveller you'll notice just how little black involvement there is in the economy. While some black people are doing well – as a result of positive discrimination in employment and because they can now participate freely in business – chances are that the only black-owned business you will deal will be a minibus taxi company.

Not surprisingly, from a white perspective the major problem is crime. Blacks also suffer from high crime rates, but most would say that their major concern is the time it is taking for economic apartheid to end. This will be a slow process. The New South Africa will really arrive when there are whites working as maids or labourers. And that's a long way off.

The Truth Commission Crimes of the apartheid era are being exposed (but not punished) by a Truth and Reconciliation Commission. As Archbishop Desmond Tutu said, 'Without forgiveness there is no future, but without confession there can be no forgiveness'. Tutu was the first chairperson of the Truth Commission, which has held sessions across the country.

The commission is a sign of the extraordinary lengths to which the new South Africa is prepared to go to achieve reconciliation. The sheer horror and casual brutality of some of the crimes confessed are sickening. Only a committed pacifist would not cry for retribution, but in appearing before the commission, the perpetrators guarantee themselves amnesty.

For the black population (against whom the vast majority of crimes were committed) the commission offers an opportunity to tell their story and, hopefully, lay ghosts to rest

Pagad & Other Hero-Villains

Rashaad Staggie's horrific (and televised) death made international news in 1996 and brought the activities of People Against Gangsterism & Drugs (Pagad) to the forefront of Western Cape politics. After a lynch mob burned then repeatedly shot the dying gangster, Pagad was labelled as a group of violent vigilantes by both white and black politicians. However the group retains strong support in the coloured community. Reactions to Pagad included a march by gangsters demanding protection of their human rights.

Pagad members are mainly coloured Muslims living in the bleak townships of Mitchell's Plain, where coloureds were dumped by the apartheid regime after being forcibly removed from their homes near central Cape Town. The group sees itself as defending the coloured community from the crooked cops and drug lords who allow gangs to control the coloured townships.

But this is South Africa and nothing is as simple as it seems. The gangs in the coloured townships grew out of a desperate need for the coloured community to organise itself against criminals from the neighbouring black townships. Gang members saw themselves as upright citizens defending their community against the apartheid-inspired resentment of blacks.

This squabbling between apartheid's victims must have been immensely satisfying to the apartheid regime, which had long practiced 'divide and rule' – given its record of dirty tricks, it's reasonable to suppose that the government helped keep the quarrels bubbling. Even the ANC had to accommodate the gangsters to ensure the safety of their electioneering teams in the coloured townships during the 1994 elections.

To further complicate the issue, Pagad is in danger of being hijacked by an Islamic fundamentalist group. The battles between Pagad and the gangsters continue, with shootings and bombings. Although Pagad is mainly a Western Cape phenomenon, Pagad-style vigilante action has flared around Jo'burg, resulting in serious riots.

Rashied, Staggie's surviving brother and leader of the Hard Livings gang, has formed a political party of 'reformed gangsters' which will stand against Pagad candidates in the 1999 elections. ∎

and allay anguish. The white population has a chance to hear the atrocities carried out in their name, and to hear the true history of their country.

The commission has partly succeeded in both these aims, although many whites still do not accept that great wrongs were done and some blacks (and whites) are bitter that torturers and murderers walk free.

However, with some exceptions, most people confessing crimes are relatively low on the chain of command. It was hoped that the chain would unravel, leading to revelations about those in government who ordered massacres and other crimes against humanity. This has not happened, and the few apartheid-era government members who have appeared have denied ordering killings or being aware that their underlings were murdering people.

GEOGRAPHY

Cape Town is at the northern end of a peninsula that juts into the Atlantic Ocean on the south-west tip of southern Africa. The peninsula has a steep, high spine of mountains, beginning at Devil's Peak in Cape Town and running all the way down to Cape Point. Table Mountain, the most prominent feature of these mountains, is more than 1km high, starting close to sea level. The escarpment running down the Atlantic (west) coast south of Table Mountain forms a striking series of buttresses known as the Twelve Apostles (although there are more than 12 of these formations).

The suburbs and towns on the Atlantic coast, and those on False Bay, west of Muizenberg, cling to a very narrow coastal strip. East of these mountains the land slopes more gently down to the Cape Flats, a sandy plain. Looking east across the Cape Flats you can see more mountain ranges rising up around Stellenbosch and, to the south-east, the Hottentots Holland area. They are sometimes snowcapped in winter. Behind these ranges are others which rise to the Great Southern African Plateau and the semi-desert of the Karoo.

There is no major river in the city area,

although there is a system of lakes north-east of Muizenberg, near the Cape Flats.

CLIMATE

Cape Town has what is described as a Mediterranean climate. This means that weather is not really a critical factor in deciding when to visit – great extremes of temperature are unknown, although it can be relatively cold and wet for a few months in winter.

One of the Cape's most characteristic phenomena is the famous Cape Doctor, a south-easterly wind that buffets the Cape and lays Table Mountain's famous tablecloth (a layer of cloud that covers the City Bowl – see The Tablecloth section following). It can be a welcome breeze in summer, but it can also be a wild gale, particularly in spring. When it really blows you know you're clinging to a peninsula at the southern end of Africa, and there's nothing between you and the Antarctic.

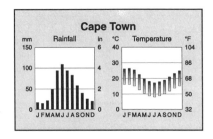

In winter, between June and August, temperatures range from 7° to 18°C, with pleasant, sunny days scattered between the gloomy ones. The prevailing winds are north-westerly. If the wind is blowing from the chilly inland mountains it can be cold, otherwise the temperature is tolerable. The rain tends to come in heavy showers, with long, fine breaks. However, it is not unknown for a rainy spell to set in and Table Mountain to be invisible for a week.

From September to November the weather is unpredictable, with anything from bright warm days to howling south-easterly storms and winds of up to 120km/h.

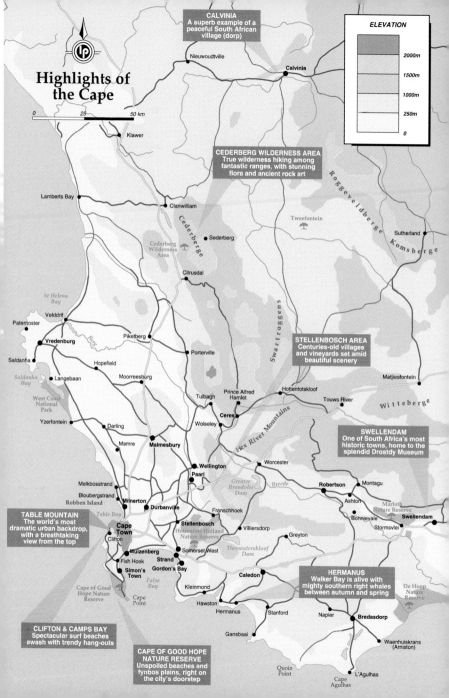

GERHARD DREYER

SUSAN STORM

Top: Table Mountain as seen from Bloubergstrand's expanse of 'reclaimed' dunes.
Bottom: Lion's Head (on the left) is the crown of a sugarloaf rock image of 'the king of
beasts' – a ridge forms the lion's body, with Signal Hill as its rump.

The wildflowers are at their best during August and September.

December to March can be very hot, although the average maximum temperature is only 26°C and the Doctor generally keeps things bearable (it is usually relatively calm in the mornings). From March to April, and to a lesser extent May, the weather remains good and the wind is at its most gentle.

The Tablecloth

As if Table Mountain was not spectacular enough in itself, for much of the summer it is capped by a seemingly motionless cloud that drapes itself neatly over the summit. An Afrikaner legend attempted to explain this phenomenon by telling of an old burgher who, fond of his pipe, tried to out smoke the devil in a competition.

Meteorologists have come up with another explanation. The south-easterly wind picks up moisture as it crosses the Agulhas current and False Bay. When it hits Table Mountain it rises and as it reaches the cooler air at about 900m above sea level, it condenses into thick, white clouds. The clouds pour over the plateau and down into the City Bowl, where they evaporate in the warmer air.

Table Mountain just happens to be at the perfect height and place, and the tablecloth is a dynamic and hypnotic sight. Although the mountain can be capped by cloud at any time, it is the avalanche of cloud pouring down into the City Bowl that makes a table-

cloth, and it generally only occurs in spring and summer.

ECOLOGY & ENVIRONMENT

The environment in this area changed drastically within a few decades of the European invasion. Dense forests that were home to lion, elephant, hippo, black rhino, buffalo, hyena and leopard vanished, and today none of these animals live anywhere near Cape Town. To replace the forests and provide wood for building, early governors encouraged settlers to plant oaks. They found, however, that the kind climate allowed the trees to grow too quickly to produce tough wood.

The characteristic tree on Table Mountain is the silver-leafed *witteboom*, which is found only in this area. The dense foliage of the Cape Peninsula is also highly localised. It is called *fynbos* (fine bush) and is part of the Cape floral kingdom. See the Cape Floral Kingdom section in the Things to See & Do chapter.

The Cape is the meeting point for two great ocean currents that have a major impact on the climate of southern Africa, and the Cape itself. The cold Benguela current (about 8°C) runs up the west side of the Cape from Antarctica.

The warm Agulhas current (about 20°C) swings around Madagascar and the east coast from the equatorial waters of the Indian Ocean and into False Bay, if you're lucky. If you're unlucky, the spring/summer south-easterly will blow in cold water.

Four centuries of close settlement and intensive (and often insensitive) agriculture mean that the indigenous flora and fauna in this area survives mainly in reserves and on agriculturally unviable land.

Just about any mountain pass you drive up has a sign warning you not to feed the baboons (and you shouldn't – they're potentially dangerous), as these steep areas are their last strongholds. Farmers shoot baboons, as they are very good at destroying crops. In Africa, hills, scrub and food (such as baboons) usually means leopards, but the few surviving big cats in the Cape are extremely wary of humans, with good reason.

continued on page 22

Do-it-yourself Forecasting

The weather in Cape Town can change rapidly and often. Many people use Table Mountain as a weather forecaster, and it's apparently quite accurate. Some things to watch for:

- if there is heavy cloud on Lions Head, rain is coming.
- if the tablecloth is on the mountain, the Cape Doctor (a south-easterly wind) is coming.
- if there is no cloud around the upper cable station (visible from all over town) there is no wind on Clifton Beach. ■

Birdlife on the Cape

Cape Town is a fine place for an aspiring birdwatcher. The unique fynbos, Table Mountain's rugged escarpment, the wetlands and the rich coastal waters all support an exciting variety of birdlife. Cape Town also makes a good base for trips further afield: there are some excellent natural areas on the very edge of the city, and numerous national parks and nature reserves are within reach of a day trip.

The unique fynbos is a botanist's delight (see the Cape Floral Kingdom section in the Things To See & Do chapter) and supports a number of equally unique birds. Those eagerly sought out by keen birdwatchers include Protea Seedeater, Cape Sugarbird and Orange-breasted Sunbird; others that are not restricted to fynbos, but are perhaps most easily seen in this habitat, include Cape Francolin and Cape Bulbul.

In and Around Town

Greater concentrations and variety of birds occur where the natural vegetation has been preserved, but even while walking around town you may notice some wild birds – this is Africa, after all. Parks and gardens are a good place to start, and among the portly pigeons being fed at lunchtime you may see the more graceful Red-eyed Dove and the smaller Laughing Dove. Among the familiar House Sparrows, a few Cape Sparrows may forage for crumbs, the males being recognisable by their striking black and white head pattern.

Sharing the view with you and the dassies at the top of Table Mountain will be a few hopeful Rock Pigeons, recognisable by their red eye patch and white-spotted wings. Noisy and garrulous Red-winged Starlings also look for handouts. Much of the vegetation at the top is fynbos, but there are also swampy patches and shallow valleys with dense scrubby vegetation. Thus, by walking one of the trails over the mountain you can encounter a variety of habitats and birds. Larger species include birds of prey, such as Black Eagle and Rock Kestrel; swifts and martins dart through the air; while the

Above: Look for the Black Eagle soaring over cliff faces as it searches for its favourite prey – rodent-like dassies. Adults are boldly marked and extremely graceful in flight.

Right: As its name suggests, the Rock Pigeon frequents the cliffs and peaks of Table Mountain. It can be readily identified by the patch of bare red skin around the eye.

iridescent green Malachite Sunbird and its pied relative the Dusky Sunbird feed on emergent flowers.

In Kirstenbosch Botanic Gardens you should encounter a few of the more common birds of the Cape among the stunning variety of plants. Be especially on the lookout for two of the region's specialities flitting among the proteas and other flowering spikes: the Cape Sugarbird and the Orange-breasted Sunbird. Both sugarbirds and sunbirds have a down-curved beak with which they probe for nectar; the male sugarbird is recognisable by his long showy tail and the male sunbird by his green iridescent plumage and orange-yellow breast.

A must for any bird enthusiast is the penguin colony at Boulders Beach, near Simon's Town. The Jackass Penguin is Africa's only penguin and so-named for its call, which resembles a braying donkey. Most of the world's penguin species inhabit the frigid Antarctic and subantarctic, but the Jackass feels quite at home in suburbia: from a few individuals the Boulders Beach colony has grown to number more than 1000 birds. This comical black and white bird spends most of its life at sea, feeding on fish and squid, but must come ashore to build its nest and breed. On land, penguin are clumsy and vulnerable to attacks by domestic pets; although superb and agile swimmers, at sea they are vulnerable to oil spills.

The Cape Sugarbird is unique to South Africa and has evolved to feed on the abundant nectar when the fynbos is in flower. Although rather nondescript in shades of brown, the male sugar-bird, shown here, is unmistakable because of his long wispy tail; the female is similar with a much shorter tail.

Further Afield

Most national parks and reserves feature a good variety of birds; a few that are particularly recommended for birdwatching are described here.

Cape of Good Hope Nature Reserve

Among the mountain fynbos and denser thickets, and along the beautiful beaches, you can expect to see some of the 240-odd species of birds recorded in this beautiful nature reserve. Its proximity to the city is an added attraction. Cormorants nest on the cliffs at Cape Point and Cape Maclear; shorebirds feeding at the water's edge can include oystercatchers, plovers and sandpipers; and you should be able to see sugarbirds and sunbirds feeding along the roadsides.

From coastal vantage points you may be lucky enough to spot a majestic albatross gliding past, particularly when onshore winds drive them close to land. Look out for marauding skuas, large, dark relatives of the gulls that harass seabirds and force them to drop their catch.

Berg River Estuary

The mouth of the Berg is near the small town of Laaiplek, north of the West Coast National Park on St Helena Bay. This area is known for its congregations of waterbirds, especially the long-distance migrants which every year complete a journey of thousands of kilometres from their breeding grounds in the Arctic tundra. These 'waders', as they are known to birdwatchers, moult from striking summer plumage to rather nondescript winter plumage. Many keen birdwatchers relish the identification challenge these drab winter plumages can present during migration.

Most waders are found near fresh or salt water, feeding along the shores on small creatures or probing intertidal mud for worms. The long-distance champions include the sandpipers and plovers; resident species include lapwings and oystercatchers. Larger waterbirds include spoonbills and flamingos.

The islands dotting the coastline here support breeding colonies for seabirds. Among the latter are the beautiful black and white Cape Gannet, which feeds by plunging from a great height after fish, and various species of fish-eating cormorants (also known as shags). Up to 30,000 pairs of gannets nest on Malgas Island, a large flat-topped granite island hardly bigger than a football field. Smaller numbers of Jackass Penguins nest and shelter among the rocks, and gulls wait to prey on unguarded eggs or chicks.

The Jackass Penguin is Africa's only breeding penguin species, although vagrants turn up from time to time on southern shores. Apart from Cape Town's colony at Simon's Town, Jackass Penguins breed on the offshore islands that dot the coast of southern Africa.

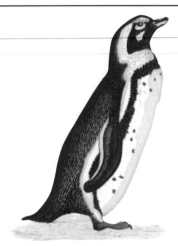

West Coast National Park

Just south of the Berg River Estuary, West Coast National Park is also famous for seabirds and waders. It shelters the lovely Langebaan Lagoon and features a good cross-section of habitats in which some 250 bird species have been recorded. This park is a popular and accessible birdwatching area. The southern end of the lagoon is particularly good for birds, and there are several colonies of the beautiful European Bee-eater around the park.

Bontebok National Park

Although this relatively small national park was declared to protect the bontebok, like many game reserves it features a good variety of birds. Habitats represented include coastal fynbos and riverine thickets, and low-lying areas are periodically flooded. Bontebok is a good place to look for Stanley's Bustard and other grassland birds such as larks, cisticolas and francolins, although they can be difficult to spot. In very wet conditions the flooded veld may attract some of southern Africa's waterbirds, such as the highly nomadic ducks.

Strandfontein Sewage Works

Only birds and the people who watch them could find sewage works attractive! Luckily, these ponds between Muizenberg and Strandfontein are no longer used for treating sewage and an impressive number of birds are attracted to these managed wetlands. It is a particularly good site to look for waterbirds such as ducks, herons, egrets and pelicans; smaller birds frequent the waterside vegetation. Flocks of up to 10,000 flamingoes once fed here, but their numbers are greatly diminished now that sewage is no longer treated.

Rondevlei Nature Reserve

Situated at Zeekoevlei, 24km south-east of Cape Town, this small nature reserve is often partially inundated and protects native marsh and dune vegetation. Hippos lived in this area 300 years ago and were reintroduced to the reserve in 1981. Facilities for birdwatchers include a waterside trail, two viewing towers and hides. Rondevlei's fluctuating water levels attract waterbirds such as egrets, herons, ducks and waders; the striking African Fish-eagle is also sometimes seen patrolling the ponds.

Birdwatching Tips

The variety of birds to be seen in southern Africa is bewildering; they are 'in your face', as the saying goes. A field guide will help with identification and a number of titles are readily available (see the Books section in the Facts for the Visitor chapter). A pair of binoculars will be a great aid to observation; basic models can be purchased quite cheaply from duty free outlets. Subtleties of plumage and form will be far more apparent through a pair of field glasses.

If you get serious about birdwatching you may want to invest in better quality optics; although expensive, brands such as Leica and Zeiss offer unrivalled quality. Both brands come in handy, pocket sized models.

If you become hooked on birdwatching you may also want to consider purchasing a spotting scope: Kowa, Swarovski and Leica are excellent examples. With a magnification usually at least twice that of binoculars, they can give stunning views. The drawback is their size (they must be mounted on a tripod for best results); on the other hand, a camera can be attached to some models and a scope then doubles as a telephoto lens.

Many birds are wide-ranging, but the vast majority have feeding, breeding or other requirements which restrict them to a habitat or group of habitats. Thus, ducks are adapted to feed in water and are rarely found far from it. Of course, creatures as mobile as birds are not totally hemmed in by their preferred environment (in fact, the habitat of some, such as swallows and swifts, could perhaps best be described as 'air'), but you will find a greater variety to look at if you walk through a few different habitats.

To help you get the most out of birdwatching, please bear the following in mind:

- An early start is advisable because most birds are generally more active during the cooler hours of the day. This is particularly so during hot weather.
- Approach birds slowly and avoid sudden movements or loud talk. Try to dress in drab clothing so as not to stand out. Many species are quite approachable and will allow opportunities for observation and photography. Birds are not usually too concerned about people in a vehicle and stunning views can often be obtained from the roadside.
- Waterbirds and waders respond to tidal movements and are usually best seen on a falling tide as they search for food.
- Be careful not to alarm guards when birding near official residences or government buildings. If you are moved on be courteous. Always ask permission before birding on private property.
- Do not disturb birds unnecessarily and never handle eggs or young birds in a nest. Adults will readily desert a nest that has been visited, leaving their young to perish.

Although the game parks are a magnet to photographers, a few of Cape Town's birds will be confiding enough for reasonable photos, especially at Table Mountain and Boulders Beach.

David Andrew

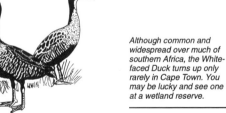

Although common and widespread over much of southern Africa, the White-faced Duck turns up only rarely in Cape Town. You may be lucky and see one at a wetland reserve.

continued from page 17

The other animals you're likely to spot are dassies. They'll spot you when you get to the top of Table Mountain, and demand food. There's a reserve for bontebok, large, handsome and extremely rare antelope, outside Swellendam (see the Excursions chapter).

The coast around Cape Town yields fish and crayfish but in much smaller quantities than it once did. Whales, however, are becoming increasingly common and the Southern Right Whale breeds in False Bay and along the southern coast (see the Hermanus section in the Excursions chapter for more information).

Another aquatic creature making a comeback is the endangered jackass penguin. There are several colonies of these relatively large penguins in the area, the most accessible at Boulders Beach near Simon's Town. Visit in late afternoon. The penguins are doing so well that local residents recently erected a penguin-proof fence to keep them out of their gardens. Unfortunately, the fence cuts across some penguin paths and it remains to be seen if it will interfere with breeding. Cape Town is a busy port and the occasional oil spill has affected the penguins.

Cape Town seems like a small city but that's because the majority of its population lives out of sight in the huge townships and squatter camps on the Cape Flats. Here, third world economic imperatives mean poor environmental standards. The most obvious sign of this is the smoke that sometimes drifts around the mountain and over the city, building up into quite heavy pollution after a few windless days. Luckily for those on the city side of the mountain, successive windless days are uncommon. The airport is close to the townships and planes sometimes have to make instrument landings because of the smoke.

Most of the smoke is from cooking and heating fires (people trudging back to the townships carrying loads of wood is a common sight on the roads east of the city) but some is from burning tyres. A few scraps of metal can be gleaned from a tyre and then sold. Yes, it's incredibly polluting, but people have to eat.

North of Cape Town at Koeberg is South Africa's only nuclear power station.

The Karoo National Botanic Garden outside Worcester is a great place to learn more about the Cape's amazing indigenous flora.

GOVERNMENT

South Africa's new constitution was passed into law in 1996. It replaced (almost unchanged) the interim constitution thrashed out at the CODESA negotiations. The constitution is one of the world's most enlightened, with an emphasis on human rights and complete freedom from discrimination on practically any grounds, 'in particular: race, gender, sex, ethnic or social origin, colour, sexual orientation, age, disability, religion, conscience, belief, culture or language'. That must cover just about everything except shoe size.

Democracy is alive and very well. Members of the new parliament who also served in the old parliament are amazed that ANC members ask ministers tricky questions, and that ANC members of parliamentary committees query legislation and actually refer it back to the people for their input.

There are two houses of parliament, a National Assembly of 400 members and a Senate of 90 members. Members of the National Assembly are elected directly using the proportional representation method – there are no constituencies – but members of the Senate are appointed by the provincial legislatures. Each province, regardless of its size, appoints 10 senators.

The head of state is the president, currently Nelson Mandela. Mandela will retire before the next elections (due in 1999) and his successor as leader of the ANC (and thus almost certainly the next president) will probably be Thabo Mbeki.

The president is elected by the National Assembly (and thus will always be the leader of the majority party) rather than directly by the people. A South African president has more in common with a Westminster system prime minister than with an American president, although as head of state he – or she –

possesses executive powers denied most prime ministers.

The current government is one of national unity, with some power-sharing arrangements. Each party winning more than 5% of the vote for the National Assembly (the Inkatha Freedom Party (IFP), the National Party and the ANC) is entitled to proportional representation in Cabinet. The Nationals have withdrawn from Cabinet to concentrate on learning how to become an effective opposition party, something that doesn't come naturally to a party which held almost dictatorial powers for almost its entire history. The IFP, with a strong Zulu base, is still pushing for a more federal system and hasn't fully endorsed the new constitution. The result is that the ANC governs pretty much alone.

Cape Town was, and remains, one of the three capitals of South Africa. Pretoria is the administrative capital, Bloemfontein is the judicial capital and Cape Town is the seat of the nation's parliament (it's also home to the legislature of Western Cape province). However, the government has decided that the administration and the parliament should be in the same city, and moving the parliament to Pretoria would be much cheaper than moving the administration to Cape Town.

Provincial Government

Under the new constitution there are provincial governments as well as the national government. Cape Town is the capital of the new province of Western Cape. Before 1994 it was the capital of Cape Province, which covered more than half of South Africa, although most of the population was concentrated in the area that is now Western Cape Province. Western Cape Province is one of only two that didn't elect an ANC provincial government. KwaZulu-Natal elected the IFP and Western Cape elected the National Party.

It seems astounding that one of the most liberal areas of South Africa should elect the party that created and enforced apartheid. However, those classified as coloured (and who still identify themselves as such) make up the largest voting group in Western Cape Province.

The coloureds are largely Afrikaans-speaking (like members of the National Party) and under apartheid they received slightly better treatment than the blacks. They didn't vote for the Nationals out of gratitude (they may have been treated better than the blacks, but that isn't saying much), but out of fear of a black government. Many blacks resented the coloureds' favoured status and perceived them as uncommitted to the struggle against apartheid. An ANC government might, the coloureds feared, seek revenge.

The Nationals played skilfully on these fears and almost went as far as implying that they regarded coloureds as sort of junior Afrikaners.

ECONOMY

South Africa's economy is a curious mixture of first and third worlds, with a marked disparity in incomes, standards of living, lifestyles, education and employment opportunities. On the one hand there is a modern industrialised and urban economy; on the other, there is a subsistence economy little changed since the 19th century.

Until the discovery of diamonds at Kimberley (1871) and of the lucrative gold reef near Johannesburg (1886), the economy was exclusively agricultural. Since then, mineral wealth has been the key to development. Mining remains central to the economy, and South Africa is the world's leading supplier of gold, chromium, manganese, vanadium and platinum.

Cape Town, as the country's first and still most important port, benefited from all these activities.

Towards the end of white minority rule, international sanctions and black mass-action destabilised the economy, which was also hit by the global recession and a serious drought. Things have improved somewhat since the 1994 election but the economy will take time to recover.

The official unemployment rate is over 30% (it is probably higher in reality) and wages for jobs associated with non-whites are very low. Low wages add some anomalies, such as most whites (and wealthier blacks) employing maids and manual labour being performed with a minimum of mechanical aids, eg sheep are still shorn with hand-clippers in many areas.

Whites do not perform manual labour (with very rare exceptions), but whites generally don't trust blacks to work unsupervised, so every road gang, plumbing job etc seems to have a beer-bellied white foreman who lazes around watching the workers. There is no white working class that you could compare with a working class in, say France or Australia. There are poor whites but they are a minority of the white population. Under the apartheid regime, whites were unofficially guaranteed jobs, but they couldn't be 'demeaning' jobs such as digging holes or cleaning offices. This meant that government-run organisations such as the railways were full of whites who couldn't get a job anywhere else.

The very large mining companies, such as Anglo-American, still dominate the economy, but industry now accounts for just 30% of GDP. Oddly, the right-wing apartheid governments developed large, state-owned companies (such as Eskom, electricity; Transnet, transport; and SASOL, oil) but the left-wing ANC government is privatising many of them.

Inflation has been a major problem but is back down to 'only' about 7.5% (the lowest rate since 1972). The economy has grown for four successive years (at a rate of 3.1% in 1996).

Western Cape has a slightly different economic mix to the rest of the country, with mining taking a back seat and financial services, agriculture (especially wine and fruit) and tourism being very important. It's a relatively wealthy province, contributing twice as much to the GDP as its population would indicate, and its economy is growing at over twice the national rate. The *average* income works out to R14,000 a year, although this is a virtually meaningless figure, as there's such a gulf between the rich and poor.

While there is tremendous poverty, on an African scale South Africa's economy is not only reasonably successful – it dwarfs all the others on the continent. This success is largely based on tremendous natural wealth and an abundance of low-paid black labour. South Africa has a well developed infrastructure and there is tremendous potential for the economy to facilitate development in the rest of southern Africa.

However, even if the economy recovers to its boom-time peak, almost the only people to immediately benefit will be whites. Non-whites have never shared in the fruits of their labour, and it will be very difficult for the new government to ensure that they do so in future. Restructuring will be a long, slow process.

POPULATION & PEOPLE
South Africa's population is about 38 million, of whom about 29 million are black, five

Unreliable Numbers
Given the apartheid regime's obsession with pigeonholing people, it's perhaps surprising to find that it was very bad at counting them. Censuses carried out during those years were extraordinarily unreliable, for a number of reasons. Figures for whites were probably fairly accurate, but for non-whites, the vast majority, it was a different story.

Blacks were not allowed to live outside their 'Homeland' unless they had a pass and a job. In reality, the shanty towns surrounding the cities were crammed with 'illegal immigrants', often the families of those lucky enough to have a job. These people would have avoided being counted, but estimates of their numbers were made. Counting in rural areas and large townships was often done by flying over in a helicopter, counting huts and multiplying by a fairly arbitrary number. Also, blacks were thought to breed prolifically, so this was also factored in.

When the first census under democratic rule was carried out in 1996, it was found that there were several million fewer blacks than had been supposed. The figures for blacks are now fairly reliable, as most realised that the census was an important tool in government planning. The figures for whites, however, are now less reliable, as many could not be bothered cooperating and some farmers would not let collectors onto their properties. ■

million are white, three million are coloured and one million are of Indian descent. Some 60% of whites are of Afrikaner descent and most of the rest are of British descent. There is a small but important Jewish population. Most are descendants of traders who arrived last century. You find synagogues (now usually disused) in the most unlikely corners of South Africa.

Cape Town and its surrounding areas present a different racial mix to the rest of the country.

The largest population group is probably still the coloureds, although the black population is increasing rapidly, with thousands arriving from the old Xhosa Homelands of Transkei and Ciskei each month. Most blacks and coloureds live on the sandy plain to the east of the mountains, known as the Cape Flats.

The last census of the Cape Peninsula was in 1985, although figures for non-whites were probably inaccurate. The census recorded 540,000 whites, one million coloureds, 280,000 blacks and 18,000 Asians. There are now probably about one million blacks.

ARTS

Although South Africa is home to a great diversity of cultures, most were suppressed during the apartheid years. To an extent, the Homelands kept alive some traditional cultures, but in a static form. The day-to-day realities of traditional and contemporary cultures were ignored, trivialised or destroyed. The most striking example of this was the bulldozing of District Six, a vibrant multicultural area in Cape Town, and Jo'burg's Sophiatown, where internationally famous musicians learned their craft in an area once described as 'a skeleton with a permanent grin'.

One of the most exciting aspects of the new South Africa is that the country has been reinventing itself and, with such a large proportion of the population marginalised from the economic mainstream, this is occurring without much input from professional image makers. The new South Africa is being created on the streets of the townships and the cities.

Many artists, black and white, were involved in the anti-apartheid campaign and some were banned. In a society where you could be jailed for owning a politically incorrect painting, serious art was forced underground and blandness ruled in the galleries and theatres. Many asked themselves whether it was ethically possible to produce art in such circumstances. For an overview of South African art during these times, see *Resistance Art in South Africa* by Sue Williamson (paperback, R97).

It will take time for the damage to be undone, but there are encouraging signs. Galleries are holding retrospectives of traditional

Cape Muslims

Cape Muslims (generally called Cape Malays by whites) are long-standing South Africans. Although many people were brought to the early Cape Colony as slaves, others were political prisoners and exiles from the Dutch East Indies. Some of the first settlers on Robben Island were Muslims. People were brought from countries as far apart as India and modern Indonesia, but their lingua franca was Malay (at the time an important trading language), which is why they came to be called Cape Malays.

A common language and religion, plus the presence of important political and religious figures, helped a cohesive community to develop. It has survived intact over the centuries, and even resisted some of the worst abuses of the apartheid decades.

Around Cape Town lies the **Circle of Karamats,** made up of the tombs of about 25 saints from the community. One of the first was Sheik Yusef, a Batavian exiled to the Cape in 1694. On the voyage out, his ship ran low on water, and the sheik obligingly turned sea water into fresh water. Another important exile was Tuan Guru from Tidor, who arrived in 1780. During his 13 years on Robben Island he wrote the *Koran* from memory (his version is apparently quite accurate) and later helped establish the first mosque.

A visit to **Bo-Kaap**, the 'Malay Quarter', is a must, and while wandering around by yourself is rewarding, it's worth taking one of the tours run by local residents. Tana-Baru Tours is highly recommended. See the Organised Tours section of the Getting Around chapter for more information. ■

and contemporary black artists, and musicians from around Africa perform in major festivals.

Although ANC-sponsored shows toured internationally during the apartheid years, and despite the fact the new government is continuing this tradition, there are relatively few opportunities to see contemporary theatre or dance within South Africa.

For more on contemporary culture, look for *ADA* (about R40), a large format design/art/culture magazine published several times a year, and *Sidelines* (R15), a quarterly literary journal.

Although Cape Town is South Africa's oldest city it is in some ways the youngest, as this is the only area of the country without a bedrock of ancient indigenous culture. Everyone here is a settler.

CULTURE
Blacks

It's a common error to see the black community as a homogeneous mass with a single culture. Most blacks in Cape Town are Xhosa and many maintain at least some cultural traditions. Xhosa culture itself is diverse, with many clan systems and subgroups. With at least one million people, it isn't surprising that the black community is as diverse as the population of any other large city – despite the fact that for blacks their city consists largely of third world slums. Politics makes an obvious division, with most people supporting the ANC but a sizeable minority supporting the more hardline Pan African Congress (PAC). There are also economic divisions, with some owning their own houses in the townships; and cul-

---

Magic & Ritual Among the Xhosa

Although there are several major and many minor groups in the traditional black cultures (depending on who's counting), they share broad similarities. All believe in a masculine deity, ancestral spirits and various supernatural forces. Marriage customs and taboos differ (but are always important) but polygamy is permitted and a *lobolo* (dowry) is usually paid. First-born males have inheritance rights. Cattle play an important part in many cultures, as symbols of wealth and as sacrificial animals.

The Xhosa who maintain a traditional lifestyle are known as red people because of the red-dyed clothing worn by most adults. Different subgroups wear different costumes, colours and bead arrangements.

The Xhosa deity is known variously as uDali, Tixo and Qwamata. This deity also figured in the San religion and it's probable that the invading Xhosa adopted it from them. There are numerous minor spirits and a rich folklore which persists in rural areas. A belief in witches (male or female) is strong and witch-burning is not unknown. Most witchcraft is malevolent, with possession of people by depraved spirits the main fear. The main source of evil is the *tokoloshe* which lives in water but is also kept by witches.

However, water is not always evil. If someone drowns and their body is not recovered, it is assumed, joyously, that they have gone to join the People of the Sea. Often those drowned are reincarnated with special knowledge and understanding.

The *igqirha* (spiritual healer) holds an important place in traditional society because he/she can deal with the forces of nature and the trouble caused by witches. The *ixhwele* (herbalist) performs some magic but is more concerned with health. *Mbongi* are the holders and performers of a group's oral history and are something like a cross between a bard and a court jester. While there is a hierarchy of chiefs the structure of Xhosa society is much looser than in Zulu society.

Many people have the top of their left little finger removed during childhood to prevent misfortune. Puberty rituals figure heavily: boys must not be seen by women during the three month initiation period following circumcision and disguise themselves with white clay or in intricate costumes made of dried palm leaves; a girl must stay in a darkened hut while her friends tour the area singing for gifts.

Marriage customs and rituals are also important. Unmarried girls wear short skirts which are worn longer as marriage approaches. Married women wear long skirts and cover their breasts. They often put white clay on their faces and wear large, turban-like cloth hats. Smoking long-stemmed pipes is also popular among married women.

Beadwork and jewellery are important. The *danga* is a long turquoise necklace which identifies the wearer to his/her ancestors. ■

tural divisions, such as with the Rastafarian community, which periodically agitates for the right to smoke *dagga* (marijuana).

Coloureds

Although the apartheid regime treated people classified as coloured marginally better than those classified as black, its racist ideology denigrated them. Racists particularly despise such people of 'mixed race', preferring 'their' natives 'pure' and 'authentic'. This, despite the fact that everyone on the planet is of 'mixed race' or is pure human race, depending on your point of view. Some of the things written about the coloureds, even in this century, are too offensive to reproduce here.

The coloured community in Cape Town – no less diverse than the black community – always provided refreshing relief to the drabber white community. This is partly a result of their East-Asian cultural heritage (not their genes). Because of this, coloureds were generally stereotyped as passionate, happy-go-lucky people with a natural gift for music (much as Mexicans were once stereotyped in the US). As with any stereotype, this perception is convenient, but it trivialises some important aspects of the community.

Whites

Superficially, the urbanised European culture of Cape Town doesn't seem to differ much from that in other western countries. There are shopping malls, freeways and all the trappings of western consumer culture. But the unique experience of white people in South Africa has given them a self-awareness that has raised culture to an issue of central importance, far beyond the arts pages of a weekend newspaper. Those of Afrikaner and British descent form distinct subgroups.

The Afrikaners' remarkable history and their geographical isolation have combined with often deliberate cultural isolation to create a unique people – often called the white tribe of Africa.

The ethnic composition of the Afrikaners is difficult to quantify, but the government estimates 40% Dutch, 40% German, 7.5% French, 7.5% British and 5% other. Some historians have argued that the '5% other' figure includes a significant number of blacks and coloureds – a claim that would still be regarded as highly offensive by many Afrikaners.

Afrikaners speak Afrikaans, the only Germanic language to have evolved outside Europe. Spoken as a mother tongue by just 5½ million people (only half of whom are actually white), it is central to the Afrikaner identity, but it has also served to reinforce their isolation from the outside world. The Afrikaners are a religious people and their brand of Christian fundamentalism based on 17th century Calvinism is still a powerful influence.

Determination and courage were required by the first trekboers who launched themselves into Africa, and again by the Boers in their long and bitter struggle against the British Empire. This history has been heavily mythologised and the concepts of culture and race are tightly fused.

Aside from the Afrikaners, the majority of European South Africans are of British extraction (about 1.9 million). The British have always held a slightly equivocal position in South African society, exemplified by a not-so-friendly Afrikaans term of abuse: *soutpiel*, literally meaning salt dick and referring to a man with one foot in South Africa and one in Britain.

The British are much more urbanised than the Afrikaners and, particularly up until the 1960s, dominated the mining, manufacturing, financial and retail sectors, much to the resentment of the Afrikaners.

Cape Town, as the seat of British power for so long, is somewhat less Afrikaner in outlook than other parts of the country. Liberal Cape Towners were regarded with deep suspicion by more conservative whites during the apartheid years, and even today the city is tantalisingly cosmopolitan in outlook. However, you don't have to venture far out of the city to find attitudes which would have been at home in the remotest Transvaal *dorp* (village) during apartheid. For instance, the appalling 'tot' system still

How & Why Colour Still Counts

In its 1986 confession of the sin of apartheid, the General Synod of the Dutch Reformed Church defined racism:

> Whoever in theory or by attitude and deed implies that one race, people, or group of people is inherently superior, or one group of people is inherently inferior, is guilty of racism. Racism is a sin which tends to take on collective and structural forms. As a moral aberration it deprives a human being of his dignity, his obligations and his rights. It must be rejected and opposed in all its manifestations because it leads to oppression and exploitation.

Not a bad definition (if sexist). In this book we make use of the old apartheid terms: white, black, coloured and Asian. We thought hard before including them, because this does in some ways perpetuate the offensive notion that skin colour is a useful or accurate distinguishing characteristic. By using these terms are we not implicitly validating a racist philosophy? Perhaps this is true to an extent, but it is impossible to pretend that these distinctions have disappeared from South Africa. It is also true that many nonracists proudly identify themselves with one or other of these groups.

The bottom line is that we have no problem with someone arguing there are cultural differences (based on language, shared beliefs, ancestry, place of birth; tribe, political belief or religion) which sometimes correlate to some degree with skin colour. We do have a problem if these generalisations do not allow for the existence of numerous individual exceptions, or if they are used to justify inequality, intolerance or prejudgement.

Visitors to South Africa will find that although the apartheid regime has been dismantled, cultural apartheid still exists. Discrimination based on economics is replacing that based on race (so most visitors will automatically gain high status) but there are people (mainly whites) who sincerely believe that a different skin colour means a radically different mindset. A few believe that it means inferiority.

If you aren't white, many white South Africans will register it, even if they don't do anything about it. This constant awareness of race is an issue, even if it doesn't result in problems, and is one constantly annoying feature of travel in South Africa, whatever your skin colour.

Racial discrimination is illegal in South Africa but it's unlikely that the overworked and under-resourced police force will be interested in most complaints. Tourism authorities are likely to be more sensitive. One or two travellers have complained about not being admitted to the caravan parks or B&Bs in rural areas. This is definitely not common but it can happen. If you think that racism has been displayed by any of the places mentioned in this book, please let us know.

White If your skin colour is white, it will be assumed by most white South Africans that you are essentially the same as them, although perhaps brainwashed by anti-apartheid propaganda. In many ways people from developed countries (whatever their skin colour) lead similar lives to white South Africans but there are some very important differences. For a start, if you've saved for your trip by, say, cleaning offices or working in a petrol station, you will get some startled reactions from whites. And don't offer to help wash the dishes. Non-white South Africans might view you with suspicion but usually this vanishes when they find out that you aren't South African.

African If you are of African descent, you will probably find some white resentment at your obvious economic status. Also, black South Africans were lowest on racism's ladder and the lies taught about them will take some time to wear off. On the other hand, do not assume a special bond with black South Africans. The various indigenous peoples of South Africa form distinct and sometimes antagonistic cultural groups. Pan-Africanism is a force in politics here, but not the dominant force. There's no special reason (other than an interest in strangers) why someone from France or the USA will receive a warmer welcome than a trader from Ghana or an illegal immigrant from Mozambique.

East Asian East Asians were a problem for apartheid – Japanese were granted 'honorary white' status, and people from other East Asian countries are probably indistinguishable from Japanese to insular South Africans. Grossly inaccurate stereotyping and cultural ignorance will probably be the main annoyances you will face.

Indian Indians in South Africa were discriminated against by the whites and were seen as collaborators by the blacks. If you are of Indian descent this could mean some low-level antagonism.

Anyone Else? People who didn't fit easily into one of the above categories were lumped together as 'coloured'. In some ways the coloureds were treated better than the blacks but they were perhaps despised more – the macho apartheid culture gave some respect to 'pure' African warrior cultures. ∎

exists in some places. Under the tot system, the coloured labourers who do most of the actual work in producing the region's acclaimed wines are partly paid in wine. The devastating health and social consequences of this compulsory alcoholism are all too visible, but many whites just don't see it as a problem for their society, much less a problem of their own making.

Remember that the majority of white South Africans had very limited exposure to western (or any other) popular culture in the 1960s and 1970s. Much of it was banned. The South African Broadcasting Commission (which was the only broadcaster) didn't play the Beatles after John Lennon said they were more popular than Jesus, and 'de-generate' bands such as the Rolling Stones, Velvet Underground and the Sex Pistols were not played in the first place. Yes, this music is outmoded but understanding much of today's popular culture depends on understanding its history. And *no* music by black artists was played on the radio or was easily available in shops. No Jimi Hendrix, no Aretha Franklin, no Diana Ross, no James Brown, no Chuck Berry ... This goes a long way to explaining the popularity of The Best of Bread and The Carpenters as background music in small-town restaurants.

ARCHITECTURE

Undoubtedly, one of the main attractions of Cape Town is its architecture – a style of

Cape Dutch Architecture

During the last years of the 17th century a distinctive Cape Dutch architectural style began to emerge. Thanks to Britain's wars with France, the British turned to the Cape for wine, so the burghers prospered and, during the 18th and 19th centuries, they were able to build many of the impressive estates that can be seen today.

Although there is no direct link between the Cape Dutch style and the Dutch style, they are recognisably related.

The building materials were brick and plenty of plaster, wood (often teak) and reeds to thatch the roof.

The main features of a Cape Dutch manor are the *stoep* (a raised platform, the equivalent of a verandah) with seats at each end, a large central hall running the length of the house and the main rooms symmetrically arranged on either side of the hall. Above the front entrance is the gable, the most obvious feature, and there are usually less elaborate gables at each end. The house is covered by a steep, thatched roof and is invariably painted white (a traveller with an eye to commerce reckoned that if you wanted to make your fortune in South Africa you would get a monopoly on white paint).

The front gable, which extends up above the roof line and almost always contains an attic window, most closely resembles 18th century Dutch styles. The large ground-floor windows have solid shutters. The graceful plaster scrolls of the gable are sometimes reflected in the curve on the top of the front door (above which is a fanlight, sometimes with elaborate woodwork) but sometimes the door has neoclassical features such as flat pillars or a simple triangle above it. This combination of styles works surprisingly well.

Inside, the rooms are large and simply decorated. The main hall is often divided by a louvred wooden screen, which probably derives from similar screens the Dutch would have seen in the East Indies. Above the ceilings many houses had a *brandsolder*, a layer of clay or brick to protect the house if the thatching caught fire. The roof space was used for storage, if at all.

Perhaps the loveliest of all the manors is **Boschendal**, near Franschhoek and Stellenbosch, although **Groot Constantia** in Cape Town is also very fine. To see the slightly different style of the Cape Dutch town-house, visit **Koopmans de Wet House**, now a museum in central Cape Town. And to get an idea of how pervasive this indigenous style is, just travel around the country and see the many imitation Cape Dutch houses, walls, gates etc.

One of the best books on Cape Dutch architecture is the modern facsimile edition of the 1900 book *Old Colonial Houses of the Cape of Good Hope* by Alys Fane Trotter, (hardcover, about R200). It includes an interesting introduction by Herbert Baker, the British architect whose work includes the Union Buildings in Pretoria. Only 1500 copies of the facsimile were printed, but you have a reasonable chance of finding one in the antiquarian bookshops in Cape Town. ■

building owing much to events in Europe, but having little to do with direct European influence.

With a few exceptions (eg the Town Hall and the Parliament), the British influence on architecture was not impressive. You can see a few remaining 'Brits in hot colonies'-style verandahs at local shopping centres (eg in Observatory) and there are a few Art Deco office blocks in the city centre.

The South African economy boomed in the 1960s, and the triumphant apartheid regime produced some hideous, almost fascist architecture. The Heerengracht area and the Civic Centre are good examples. Until very recently this remained the dominant style, partly for political reasons and partly because of the economy's decline due to international sanctions and burgeoning military spending.

There are plenty of examples of third world shack houses, products of crushing poverty and ingenuity, in the vast townships on the Cape Flats.

SOCIETY & CONDUCT

On first impressions Cape Town is much like any small western city, with similar rules of behaviour. After spending a day or two here, you'll find that this isn't quite so. The major differences are, unfortunately, hangovers from the apartheid days.

Most obviously there is an obsession with personal security, and while you need not go to the same extremes as the white population, you should take care. See Dangers & Annoyances in the Facts for the Visitor chapter for more information.

Another set of rules, which you might well want to ignore, pertain to the unspoken master/servant relationship between whites and non-whites. It's annoying that the question of skin colour even arises, but it does. Even though Cape Town is the most liberal of South Africa's cities, visitors will find it difficult to meet non-whites socially.

If you happen to share skin colour with white South Africans it's dangerously easy to be lead into seeing all non-whites as potential muggers; regarding places and services used by non-whites as not quite good enough; and treating domestic servants as children. The role-playing of the apartheid years hasn't disappeared and the non-white community's poverty reinforces it, despite the change of government and an enlightened constitution.

For a brief rundown on attitudes towards women in South Africa, see the Women Travellers entry in the Facts for the Visitor chapter.

RELIGION

Most South Africans are Christian, but among Christians there is enormous diversity, from the 4000 independent indigenous churches to the racist sub-sects which have split from the Dutch Reformed Church. The indigenous churches are run by and for blacks, independent of the mainstream churches. They broadly follow either the Ethiopian line, which split from the early Methodist missions, or the later Zionist line, which developed as a result of the activities of American Pentecostal missions early this century.

The Dutch Reformed Church covers at least three major groups of Afrikaner churches, all conservative. The Church of England is also represented; it has a high profile because of Archbishop Desmond Tutu's brave stand against apartheid.

Hindus make up about 70% of South Africa's Indian population, and Muslims account for about 20%. In Cape Town there are few Indians but there is a large and important Muslim population that is not of recent Indian descent. See the earlier Cape Muslims boxed text for more information.

A minority of blacks follow traditional religions. Beliefs and practices vary among different peoples, though there is usually a belief in a supreme deity and an emphasis on 'ancestor worship'. The distinction between religion and what would be considered folklore in western societies is blurred on a day-to-day level. Many blacks have no problem combining Christianity with traditional beliefs in much the same way that Christianity adopted 'pagan' rituals as it spread through Europe.

LANGUAGE

South Africa's official languages were once English and Afrikaans but nine others have been added: Ndebele, North Sotho, South Sotho, Swati, Tsonga, Tswana, Venda, Xhosa and Zulu.

Forms, brochures and timetables are usually bilingual (English and Afrikaans); road signs alternate (see the Road Signs boxed text in the Getting Around chapter). Most Afrikaans speakers also speak good English, but this is not always the case in small rural towns and among older people. However, it's not uncommon for blacks in cities to speak at least six languages – whites can usually speak two.

In the Cape Town area only three languages are prominent: Afrikaans (spoken by many whites and coloureds), English (spoken by nearly everyone) and Xhosa (spoken mainly by blacks).

> If you're completely lost for words, remember that 'thumbs-up' is a virtually universal gesture of goodwill, and can have an amazingly positive effect.

Afrikaans

Although Afrikaans has been closely associated with the tribal identity of the Afrikaners, it is also spoken as a first language by many coloureds. Ironically, it was probably first used as a common language by the polyglot coloured community of the Cape, and passed back to whites by nannies and servants. Some 5½ million people speak the language, roughly half of whom are Afrikaner and half coloured.

Afrikaans developed from the High Dutch of the 17th century. It has abandoned the complicated grammar and incorporated vocabulary from French, English, indigenous African languages and even Asian languages (as a result of the influence of East-Asian slaves). It's inventive, powerful and expressive, but it was not recognised as one of the country's official languages until 1925; before then it was officially a dialect of Dutch.

Afrikaans is a phonetic language and words are generally pronounced as they are spelt, with the characteristic guttural emphasis and rolled 'r' of Germanic languages.

> The Afrikaans Language Museum in Paarl has much more on the history of Afrikaans.

The following pronunciation guide is not exhaustive, but it includes the more difficult sounds that differ from English.

a	as the 'u' in pup
e	as in hen
i	as the 'e' in angel
o	as the 'o' in fort, or 'oy' in boy
u	as the 'e' in angel but with lips pouted
r	should be rolled
aai	as the 'uy' in buy
ae	like 'ah'
ee	as in deer
ei	as in play
oe	as the 'oo' in loot
oë	as the 'oe' in doer
ooi	as the 'oi' in oil, preceded by 'w'
oei	as in phooey, preceded by 'w'
tj	as the 'ch' in chunk

Greetings & Civilities

Hello.	*Hallo.*
Good morning, sir.	*Goeie môre, meneer.*
Good afternoon, madam.	*Goeie middag, mevrou.*
Good evening.	*Goeienaand.*
Good night.	*Goeie nag.*
Please.	*Asseblief.*
Thank you.	*Dankie.*
How are you?	*Hoe gaan dit?*
Good thank you.	*Goed dankie.*
Pardon.	*Ekskuus.*

Useful Words & Phrases

Yes.	*Ja.*
No.	*Nee.*
What?	*Wat?*
How?	*Hoe?*
How many/ how much?	*Hoeveel?*
Where?	*Waar?*
When?	*Wanneer?*
today	*vandag*
tomorrow	*môre*

yesterday	*gister*	19	*negentien*
soon	*nou-nou*	20	*twintig*
emergency	*nood*	21	*een en twintig*
		30	*dertig*
Do you speak English/Afrikaans?	*Praat u Engels/u Afrikaans?*	40	*veertig*
		50	*vyftig*
I only understand a little Afrikaans.	*Ek verstaan net 'n bietjie Afrikaans.*	60	*sestig*
		70	*sewentig*
Where do you live?	*Waar woon u?*	80	*tagtig*
What is your occupation?	*Wat is jou beroep?*	90	*negentig*
		100	*honderd*
Where are you from?	*Waarvandaan kom u?*	1000	*duisend*

Days of the Week

from ...	*van ...*	Monday	*Maandag* (abbreviated to *Ma*)
overseas	*oorsee*		
Isn't that so?	*Né?*	Tuesday	*Dinsdag (Di)*
sons	*seuns*	Wednesday	*Woensdag (Wo)*
daughters	*dogters*	Thursday	*Donderdag (Do)*
wife	*vrou*	Friday	*Vrydag (Vr)*
husband	*eggenoot*	Saturday	*Saterdag (Sa)*
mother	*ma*	Sunday	*Sondag (So)*
father	*pa*		
sister	*suster*	**Travel Terms**	
brother	*broer*	am	*vm*
nice/good/pleasant	*lekker*	pm	*nm*
bad	*sleg*	travel	*reis*
cheap	*goedkoop*	daily	*daagliks*
expensive	*duur*	departure	*vertrek*
party/rage	*jol*	arrival	*aankoms*
		to	*na*

Numbers

1	*een*	from	*van*
2	*twee*	public holiday	*openbare vakansiedag*
3	*drie*		
4	*vier*	ticket	*kaartjie*
5	*vyf*	single	*enkel*
6	*ses*	return	*retoer*
7	*sewe*		
8	*agt*	**Getting Around – Town**	
9	*nege*	art gallery	*kunsgalery*
10	*tien*	building	*gebou*
11	*elf*	church	*kerk*
12	*twaalf*	at the corner	*op die hoek*
13	*dertien*	avenue	*laan*
14	*veertien*	road	*pad*
15	*vyftien*	street	*straat*
16	*sestien*	traffic light	*robot*
17	*sewentien*	city	*stad*
18	*agtien*	city centre	*middestad*
		town	*dorp*

The New Blue Train

The *Blue Train*, synonymous with luxury train travel in South Africa, has undergone a R70 million face-lift that has given it a claim to the title of the world's most luxurious train. (Nelson Mandela himself blew the first whistle, flanked by some of the world's most beautiful people, including Naomi Campbell, Imran and Jemima Khan, Quincy Jones and Mia Farrow.)

A splendid hotel on rails, the *Blue Train* indulges its guests with sumptuous interiors, personal butlers and award-winning wines and food – all included in the ticket cost.

This is the train's third incarnation. The first luxury rail service between Jo'burg and Cape Town began in 1928; known even then as 'the blue train' for its sapphire-blue carriages, the name became official in 1946. The train was upgraded in the 1970s, but the renovations were minor compared with the new service, which began on 1 August 1997.

The train accommodates 84 passengers in elegant compartments (with bulletproof windows) that include their own *en suite* with bath or shower. The *Blue Train* travels weekly between Pretoria and Victoria Falls, Zimbabwe (R10,800 per suite) or three times a week between Pretoria and Cape Town (R9000).

The Zimbabwe Spectacular route (two nights) stops in historic Bulawayo on the way to Victoria Falls; the return trip includes a wildlife-viewing break at Hwange Game Reserve. The 1600km Cape route (one night) takes in Witwatersrand's gold fields, the eerie expanse of sunbaked Karoo and the verdant valleys of the wine region, before rolling into Cape Town.

Bookings can be made in Jo'burg on ☎ (011) 773 7631; fax 773 7643. Short hops are now strictly déclassé – forget about climbing aboard for a quick look and lunch.

If you want more champagne while in your bubble bath, the butler on the other end of your telephone will come and oblige.

Susan Storm and Russ Kerr

Left: Cecil Rhodes' imperial dream of a railway running all the way from Cairo to Cape Town didn't materialise. But ironically, the opulent train he might have imagined plying the route has become real in postcolonial South Africa.

Right: David Robbins' book, The Blue Train, tells some of the stories this carriage has heard. If chess is your game, the butler might also suggest some good moves to make.

COURTESY OF BLUE TRAIN

COURTESY OF BLUE TRAIN

Top: Groot Constantia's Jonkerhuis restaurant on a quiet day.
Bottom: Don't miss the bright, terraced beauty of the Muslim Quarter (Bo-Kaap), where a unique community has survived and prospered.

rooms	*kamers*
enquiries	*navrae*
exit	*uitgang*
left	*links*
right	*regs*
office	*kantoor*
pharmacy/chemist	*apteek*
station	*stasie*
information	*inligting*
tourist bureau	*toeristeburo*

Getting Around – Country

bay	*baai*
beach	*strand*
caravan park	*woonwapark*
field/plain	*veld*
game reserve	*wildtuin*
hiking trail	*wandelpad*
marsh	*vlei*
mountain	*berg*
point	*punt*
river	*rivier*
road	*pad*
utility/pick-up	*bakkie*

Food & Drink

barbecue	*braaivleis/braai*
beer	*bier*
bread	*brood*
cheese	*kaas*
cup of coffee	*koppie koffie*
dried & salted meat	*biltong*
farm sausage	*boerewors*
fish	*vis*
fruit	*vrugte*
glass of milk	*glas melk*
hotel bar	*kroeg*
meat	*vleis*
vegetables	*groente*

wine	*wyn*

Xhosa

The language of the Xhosa people is Xhosa, the dominant indigenous language in Western Cape Province.

Good morning.	*Molo.*
Good night.	*Rhonani.*
Do you speak English?	*Uyakwazi ukuthetha isiNgesi?*
father (term of respect for older man)	*bawo*
Are you well?	*Uphilile namhlanje?*
Yes, I am well.	*Ewe, ndiphilile.*
Where do you come from?	*Uvela phi na?*
I come from ...	*Ndivela e ...*
When do we arrive?	*Siya kufika nini na?*
The road is good.	*Indlela ilungile.*
The road is bad.	*Indlela imbi.*
I am lost.	*Ndilahlekile.*
Is this the road to ...?	*Yindlela eya ...?*
Would you show me the way to ...?	*Ungandibonisa indlela eya ...?*
Is it possible to cross the river?	*Ungaweleka umlambo?*
How much is it?	*Yimalini?*
day	*usuku*
week	*iveki*
month (moon)	*inyanga*
east	*empumalanga*
west	*entshonalanga*

 Xhosa phrasebooks are readily available, although the older ones include phrases such as 'You must wash the dishes now'.

Facts for the Visitor

WHEN TO GO

There's not really any best or worst time to visit, although different seasons have their advantages.

From late December to the end of January accommodation can be hard to find and prices rise. Easter and the other school holidays are also busy times. You're more likely to encounter one of the famous south-easterly gales during spring (September to November), but this might be an attraction, with huge waves rolling up from the Antarctic and pounding the coastline. In winter (June through August) the weather can be bit gloomy and, if the wind blows from the snowy peaks inland, chilly. However there are plenty of clear days and the crowds have gone.

Pricing Seasons

Peak season is from Christmas to late January. High season is the rest of summer (November through February) and sometimes October and March as well. Easter is also high season. The non-summer school holidays (see the Public Holidays & Special Events entry later in this chapter) are considered high season at some places, mid-season at others. Low season is winter (June through August). Mid-season is the rest of the year, eg not summer or winter.

ORIENTATION

On first impressions, Cape Town is surprisingly small. The city centre lies to the north of Table Mountain and to the east of Signal Hill, and the old inner city suburbs of Tamboerskloof, Gardens and Oranjezicht are all within walking distance. This area is sometimes referred to as the City Bowl. On the western slope of the City Bowl is Bo-Kaap, the old Cape Muslim area that survived apartheid's bulldozers.

To the north of the city centre is the Victoria & Alfred Waterfront. The Waterfront is a popular area, although it's probably too far to reach on foot from the city centre. Those tempted to try will find the walk quite dull – there is little of interest along the way – and at night it cannot be considered safe.

On the other side of Signal Hill, Sea Point is another older suburb, densely populated, with high-rise flats, apartments, hotels, restaurants and bars.

The main white dormitory suburbs spread north-east of the city (either side of the N1 to Paarl, including Goodwood, Parow, Bellville and Kraaifontein) and to the south, skirting the eastern flank of the mountains

---

What's in a Name?

Well, plenty, especially if the name invokes unpleasant memories. It's not uncommon for streets, buildings, bridges and airports honouring colonial masters to be renamed once former subjects gain a say in such matters. By now you may have forgotten that Zimbabwe was once named after Cecil Rhodes; the new South Africa faces a similar issue.

The ANC government is renaming some concrete reminders of apartheid, especially those named after politicians like Daniel Malan, JG Strijdom and Hendrik Verwoerd. As a result, Cape Town's international airport is no longer DF Malan airport, and the Nico Malan complex in the city centre has dropped the dynastic surname. Some streets may undergo a similar transformation.

The changes are understandable, even necessary, though change too comes with a price. As Salman Rushdie once observed of his native Bombay (now Mumbai), renaming the street one grew up in means moving one's childhood to a new neighbourhood – another dislocation to add to the rest.

But it's worth noting that the ANC has made an effort to minimise the price – unlike what usually accompanies major changes in a state, South African towns don't have a new Mandela, Biko or Liberation Blvd. And, since they were named long ago, the names of the Cape are less tainted by recent history; Adderly, Riebeeck, Stellenbosch etc will probably live on.

Russ Kerr

---

and running down to False Bay (from Observatory to Rosebank, Rondebosch, Constantia and through to Muizenberg). These are known as the Southern Suburbs.

The sandy plain east of Table Mountain is known as the Cape Flats, and it's here that most Cape Towners live, in vast 'townships' and squatter camps.

Small towns and suburbs cling to the coast. On the Atlantic side, the exclusive suburbs of Clifton and Camps Bay are accessible by coastal road from Sea Point or through Kloof Nek, the pass between Table Mountain and Lion's Head. Camps Bay is a 10 minute drive from the city centre.

The towns further south (Llandudno, Hout Bay and Kommetjie) are less accessible by public transport than those on False Bay (from Muizenberg to Simon's Town), which can all be reached by rail.

The spectacular Cape of Good Hope (which is not Africa's southernmost point – see Cape Agulhas in the Excursions chapter later in this book) is 70km by road to the south of the city centre. Its extraordinary indigenous flora is protected within the Cape of Good Hope Nature Reserve. This area is also commonly known as Cape Point.

MAPS
The Map Studio (☎ 462 4360), Struik House, 80 McKenzie St, Gardens, sells its own wide range of maps as well as others, including Michelin maps and government topographic maps. If you're staying for more than a week or so and have a car, consider buying the Map Studio's *Cape Town Street Guide* (R76 or R51 for the smaller A-Z version) at all CNA bookshops.

Lonely Planet also publishes a *South Africa, Lesotho & Swaziland travel atlas*.

TOURIST OFFICES
Local Tourist Offices
At the Tourist Rendezvous, at the main train station, you'll find the Captour desk (Map 8) (☎ (021) 418 5214/5) and many other desks of interest to visitors, including car hire, accommodation and adventure activities.

Captour is the body which oversees tourism in and around Cape Town, but it's a private organisation and lists only those businesses which pay membership fees. This includes pretty much all the major places but for more obscure information (such as minibus taxi routes) Captour cannot help.

The Tourist Rendezvous complex is open from 8.30 am to 6 pm on weekdays, to 3 pm on Saturday and from 9 am to 1 pm on Sunday.

Captour has an informative Web site at www.africa.com/captour/captour.htm.

Tourist Offices Abroad
Satour Satour, the South African government tourism promotion organisation, has offices in several countries. It's worth contacting them before you leave home, not least because they can give you (free) some good brochures which you have to pay for in South Africa.

Satour's Web site can be found at www.africa.com/satour/index.htm.

Its head office is in Pretoria at 442 Rigel Ave South, Erasmusrand 0181 (☎ (012) 347 0600; fax 45 4889). Satour offices abroad include:

Australia
    Level 6, 285 Clarence St, Sydney NSW 2000 (☎ (02) 9261 3424; fax 9261 3414)
Austria
    Stefan-Zweig-Platz 11, A-1170, Vienna (☎ (0222) 4704 5110; fax 4704 5114)
Canada
    Suite 2, 4117 Lawrence Ave East, Scarborough, Ontario M1E 2S2 (☎ (416) 283 0563; fax 283 5465)
France
    61, rue La Boëtie, 75008 Paris (☎ 01 45 61 01 97; fax 01 45 61 01 96)
Germany
    Alemannia Haus, An der Hauptwache 11, D-60313 Frankfurt/Main 1, Postfach 101940, 60019 Frankfurt (☎ (069) 929 1290; fax 28 0950)
Israel
    14th floor, Century Towers, 124 Ibn Gvirol Street, PO Box 3388, Tel Aviv (☎ (03) 527 2950/2351; fax 527 1958)
Italy
    Via Durini 24, 20122 Milan (☎ (02) 79-4100; fax 79-4601)

Japan
> Akasaka Lions building, 2nd floor, 1-1-2 Moto Akasaka, Minato-ku, Tokyo 107 (☎ (03) 3478 7601; fax 3478 7605)

Netherlands
> Josef Israelskade 48, Postbus 75360, 070 AJ, Amsterdam (☎ (020) 662 43 60; fax 662 97 61)

Switzerland
> Seestrasse 41, CH 8802 Kilchberg/Zurich (☎ (01) 715 18 15/6/7; fax 715 18 89)

Taiwan
> Room 1204, 12th floor, Bank Tower building, 205 Tun Hua North Rd, Taipei 10592 (☎ (02) 717 4238; fax 717 1146)

UK
> 5 Alt Grove, Wimbledon, London SW19 4DZ (☎ (0181) 944 8080; fax 944 6705)

USA
> 500 Fifth Ave, 20th floor, Suite 2040, New York, NY 10110 (☎ (212) 730 2929, 800 822 5368 (toll-free); fax (212) 764 1980)
>
> Suite 1524, 9841 Airport Blvd, Los Angeles, CA 90045 (☎ (310) 641 8444, 800 782 9772 (toll-free); fax (310) 641 5812)

Zimbabwe
> Offices 9 and 10, Mon Repos building, Newlands Shopping Centre, Harare (☎ (04) 70 7766; fax 78 6489)

DOCUMENTS
Visas

Visa regulations have changed several times in the last few years and could change again, so check before you arrive.

Entry permits are issued on arrival to tourists from many Commonwealth countries, including Australia, Canada, New Zealand and the UK, and from other countries including Germany, Ireland, Japan and the USA. You are entitled to 90 days but you might get less, as the immigration officer will write the date of your flight home as the date of expiry. If you expect to change your flight to a later one, tell the immigration officer.

If you aren't entitled to an entry permit you'll need a visa. Visas are not issued at the border so apply for one before you leave home and allow sufficient time for processing. Tourist visas are free of charge.

Note that if you do need a visa (rather than an entry permit), it must be multiple-entry if you plan to travel to a neighbouring country, including Lesotho and Swaziland, and return to South Africa.

On arrival you might have to satisfy an immigration officer that you have sufficient funds for your stay in South Africa. Obviously, 'sufficient' is open to interpretation, so it pays to be neat, clean and polite.

You must have an onward ticket of some sort. An air ticket is best but an overland one seems acceptable.

Visa Extensions

You can apply for visa extensions or a re-entry visa at the Department of Home Affairs (Map 8) (☎ 462 4970), 56 Barrack St, city centre. Extensions cost a massive R360.

Photocopies

It's a good idea to make photocopies of vital documents and to keep them separate from the originals – if anything goes missing, a photocopy makes it much easier to replace. You might also consider leaving copies with someone back home. Documents you should consider photocopying include your passport (the data pages), air tickets, birth certificate and driving licence. Similarly, keep records of all credit card numbers and the serial numbers of travellers cheques. While you're at it, an emergency stash of cash can be handy too.

Driving Licences & Permits

As a visitor, you can use any foreign driving licence that carries your photo. You might experience difficulties if the licence is in a language that a traffic officer cannot easily read. It's best to carry other forms of ID as well.

Travel Insurance

A travel insurance policy to cover theft, loss and medical problems is a good idea. Although there are excellent private hospitals in South Africa, the public health system is underfunded and overcrowded, and is not free. Services such as ambulances are often run by private enterprise and are expensive. There is a wide variety of policies and your travel agent will have recommendations.

The policies handled by STA Travel and other youth-oriented travel organisations are usually good value. Some policies offer lower and higher medical-expense options; the higher ones are chiefly for countries such as the USA which have extremely high medical costs. There is a wide variety of policies available so check the small print.

Some policies specifically exclude 'dangerous activities', which can include scuba diving, motorcycling, even trekking. If such activities are on your agenda you don't want that sort of policy. A locally acquired motorcycle licence is not valid under some policies.

You may prefer a policy which pays doctors or hospitals direct rather than you having to pay on the spot and claim later. If you have to claim later make sure you keep all documentation. Some policies ask you to call back (reverse charges) to a centre in your home country where an immediate assessment of your problem is made. Check that the policy covers ambulances or an emergency flight home. If you have to stretch out you will need two seats – somebody has to pay for them.

Hostelling International Card
You'll save a few rand at Hostels Association Southern Africa (HASA) hostels (there are three in the area) with a Hostelling International (HI) card. Most hostels, whatever their affiliation (or lack of it), arrange discounts with local businesses.

Student & Youth Cards
There's no real advantage in having a student card, although determined travellers might be able to bluff their way to discounts.

EMBASSIES
South African Embassies, High Commissions & Consulates
South Africa once had a limited number of embassies and consulates, especially within Africa. That is changing rapidly, and you can expect more to open in the near future.

Australia
 Rhodes Place, Yarralumla, Canberra ACT 2600 (☎ (06) 273 2424; fax 273 2669)

Brazil
 Rua Lauro Muller 116/1107 (Torre Rio Sul), Botafogo 22299, Rio de Janeiro (☎ (021) 542 6191; fax 542 6043)
Canada
 15 Sussex Drive, Ottawa K1M 1M8 (☎ (613) 744 0330; fax 744 8287)
 Suite 2515, Exchange Tower, Toronto M5X 1E3 (☎ (416) 364 0314; fax 363 8974)
Denmark
 1st floor, Montergade 1, Copenhagen DK-1011 (☎ (01) 18 0155)
France
 59 Quai d'Orsay, Paris 75007 (☎ 01 45 55 92 37; fax 01 45 51 88 12)
Germany
 Auf der Hostert 3, Bonn 5300 (☎ (0228) 82010; fax 35 2579)
Israel
 Yakhin House, 2 Kaplan St, Tel Aviv 64734 (☎ (03) 525 2566)
Malawi
 Mpico building, City Centre, Lilongwe 3 (☎ (09265) 73 3722)
Netherlands
 Wassenaarseweg 40, The Hague (☎ (070) 392 4501; fax 45 8226)
Réunion
 Immeuble Cie des Indes, 20 Rue de la Compagnie BP 1117, 97482 St-Denis Cedex (☎ (09262) 21 5005; fax 41718)
Spain
 Edificio Lista, Calle de Claudio Coello 91-6 (☎ (01) 435 6688; fax 593 1384)
Sweden
 Linnégatan 76, 11523 Stockholm (☎ (0946) 24 3950; fax 660 7136)
UK
 South Africa House, Trafalgar Square, London WC2N 5DP (☎ (0171) 930 4488; fax 839 1419)
USA
 3051 Massachusetts Ave NW, Washington DC 20008 (☎ (202) 232 4400; fax 265 1607)
 Suite 300, 50 North La Cienega Blvd, Beverly Hills, CA 90211 (☎ (213) 657 9200; fax 657 9215)
Zimbabwe
 Temple Bar House, Baker Ave, Harare (☎ (04) 75 3150)

Foreign Consulates in Cape Town
Most countries have their main embassy in Pretoria, with an office or consulate in Cape Town that becomes their official embassy during Cape Town's parliamentary sessions. A surprising number of countries also maintain consulates (which can arrange visas and

passports) in Jo'burg. Some consulates, like Mozambique and Zimbabwe, only have representation in Jo'burg.

The following is not a comprehensive list. If your consulate is not listed, consult the Cape Town Yellow Pages telephone directory under 'consulates and embassies'. Many are only open in the morning.

Most diplomatic offices listed below are in the city centre (Map 8).

Australia
  14th floor, BP Centre, Thibault Square (☎ (021) 419 5425)
Belgium
  Vogue House, Thibault Square (☎ (021) 419 4960)
Canada
  Reserve Bank building, Hout St (☎ (021) 23 5240)
France
  2 Dean St, Gardens (☎ (021) 23 1575)
Germany
  825 St Martini Gardens, Queen Victoria St (☎ (021) 24 2410)
Japan
  Standard Bank Centre, Heerengracht St (☎ (021) 25 1695)
Netherlands
  100 Strand St (☎ (021) 21 5660)
UK
  Southern Life Centre, 8 Riebeeck St (☎ (021) 25 3670)
USA
  4th floor, Broadway Centre, Heerengracht St (☎ (021) 21 4280)

CUSTOMS

South Africa, Botswana, Swaziland and Lesotho are all part of the South African Customs Union, which means the internal borders are effectively open from a customs point of view. When you enter the union, however, you're restricted to the usual duty-free quota per person: 1L of spirits, 2L of wine and 400 cigarettes. Motor vehicles must be covered by a carnet. For information contact the Department of Customs & Excise in Pretoria (☎ (012) 28 4308).

MONEY
Cash

When you change money it's best not to accept R200 notes. There have been forgeries so some businesses don't like accepting them, and anyway they don't like making change on R200. Even R100 or R50 notes can present difficulties for small purchases. This means that you're likely to end up with a big wad of small denominations. Nearly all accommodation types (including hostels) have safes and you're advised to use them. Be a little wary of showing a wallet full of notes in the street. Keep some coins handy for giving to buskers, beggars and bus conductors.

Travellers Cheques

Most banks change travellers cheques in major currencies, with various commissions. The First National Bank (BOB) is associated with Visa and isn't supposed to charge commission when changing Visa travellers cheques, but many branches do not know this. Rennies Travel is the agent for Thomas Cook and has a number of foreign exchange offices, including on the corner of St George's Mall and Hout St (Map 8) (☎ (021) 26 1789), open Monday to Friday from 8.30 am to 4.30 pm, and Saturday morning; 182 Main Rd, Sea Point (☎ (021) 439 7529); and at the Waterfront (☎ (021) 418 3744). Rennies does not charge commission.

American Express is on Thibault Square (at the end of St George's Mall) (Map 8) (☎ (021) 21 5586) and in the arcade at the Victoria & Alfred Hotel at the Waterfront (☎ (021) 21 6021). The Waterfront office is open from 10 am to 5 pm daily.

ATMs

You can use the automatic teller machines at First National banks for Visa cash advances – there's a handy branch in St George's Mall on the corner of Shortmarket St and a machine at the main train station. Some ATMs will give Visa and MasterCard cash advances.

Credit Cards

Credit cards, especially Visa and Master-Card, are widely accepted. You will need a credit card if you plan to hire a car.

International Transfers

International electronic transfers theoretically take a couple of days, but if you deal with the branch of a major bank (eg a big branch in the city centre), it might be faster. There's a fee of around R40.

Currency

The unit of currency is the rand (R), which is divided into 100 cents. The import and export of local currency is limited to R500. There is no black market.

South Africa introduced new coins and notes ('Mandela money') a few years ago. The only old note you might see is the R5 (which has been replaced by a coin) but old coins are common, making it difficult to establish familiarity. The coins are: 1, 2, 5, 10, 20 and 50 cents; 1, 2 and 5 rand. The notes are: 10, 20, 50, 100 and 200 rand. The R200 note looks a lot like the R20 note, so take care.

Currency Exchange

The rates given here are those offered for travellers cheques in South Africa while this guide was being researched. It's likely that the rand will continue to devalue (ie you will get more rands for your dollar or whatever), but prices, especially for accommodation, tend to rise to compensate for devaluation.

Australia	A$1	=	R3.63
Canada	C$1	=	R3.38
France	FF1	=	R0.88
Germany	DM1	=	R2.99
Italy	L100	=	R0.30
Japan	¥100	=	R4.08
Sweden	Skr1	=	R0.69
UK	UK£1	=	R7.22
USA	US$1	=	R4.56

Changing Money

You can change money at the airport although the rates aren't as good as you'll get in town. Money can be changed at any commercial bank; they're open from 9 am to 3.30 pm on weekdays and many larger branches are also open on Saturday morning.

Keep at least some of the receipts you get when you change money (or travellers cheques) as you'll need to show them to convert your rands when you leave.

Costs

Although South Africa is not as cheap to travel in as many other African countries, it is very good value by European, American and Australian standards. This is due, in large part, to the collapse of the rand's value, which gives those converting from a hard currency a major advantage.

On the negative side, at the time of this book's publication inflation was running at well over 7%, so the prices in this book can be expected to change at a corresponding rate. In such circumstances, however, the rand is also likely to continue to devalue, so inflation and devaluation may well cancel each other. Don't expect imported or manufactured goods (including books) to be cheap.

Cape Town, with its current popularity as a destination for foreign visitors, tends to be a little more expensive than the rest of the country but it still isn't prohibitive. The exception is top-end accommodation. It is not especially expensive compared to, say London or Tokyo, but is way overpriced when you consider average incomes in South Africa.

What You Can Expect to Pay

Hostel dorm bed – average R35
Hostel double room – about R100
Cottage, sleeping two – from R90 (rural areas)
Cheap B&B – R90 per person
Three star hotel room – from R250/300 a single/
   double
Four star hotel room – from R350/450 a single/
   double
Five star hotel room – from R900 a room
Hamburger and chips – R18
Steak – from R30
Stubby beer – R3.50
One-way economy air ticket from Jo'burg to
   Cape Town – R790
Deluxe bus from Jo'burg to Cape Town – R340
Minibus taxi from Jo'burg to Cape Town – about
   R170

Tipping

Tipping in bars and restaurants is usual; 10 to 15% is reasonable. Staff are often paid very low wages (or even no wages). This results in over-friendly service, which can be irritating. Tipping taxi drivers, petrol-pump attendants and so on, is also common. A rand or two is sufficient.

Bargaining & Discounts

Although bargaining is not a South African habit, you'll often find that you can lower the price of accommodation and perhaps other expenses when business is slow. It's definitely worth asking about special deals whenever you're inquiring about accommodation. When buying handicrafts from street hawkers, bargaining is expected, but it isn't usually the sophisticated game that it is in Asia. Don't press too hard.

Taxes & Refunds

A Value Added Tax (VAT) of 14% is slapped onto nearly all goods and services, but foreign visitors can reclaim some of their VAT expenses on departure. This applies only to goods that you are taking out of the country; you can't claim back the VAT you've paid on food or car rental, for example. Also, the goods must be bought at a shop participating in the VAT Foreign Tourist Sales scheme.

To make a claim you need the tax invoices (usually the receipts, but make sure that the shop knows that you want a full VAT receipt). They must be originals – not photocopies. You also have to fill in a form or two and show the goods to a customs inspector when you depart. The total value of the goods must exceed R250. You either get a refund cheque on the spot or, if your claim comes to more than R3000, customs will mail the cheque to your home address.

You can claim only at the international airports in Cape Town, Durban and Jo'burg, at the Beit Bridge (heading to Zimbabwe) and Komatipoort (heading to Mozambique) land borders, and at major harbours. At airports, make sure you have the goods checked by the inspector *before* you check in your luggage. You make the actual claim after you have gone through immigration.

POST & COMMUNICATIONS

Post

Most post offices are open from 8.30 am to 4.30 pm on weekdays and from 8 am to noon on Saturday. Aerograms (handy, pre-paid letter forms) and standard size postcards cost R1. Airmail letters cost R1.40 per 10g (R1 to southern African countries). Internal letters cost 60c. Internal delivery can be very slow and international delivery isn't exactly lightning fast. If you are asking someone in South Africa to mail you something, even a letter, emphasise that you need it sent by airmail, otherwise it will probably be sent by sea mail and it could take months to reach you.

The main post office (Map 8) is on the corner of Darling and Parliament Sts and has a poste restante counter in the Main Hall (identification is theoretically required).

Telephone

You'll notice that phone books carry long lists of numbers that are due to change. The phone system seems to be perpetually upgrading and there's a good chance that many of the numbers (including some area codes) in this guide will have changed by the time you get to South Africa.

Except in remote country areas, telephones are automatic, with direct-dialling facilities to most parts of the world. Long distance and international telephone calls are expensive.

Local calls are timed and although you get a reasonable amount of time for each R0.30 unit, you might go through a few of these if you're calling a government department. Most public phones accept both new and old coins, and most accept phone cards, which are sold by many small shops.

When using a coin phone you might find that you have credit left after you've finished a call. If you want to make another call don't hang up or you'll lose the credit. Press the black button under the receiver hook.

Card phones are even easier to find than coin phones, so it's certainly worth buying a phonecard if you're going to make more than just the odd call. Cards are available in R10, 20, 50, 100 and 200 denominations.

If you are staying in a hotel, beware of the hefty surcharge that is added to phone calls – often 100%, sometimes more. Many slug you R5 or more just to use your Home Direct service.

Finding a Phone The public phones in the main post office are open 24 hours, but they're often very busy. There are also plenty of privately run public phone businesses, where you can make calls (and usually send faxes) without coins. Check their rates first; they are much more expensive than a normal public phone. A handy office is Postnet (Map 8), on Hout St between Adderley St and St George's Mall. You can use the phone and fax, and send Federal Express parcels. If you're looking for a quiet public phone in the city centre, there's one in the foyer of the Cultural History Museum (Map 8).

You can make international phone calls from Connection Internet C@fé (Map 8) (see the following Email & Internet section) at Telkom rates, which are *much* lower than the rates charged in hotels or at other private phone services. Standard rates are charged from 8 am to 8 pm on weekdays, all other times are charged at an economy rate.

Mobile Phones Mobile phones can be rented from a number of dealers. You can bring your own GSM phone if your service provider has an agreement with a local company. Vodacom (associated with Vodaphone) charges about R2.50 per minute for GSM calls within South Africa.

Enquiries
National and International	1025
Local	1023

Collect Calls
National	0020
International	0090

Area Codes Cape Town's area code is 021, as is Stellenbosch's. If a number given in this book doesn't have an area code, you can assume that it is in the 021 area.

International Codes Dial 09 (the South African international access code) followed by the relevant international code:

Australia	61
Botswana	267
Canada	1
Denmark	45
France	33
Germany	49
Japan	81
Netherlands	31
New Zealand	64
Spain	46
Sweden	46
UK	44
USA	1

International Rates Rates per minute for international calls include:

To	Standard	Economy
Australia	R4.69	R3.99
France	R7.84	R4.88
Germany	R8.59	R7.07
UK	R6.39	R4.88
USA/Canada	R5.33	R4.43

Home Direct Dialling a home direct number will take you straight through to your home-country telephone operator, and you can then make a reverse-charge telephone call or charge the call to a telephone company credit card if you have one. Home direct calls can be made from any telephone, including pay phones.

Australia Direct	0800 990061
Belgium Direct	0800 990032
Canada Direct	0800 990014
Denmark Direct	0800 990045
Ireland Direct	0800 990353
Japan Direct	0800 990081
Netherlands Direct	0800 990031
New Zealand Direct	0800 990064
UK Direct – BT	0800 990044
UK Direct – Call UK	0800 990544

USA Direct – AT&T	0800 990123
USA Direct – MCI Call USA	0800 990011
USA Direct – Sprint Express	0800 990001

Fax

Most businesses and places to stay have fax facilities. One good feature of South African telephone directories is that they include fax numbers.

Email & Internet

There are a couple of Internet cafés in the city centre which provide email and Internet services. Connection Internet C@fé (Map 8) (☎ (021) 419 6180; fax 419 6208; email mandy@postman.co.za) is on Heerengracht St between Hans Strijdom and Coen Stydler (across from the US embassy). It opens at 9 am on weekdays, 10 am on Saturday and 2 pm on Sunday. Closing time is around 9 pm. Internet access costs from R10 for half an hour. There's another cyber café, iCafé (Map 8), on Long St near the Long St Baths.

Lonely Planet on The Net Though you're carrying LP's latest 'treeware' on Cape Town, the Lonely Planet Web site (www. lonelyplanet.com) contains cyber-speed information on travel, travellers' letters, a bulletin board and more – check it out.

The Cape on The Net South Africans are very quick to pick up on new technology, and there many useful Web sites emanating from the country. The Internet country code for South Africa is za.

For more general tourist information and some links, the South African embassy in the USA has a useful site:

www.safrica.net

Check out SAA (South African Airways) routes on the web at

www.is.co.za/saa/pak/

Spoornet (the company that runs passenger trains) has routes and timetables and a good email contact address at

www.spoornet.co.za/

As well as the Spoornet site, there's a good site run by a dedicated railways enthusiast, with useful information and news, plus some very esoteric items and details of steam train options:

www.ru.ac.za/departents/iwr/staff/daf/sartrain.html

For backpacker-oriented tours and services, check out the Africa Travel Centre's site:

www.kingsley.co.za/millennia/bp&atc.htm

A great way to keep up with news and entertainment listings is to visit the *Weekly Mail & Guardian*'s home page:

www.mg.co.za/mg/

Arthur Goldstuck is a collector of South African urban legends (his books include *The Leopard in the Luggage*) and is a connoisseur of the Net, with a Web site at

www.web.co.za/arthur/longlist.htm

For an interesting list of South African organisations (including detailed news from the ANC), go to

http://minotaur.marques.co.za/saorg.htm

DOING BUSINESS

South Africa has a free-enterprise economy which is recovering from the distortions imposed on it by apartheid governments. The ANC government is privatising many of the huge state-owned monopolies and the very cosy relationship between these and favoured contractors is disappearing.

The tax system won't be unfamiliar to businesspeople from developed countries, nor will commercial practice. Labour unions are well-organised in some industries. South Africans complain loudly about the unions – until recently strikes in South Africa were seen as a weapon in a revolution – but they are probably less disruptive than in many other countries.

The Reconstruction & Development Programme (RDP) is the government's major tool in opening up the economy to people previously shut out. Small (and tiny) businesses owned by 'the disadvantaged sector' (non-whites) are the main beneficiaries.

At the small-business end, this is pretty much a 'me too' economy. Good ideas, such as franchised pubs, are seized upon and quickly done to death. There is room for new ideas but there are pitfalls for outsiders. The white community (which still controls most business) is so small that it's easy for foreigners to network but hard for them to become established.

Until recently there were two units of currency, the tightly controlled Financial Rand and the Commercial Rand, which were used internationally and domestically, respectively. The Financial Rand has been abolished but there are still currency controls on international transactions. It is expected that these will ease as the economy improves.

Price Waterhouse (☎ (021) 410 5800; fax 418 1337), 11th floor, Metlife Centre, 7 Coen Stydler Ave, produces a useful small book, *Doing Business in South Africa*, although the rapid changes taking place sometimes leave it behind. Other business contacts include:

Cape Chamber of Commerce & Industry
  (☎ (021) 418 4300; fax 418 1800)
Development Bank of South Africa
  (☎ (011) 313 3911; fax 313 3086)
Institute of Administration & Commerce
  (☎ (021) 461 7340; fax 45 3581)
South African Franchise Association
  (☎ (021) 913 1822; fax 913 1864)

BOOKS

Most books are published in different editions by different publishers in different countries. As a result, a book might be a hardcover rarity in one country while it's readily available in paperback in another. Fortunately, bookshops and libraries search by title, author or subject, so your local bookshop or library is best placed to advise you on the availability of the following recommendations.

Although there are surprisingly few books devoted entirely to Cape Town, there are many excellent writers who can help unlock something of South Africa's soul. Not least among them is Nadine Gordimer, who won the 1991 Nobel Prize for literature. The South African publishing industry churns out high-quality coffee table books.

Lonely Planet
If you want to venture further into Africa, check out Lonely Planet's *South Africa, Lesotho & Swaziland*, *Africa – the South* or *Zimbabwe, Botswana & Namibia*. *Africa on a shoestring* covers the whole continent. The *South Africa, Lesotho & Swaziland travel atlas* is a handy addition to your glove-box.

Guidebooks
This book will be sufficient for most visitors, but if you want even more, Satour produces two guides to accommodation in South Africa and the Portfolio organisation has brochures detailing some excellent accommodation. See the Places to Stay chapter for more information on these.

Special Interest
These are some of the better specialist guides to the Cape area:

Animals *Field Guide to the Mammals of Southern Africa* (paper, R101) by Chris and Tilde Stuart has a great deal of information and many excellent photos. *Whale Watching in South Africa* (paper, R17) by Peter Best contains handy information about the leviathans you have a good chance of seeing.

Birds *Newman's Birds of Southern Africa* (paper, R94; hard, R117) by Kenneth Newman is an excellent, comprehensive field guide with full-colour illustrations.

Ian Sinclair's pocket-sized *Southern African Birds* (paper, about R50) is another excellent guide with full-colour photos, and is particularly suitable for short-term visitors as it doesn't cover obscure birds.

Flora *Southern African Trees* (paper, R54) by Piet van Wyk is a handy little guide full of information and photos. *Namaqualand in Flower* (paper, R60) by Sima Eliovson is a detailed book with excellent colour plates on Namaqualand's flora.

Reserves *Guide to Southern African Game & Nature Reserves* (paper, R70) by Chris & Tilde Stuart is a comprehensive guide to every game and nature reserve, with lots of maps and photos. It's very good, but much more than you'll need for a visit to Cape Town.

Stars Visitors from the northern hemisphere might want a celestial guidebook to help chart a course through unfamiliar constellations. Try the *Struik Pocket Guide to the Night Skies of South Africa* (paper, about R35).

Surfing *Surfing in South Africa* (paper, R30) by Mark Jury is one of the best surfing guides around, with good tips and maps. This book is out of print, but you might find a second-hand copy.

Walking *Western Cape Walks* (paper, R50) by David Bristow details 70 walks of varying length and standard. Many other small books also detail walks in the Cape Town area. Have a look at *Best Walks in the Cape Peninsula* by Mike Lundy (paper, R53).

Wine *John Platter's South African Wine Guide* (paper, about R50), updated annually, is incredibly detailed, covering all available wines, and includes information on visiting vineyards. It's highly recommended. More down-to-earth is *The South African Plonk Buyer's Guide* (paper, about R20) by David Briggs.

History & Politics

For a brief introduction, Kevin Shillington's *History of Southern Africa* (paper, about R60) is good, although it is intended as a school text. For a more partisan, but nonetheless accurate, view try *Foundations of the New South Africa* (paper, R35) by John Pampallis. Originally written as a textbook for exiled South African students in Tanzania, it presents South African history from the ANC's point of view.

A History of the African People of South Africa (paper, about R40) by Paul Maylam is a detailed and fascinating book.

The best introduction to white South African history is *The Mind of South Africa*

(paper, R40) by Allister Sparks. It's opinionated but readable and insightful – highly recommended. Allister Sparks' latest book, *Tomorrow is Another Country* (paper, R61), is the inside story of the CODESA negotiations. Also good is *The Afrikaners – Their Last Great Trek* (paper, R40) by Graham Leach. This book provides a detailed analysis of the Afrikaner people and their political development.

For a history of the ANC, read *South Africa Belongs to Us* (paper, R68) by Francis Meli.

If you're at all interested in the political process, buy *Election '94 South Africa* (paper, R40), edited by Andrew Reynolds, which gives a fascinating and detailed account of the parties and that election. *Reconciliation Through Truth* by Asmal, Asmal & Roberts (paper, R53) concerns the Truth Commission, which is perhaps the best hope for South Africa to overcome its deep wounds.

If you find that contemporary history is too omnipresent (it's exciting but draining to be in a country where many of the major historical figures are still active and some of the most important events are still taking place), sink into a bit of old history, such as *Rhodes – the Race for Africa* by Anthony Thomas (paper, R91) or *Jan Smuts: Memoirs of the Boer War*, edited by Spies & Nattras (hard, R90).

General

Culture *Indaba My Children* (paper, R68) is an interesting book of folk tales, history, legends, customs and beliefs, collected and told by Vusamazulu Credo Mutwa (an important *sangoma* – traditional healer). Mutwa has also written *Isilwana – the Animal* (paper, R61). *Religion in Africa* (paper, R122), published by the David M Kennedy Centre at Princeton University, is thick and scholarly, but it is one of the few books providing an overview of this subject.

Women & Art in South Africa by Marion Arnold (paper, R101) is interesting and *Resistance Art in South Africa* by Sue Williamson (paper, R97) tells the story of the apartheid years from the point of view of South African artists. This book is highly recommended.

Literature Nadine Gordimer was awarded the Nobel Prize for literature in 1991. Her first novel, *The Lying Days*, was published in 1953. In subsequent novels she has explored South Africa, its people and their interaction. *The Conservationist* was joint winner of the 1974 Booker Prize. Her more recent work explores the interracial dynamics of the country. Look for *July's People* and *A Sport of Nature*.

JM Coetzee is another contemporary writer who has received international acclaim; *The Life & Times of Michael K* won the 1983 Booker Prize, and is set partly in a chaotic Cape Town of the future – a future that didn't come to pass.

Being There (paper, R35), edited by Robin Malan, is a good introductory collection of short stories from southern African authors, including Doris Lessing and Nadine Gordimer.

The most famous exponent of the short story in South Africa is Herman Charles Bosman. He wrote mainly in the 1930s and 40s and is reminiscent of Australia's Henry Lawson. Bosman is an accessible writer and is widely popular for stories that blend humour and pathos, and capture the essence of rural South Africa. The most popular collection is *Makeking Road*, but several compilations are available.

Alan Paton was responsible for one of the most famous South African novels, *Cry the Beloved Country* (paper, R38), an epic that follows a black man's sufferings in a white, urban society. This was written in 1948. Paton returned to the theme of apartheid in *Ah, but Your Land is Beautiful*. André Brink is another noted South African author worth reading.

Olive Schreiner (1855-1920) wrote *The Story of an African Farm* (published 1883), which was immediately popular and established her enduring reputation as one of South Africa's seminal novelists. Although her novel was adopted as part of white South Africa's folk heritage, Olive Schreiner

herself was a feminist, an antiracist (to an extent) and held left-wing political views.

Literature by non-white authors is in short supply, but that will certainly change.

My favourite Bosman is the novella *Wilemsdorp*. It is set in a narrow-minded Transvaal town, but one which is seething with sex (seduction, adultery and illegal 'miscegenation'), murder and suicide. And dagga – it contains 'stoned and on the run' scenes unmatched until Hunter S Thomson. The ostensible theme is that a white man is brought dreadfully low by associating with a non-white woman and by smoking dagga (the drug of choice of the 'natives'), but you get the feeling that Bosman was much more ambivalent. On the other hand, most of Bosman's humorous short stories set in Jurie Steyn's post office in Drogevlei (a fictitious hamlet in the Zeerust area of Transvaal) contain gratuitous and extremely offensive jokes about the 'natives'.

Jon Murray

Personal Accounts Some books have such a powerful sense of place they become compulsory reading for foreign visitors. There can be no more obvious or important example than Nelson Mandela's autobiography, *Long Road to Freedom* (hard, R100; R500 for an autographed copy), despite the fact that the man was behind bars for 27 years.

If you want to read more of Mandela's words, look for the collections of his writings and speeches in *The Struggle is My Life* and *Nelson Mandela Speaks* (paper, about R50 each). They can be rather dry, but offer an insight into the steadfastness of this amazing man – and also how he focussed his message to suit the particular audience he addressed. Mandela might be a hero of the people, but he is also a consummate politician.

For a white perspective on the apartheid years read *My Traitor's Heart* (paper, R46) by Rian Malan. This is an outstanding autobiography of an Afrikaner attempting to come to grips with his heritage and his future. Breyten Breytenbach, a political prisoner and exile under the apartheid regime, writes of his return to South Africa in *Return to Paradise* (paper, R45). It's a very personal and rather poetic account.

NEWSPAPERS

There are two English-language broadsheets, the *Cape Times* (morning) and *The Argus* (afternoon). The *Cape Times* is marginally more serious, but both papers are relatively skimpy. For an insight into conservative white thinking, buy the tabloid *The Citizen*.

The Sowetan is the biggest-selling paper in the country, and although it is primarily concerned with Jo'burg issues, it does make interesting reading. Some of the vendors in the city centre sell it. Despite catering to a largely poorly educated audience, it has a much more sophisticated political and social outlook than the major white papers.

IMVO (roughly, My View) is published weekly in both English and Xhosa editions. It is concerned mainly with issues in Eastern Cape Province, but because of Cape Town's large Xhosa-speaking population you can sometimes find copies here. The paper was founded in 1884.

The best newspaper/magazine for investigative journalism, sensible overviews and high-quality columnists, not to mention a week's worth of Doonesbury and a good entertainment section, is *The Weekly Mail & Guardian*, published each Thursday. It also includes a shortened version of the British *Guardian*'s international edition, which itself includes features from *Le Monde* and the *Washington Post*.

TV & RADIO

The monolithic and conservative South African Broadcasting Corporation (SABC) used to be the government's mouthpiece and, though times have changed, you'll still find most of its fare rather timid. There are a few exceptions, such as the flamboyant Dali Tambo's innovative talk show *People of the South*. (Dali is son of ANC legend Oliver Tambo, and his impending marriage to a white woman is raising eyebrows across the country.)

Soap-opera fans are in for a treat, as US daytime soaps are shown during prime time, and Brits and Aussies hooked on *Home & Away* can catch some very early episodes.

Melrose Place dubbed into Afrikaans is very weird.

Most programmes are in English or Afrikaans but with 11 official languages to accommodate, that will change. Unfortunately, subtitling is rare.

As well as the SABC there is also the pay channel M-Net, which shows some good movies. A few experimental community TV licences have been granted, although the stations aren't really on their feet yet.

Most radio stations are FM, which means a lot of dial-switching as you drive around the hilly Cape Peninsula.

Most SABC radio stations play dreary music interspersed with drearier chat about recipes and the like. Stations geared to black audiences often play good music. Radio Lotus caters to South Africans of Indian descent and plays Indian film music. Cigarette ads are still aired and some gems sound as if they were made in the 1950s. Some non-SABC radio licences have been granted but standards haven't risen much. The popular Jo'burg talk station, 702, is about to start a similar station in Cape Town. If it's anything like the original it will be worth listening to for insights into middle-of-the-road white attitudes.

PHOTOGRAPHY & VIDEO
Photography

Cape Town and the Winelands are very photogenic. Remember the harsh midday sun will wash out colours. Morning and evening are the best times to take photos. Keep your film cool and have it processed promptly.

One-hour photolabs offering print-film processing and printing are scattered throughout Cape Town. Prices vary from one outlet to another, but processing a 24-exposure film typically costs about R40 and processing and printing is another R45. Prolab (Map 8), 177 Bree St (on the corner of Pepper St), does excellent slide processing and mounting in two hours for less than R35 for 36 slides.

Camera Care (Map 8), on Castle (Kasteel) St between Burg St and St George's Mall, repairs cameras.

Video

Properly used, a video camera can give a fascinating record of your holiday. As well as videoing the obvious things – sunsets, spectacular views – remember to record some of the ordinary everyday details of life in the country. Often the most interesting things occur when you're actually intent on filming something else. Remember too that, unlike still photography, video 'flows' – so, for example, you can shoot scenes of countryside rolling past the train window, to give an overall impression that isn't possible with ordinary photos.

Video cameras these days have amazingly sensitive microphones, and you might be surprised how much sound will be picked up. This can also be a problem if there is a lot of ambient noise – filming by the side of a busy road might seem OK when you do it, but viewing it back home might simply give you a deafening cacophony of traffic noise. One good rule to follow for beginners is to try to film in long takes, and don't move the camera around too much. Otherwise, your video could well make your viewers seasick! If your camera has a stabiliser, you can use it to obtain good footage while travelling on various means of transport, even on bumpy roads. And remember, you're on holiday – don't let the video take over your life and turn your trip into a Cecil B de Mille production.

Remember to follow the same rules regarding people's sensitivities as for still photography – having a video camera shoved in their face is probably even more annoying and offensive for locals than a still camera is. Always ask permission first.

TIME

South African Standard Time is two hours ahead of GMT (at noon in London it's 2 pm in Cape Town), seven hours ahead of USA Eastern Standard Time (at noon in New York it's 7 pm in Cape Town) and eight hours behind Australian Eastern Standard Time (at noon in Sydney it's 4 am in Cape Town). There is no daylight saving.

ELECTRICITY

The electricity system is 220/230 volts AC at 50 cycles per second. Appliances rated at 240 volts AC will work. Plugs have three round pins. Although hardware stores and some travel agencies sell adaptors, most are designed for South Africans going overseas, not for visitors.

You'll probably be able to find an adaptor for UK plugs, but for others you will have to search hard. As a last resort, have a South African plug wired onto your lead. I found a South African lead that fitted my computer's charger at Audio Sound (Map 8), on Longmarket St, between Long and Loop Sts. Staff there are helpful and knowledgeable.

LAUNDRY

There are laundrettes scattered throughout the suburbs, although if you're staying in any sort of budget accommodation there will probably be a laundry on the premises.

Rather than sitting in a laundrette feeding a machine coins, it's simpler to do a bag wash for about R20 (you drop off your washing and staff do the loading and unloading). Nannucci Dry Cleaners does same-day laundry and has branches everywhere, including Shop 35, ground floor, Golden Acre Centre; Unity House, Long St; 57 Main Rd, Green Point; 152A Main Rd, Sea Point; and 67 Station Rd, Observatory.

WEIGHTS & MEASURES

South Africa uses the metric system. See the Metric Conversion table on the inside back cover for more.

HEALTH

Unless you venture into areas of the country where malaria and bilharzia occur (see later in this section), you can assume that health problems are the same as in any first world country.

You should ensure that your tetanus, diptheria and polio vaccinations are up to date. Particularly if you are travelling to remote villages, you should consider vaccinations against typhoid and hepatitis A, which are food-borne diseases.

People who have travelled through the yellow fever zone in Africa (or South America) must have an International Certificate of Vaccination against yellow fever before entering South Africa.

South Africa is probably not as badly affected by HIV/AIDS as some areas of Africa and a belated public awareness campaign has begun. However, AIDS is certainly present and widespread in the heterosexual community.

Malaria is mainly confined to the eastern half of South Africa, especially on the low veld, ie far from the area covered in this book. Bilharzia is also found mainly in the east but outbreaks do occur in other places, so you should always check with knowledgeable local people before drinking water or swimming in it.

When hiking, don't drink untreated water from streams unless someone reliable tells you that it is safe.

A hazard of the mountains is ticks, which might hitch a ride when you brush past bushes. A strong insect repellent can help, and serious hikers should consider having their boots and trousers impregnated with benzyl benzoate and dibutylphthalate.

You should always check all over your body if you have been walking through a potentially tick-infested area as ticks can cause skin infections and other more serious diseases, including typhus. You should seek medical advice if you think you may have any of these diseases.

If a tick is found attached, press down around the tick's head with tweezers, grab the head and gently pull upwards. Avoid pulling the rear of the body as this may squeeze the tick's gut contents through the attached mouth parts into the skin, increasing the risk of infection and disease. Clean and apply pressure if the point of attachment is bleeding. Smearing chemicals on the tick will not make it let go and is not recommended.

There are also some poisonous snakes in the area, although they are rarely aggressive and will generally get out of your way if they sense you coming. But to minimise your chances of being bitten, wear boots, socks and long trousers when walking through undergrowth where snakes may be present. Don't put your hands into holes and crevices, and be careful when collecting firewood. See the Surviving a Snake Bite boxed text in this section.

Travel with Children by Maureen Wheeler is a Lonely Planet guide which includes advice on travel health for young children.

Surviving a Snake Bite
Snake bites do not cause instantaneous death and antivenins are usually available. Keep the victim as calm and still as possible to prevent dissemination of the venom via the lymphatics. Wrap the bitten limb very tightly, as you would for a sprained ankle, and attach a splint to immobilise it. Then seek medical help.

If the snake is definitely *dead* take it along for identification. Do *not* attempt to catch the snake if there is even a remote chance of being bitten. ■

Medical Services
Medical services are of a high standard in Cape Town. Many doctors will make house calls. Doctors are listed under 'medical' in the phone book, and they will generally be able to arrange for hospitalisation.

In an emergency you can go direct to the casualty department of Groote Schuur Hospital (Map 6) (☎ 404 9111), the same hospital where in 1967 Christiaan Barnard made the first 'successful' heart transplant. It's at the intersection of De Waal (M3) and the Eastern Boulevard (N2), to the east of the city. Ring the police (☎ 10111) to get directions to the nearest hospital.

The Glengariff Pharmacy (Map 3), Main Rd, Sea Point, is open until 11 pm daily. There's another pharmacy open until 11 pm daily, in the city centre on Darling St between Plein and Parliament Sts.

For vaccinations, the British Airways Travel Clinic (Map 8) (☎ 419 3172; fax 419

3389), is at Room 1027 in the Medical Centre, Adderley St.

Medical Kit
Pharmacies in Cape Town stock all the items you will need, but it isn't a bad idea to carry a basic medical kit. Consider taking:

Aspirin or **paracetamol** (acetaminophen in the US) – for pain or fever.

Antihistamine (such as Benadryl) – useful as a decongestant for colds and allergies, to ease the itch from insect bites or stings, and to help prevent motion sickness. Antihistamines may cause sedation and interact with alcohol so care should be taken when using them; take one you know and have used before, if possible.

Loperamide (eg Imodium) or Lomotil for diarrhoea; prochlorperazine (eg Stemetil) or metaclopramide (eg Maxalon) for nausea and vomiting.

Rehydration mixture – for treatment of severe diarrhoea; particularly important for travelling with children.

Antiseptic such as povidone-iodine (eg Betadine) – for cuts and grazes.

Calamine lotion or **aluminium sulphate spray** (eg Stingose) – to ease irritation from bites or stings.

Bandages and **Band-Aids**.

Scissors, tweezers and a **thermometer** (note that mercury thermometers are strictly prohibited by airlines).

Cold and flu tablets and throat lozenges. Pseudoephedrine hydrochloride (Sudafed) may be useful if flying with a cold to avoid ear damage.

Insect repellent, sunscreen, chap stick and, if you're planning a remote-area hike, **water purification tablets.**

Women's Health
Gynaecological Problems Sexually transmitted diseases are a major cause of vaginal problems. Symptoms include a smelly discharge, painful intercourse and sometimes a burning sensation when urinating. Male sexual partners must also be treated. Medical attention should be sought and remember in addition to these diseases HIV or hepatitis B may also be acquired during exposure. Besides abstinence, the best thing is to practise safe sex using condoms.

Antibiotic use, synthetic underwear, sweating and contraceptive pills can lead to fungal vaginal infections when travelling in hot climates. Maintaining good personal hygiene, and wearing loose-fitting clothes and cotton underwear will help to prevent these infections.

Fungal infections, characterised by a rash, itch and discharge, can be treated with a vinegar or lemon-juice douche, or with yoghurt. Nystatin, miconazole or clotrimazole pessaries or vaginal cream are the usual treatment.

Pregnancy It is not advisable to travel to some places while pregnant as some vaccinations

FACTS FOR THE VISITOR

normally used to prevent serious diseases are not advisable in pregnancy, eg yellow fever. In addition, some diseases are much more serious for the mother (and may increase the risk of a stillborn child) in pregnancy, eg malaria.

Most miscarriages occur during the first three months of pregnancy. Miscarriage is not uncommon, and can occasionally lead to severe bleeding. The last three months should also be spent within reasonable distance of good medical care. A baby born as early as 24 weeks stands a chance of survival, but only in a good modern hospital. Pregnant women should avoid all unnecessary medication, vaccinations and malarial prophylactics should still be taken where needed. Additional care should be taken to prevent illness and particular attention should be paid to diet and nutrition. Alcohol and nicotine, for example, should be avoided.

TOILETS

Toilets are standard western style (although the flush will be unfamiliar to North Americans). There aren't many public toilets but there are plenty of hotels and restaurants which will let you use their facilities. The main long-distance bus lines have on-board toilets.

WOMEN TRAVELLERS

If you want to find out what life for women was like in western countries in the 1950s, talk to well-off white women in South Africa. Women who do anything technical or physical (including sport) are invariably referred to as 'guys', serious newspapers have 'pretty miss' photos and you'll be expected to take an interest in beauty contests. Until recently, modelling was one of the few prestigious careers open to most white South African women.

The situation in cosmopolitan Cape Town is not as extreme, but you'll encounter plenty of paternalism. The statistics for sexual assault in South Africa are horrendous, but Cape Town is safer than other cities. Many

women travel alone safely in southern Africa.

It's essential to exercise common sense and caution, particularly at night. The risk varies depending on where you go and what you do. Hitching alone is extremely foolhardy, for instance. Particularly in the current environment of rapid change, the best advice on what can and can't be undertaken safely will come from local women. Unfortunately, many white women are likely to be appalled at the idea of travelling on your own and will do their best to discourage you with horrendous stories, often of dubious accuracy.

The risks, however, are significantly reduced if two women travel together or, even better, if a woman travels as part of a mixed-sex couple or group. Note that however you travel, especially inland, it's best to behave conservatively.

Women in traditional black cultures often have a very tough time, but to a certain extent this is changing because a surprising number of girls are staying at school, while the boys are sent away to work. It always seems to be women who get reforms underway in the townships. Women played a vital role in ending minority rule.

As a result of affirmative action programmes, educated black women can be found staffing government office counters. Their outlook on life may more closely align with yours (whatever the colour of your skin) than with that of the manicured white staff.

GAY & LESBIAN TRAVELLERS

The gay and lesbian scene is small but healthy, with a few clubs, bars and cafés catering to gays, or at least describing themselves as gay-friendly. For details, see under Gay Scene in the Entertainment chapter later in this book. Gay esCape, an excellent travel agency, has information on good places to stay and gay-friendly tours etc. See the Travel Agents section of the Getting There & Away chapter.

Although the new South African constitution guarantees freedom of choice regarding sexuality (it's the world's first constitution to do so), redneck attitudes persist. And, amazingly, some anti-gay laws are still on the books, despite the fact that they are now unconstitutional. It's highly unlikely that the laws will be enforced and even less likely that they would be enforced against foreign visitors.

DISABLED TRAVELLERS
Cape Town is not especially well equipped to help disabled travellers, but nor is it especially large or fast, so most problems can be overcome. There are no wheelchair-friendly public transport vehicles and few ramps, but you can pre-arrange a wheelchair ramp and assistance at some train stations.

SENIOR TRAVELLERS
Much of the tourist infrastructure (which has been, until recently, geared to domestic tourism) caters to older visitors. Comfort and convenience are high priorities.

Nonetheless, you won't find seniors' discounts, special tours or other 'grey power' goodies. There's a marked divide in South Africa between wealthy seniors, who have servants to help them get around, and poor seniors, who can't afford to travel.

Still, there is some good news – despite the fact that South Africa does badly in international surveys of service levels, you'll find more personalised service here than in many other countries. If you stay in some of the more upmarket guesthouses the service is very good indeed, and even the less expensive hotels tend to have porters.

CAPE TOWN FOR CHILDREN
There aren't very many children's attractions in Cape Town, but South Africans (of all colours) are family oriented, so most places cope easily with kids' needs. 'Family' restaurants, such as the Spur chain, offer children's portions, as do some of the more upmarket places.

Many of the sights and attractions of interest to parents will also entertain kids. The Table Mountain cableway, the attractions at the Waterfront (especially the seals, one of which can usually be seen at Bertie's Landing) and Cape Point with its baboons will delight kids. Dragging children around museums might cause some strain, although the South African Museum has plenty to offer younger visitors.

Many of the surf beaches will be too rough for children (and even adults at times), but there are some quiet rock pools as well as some family beaches. The Things to See & Do chapter later in this book has information on many beaches in Cape Town.

There are few services such as nappie changing facilities in large stores (many don't even have public toilets), and short-term daycare is almost unheard of – kids whose parents can afford that sort of thing tend to have nannies.

However, your hotel should be able to arrange a baby-sitter, or you can contact an outfit such as Supersitters (☎ 439 4985).

For tips on having happy children (and parents) on the road, check out Lonely Planet's *Travel with Children* by Maureen Wheeler.

USEFUL ORGANISATIONS
In addition to a desk at the Tourist Rendezvous, the National Parks Board (Map 8) has offices in a restored Victorian building on the corner of Long and Hout Sts, open weekdays from 9 am to 4 pm. If you're heading to any of the national parks and want to be sure of accommodation, you must book. Outside of school holidays it's not necessary to book camp sites. For bookings and inquiries phone (☎ 22 2810; fax 24 6211) or write (PO Box 7400, Roggebaai 8012).

For information on the extensive and excellent provincial parks contact Cape Nature Conservation (Map 8) (☎ 483 4051), 1 Dorp St (not far from the corner of Long St).

The Mountain Club (☎ 45 3412), 97 Hatfield St, has useful information for climbers.

EMERGENCIES
In case of emergency contact the following:

Ambulance	☎ 10177
Police	☎ 10111
Tourist Police	☎ 418 2852

Fire Brigade	☎ 461 4141
Automobile Association (AA)	☎ 21 1550
Lifeline	☎ 461 1111
Rape Crisis Centre	☎ 47 9762

DANGERS & ANNOYANCES
Crime

Cape Town is perhaps the most relaxed city in Africa, which can instil a false sense of security. People who have travelled overland from Cairo without a single mishap have been known to be cleaned out in Cape Town – generally doing something stupid like leaving their gear on a beach while they go swimming.

Paranoia is not required – but common sense is. There is tremendous poverty on the peninsula and informal redistribution of wealth is reasonably common. The townships on the Cape Flats have an appalling crime rate and unless you have a trustworthy guide they are off-limits. If violence on the flats gets out of control even the N2 can become unsafe – it's probably best not to drive on the N2 late at night when traffic is sparse.

The rest of Cape Town is reasonably safe. Care should be taken in Sea Point and the city centre late at night, and walking to/from

---

Life on the Streets

Young black kids living on the streets are blamed for a lot of crime, and they do commit petty thefts. You'd have to suspect, though, that whites' annoyance with the kids stems from the fact that they are visible and sometimes cheeky.

The response to street kids has been typically inappropriate. 'Cleaning-up' the city centre has seen businesses club together to employ security guards with guard dogs to harass the kids.

Most of the kids, who are obviously sleeping rough, are boys. There are also many girls, but they usually eschew the standard street kid uniform of ragged clothes and a jumper with dangling sleeves – or they disguise themselves as boys. Many girls quickly become caught up in prostitution. ■

---

the Waterfront once it starts to get dark is not recommended. As always, listen to local advice, and remember that there is safety in numbers.

There's a police Tourism Assistance Unit on the corner of Riebeeck St and Tulbagh Square, although the police booth on the lower end of St George's Mall is more central. The main city centre police station is on Buitenkant St between Albertus and Barrack Sts. There are always police at the main train station and at the Waterfront.

Natural Hazards

All the Cape beaches are potentially hazardous, especially for people inexperienced in surf. Check for signs warning of rips and rocks, and unless you really know what you're doing, only swim in patrolled areas.

The mountains in the middle of the city are no less dangerous just because they're in the middle of the city. Occasionally there are deaths. Weather conditions can change rapidly, so warm clothing, a good map and a compass are always necessary.

LEGAL MATTERS

South Africa's legal system is a blend of the Dutch-Roman and British systems. The British influence seen most strongly in criminal justice procedures. Cases are tried by magistrates (*landdrost*) or judges without juries, at the instigation of police 'dockets' or private actions. Clients are represented by solicitors (*prokureurs* in Afrikaans) and advocates (*advokates* – the equivalent of barristers).

Under apartheid, South Africa was a police state. A police force that had virtually unlimited power and existed to serve the interests of a small minority while brutally suppressing the majority is not likely to have picked up many skills in policing in a free society. And that's painfully obvious. Not surprisingly, private security firms are in high demand and many people own firearms and attack dogs.

The police force is far too busy sorting out its own problems to prosecute petty breaches of the law. This might sound like a pleasant state of affairs, but after you've encountered a few speeding drunk drivers or some brawling up-country farmers on a spree, strict cops seem attractive. If your skin colour isn't white you might receive less than courteous treatment if, say, you're pulled over for a traffic violation, but a foreign passport should fix things quickly.

BUSINESS HOURS
Banking hours vary, but are usually from 9 am to 3.30 pm on weekdays. Many branches also open from 8.30 to 11 am on Saturday. Post offices usually open from 8 am to 4.30 pm on weekdays and until noon on Saturday. Both banks and post offices close for lunch in small towns.

Most shops are open between 8.30 am and 5 pm on weekdays, and on Saturday morning. Many pubs and bars stay open way past midnight and there are a few that stay open 24 hours.

PUBLIC HOLIDAYS & SPECIAL EVENTS
Public holidays underwent a shake-up after the 1994 elections. For example, the Day of the Vow, which marked the massacre of Zulus, has become the Day of Reconciliation. The officially ignored but widely observed Soweto Day, marking the student uprisings which eventually led to liberation, is now celebrated and officially acknowledged as Youth Day. Public holidays and approximate dates are:

New Year's Day
    1 January
Human Rights Day
    21 March
Good Friday
    (varies)
Family Day
    17 April
Constitution Day
    27 April
Workers' Day
    1 May
Youth Day
    16 June
Women's Day
    9 August
Heritage Day
    24 September

Cape Minstrel Carnival
The Cape Minstrel Carnival was called, until a year or so back, the Coon Carnival. The Coon Carnival was a long-standing festival involving the coloured community, celebrated around the New Year. *Coon* Carnival? Yes, but the name derives from a side alley of racism, not the apartheid highway. It seems that the coloured community was impressed by a touring black-and-white minstrel show and decided to emulate it. Traditionally, the Coon Carnival allowed some licence, and revellers would grab passers-by and black their faces with boot polish. During the apartheid era, the carnival was moved to a stadium, away from the streets, so that this sort of thing couldn't happen. ■

Day of Reconciliation
    16 December
Christmas Day
    25 December
Day of Goodwill
    26 December

The Cape Festival, which used to be held annually early in March, featured a range of music, from classical to jazz and everything in between. However, it's uncertain whether the festival will continue.

Perhaps the biggest party in town is held by the Cape Town Queer Project in mid-December, usually at the River Club (see the Entertainment chapter). It has a different theme each year and outrageous fancy dress is compulsory. Straights are welcome.

A food and wine festival is held in Stellenbosch in October; Calvinia has a Meat Festival in August; and Hermanus holds a Whale Festival in late September or early October.

School Holidays
It's useful to know school-holiday dates, as accommodation at reserves and resorts – especially beach resorts in summer – is at a premium during these times. Cape Town also experiences a big influx of domestic tourists in the summer school holidays.

The dates differ slightly from year to year and between provinces, but the times are roughly mid-April (two weeks), late June to mid-July (three weeks), late September to early October (about one week) and early December to early February (about eight weeks). Peak time occurs from just before Christmas to mid-January. Contact Satour for the exact dates.

WORK

High unemployment and fears of illegal immigration from the rest of Africa mean that employers taking on foreigners without work permits face tough penalties. Work permits are hard to get, and it's extremely unlikely anyone after a holiday job will get one.

So far this doesn't seem to have stopped foreigners getting jobs in restaurants or bars (where their services are valued, especially Australians) but this might change. Don't expect generous pay – about R5 to R10 per hour plus tips is usual. You might even be offered work for no wages at all, just tips. The best time to look for work is between October and November, before the summer season starts and before university students begin holidays.

Hostels might know of some fruit-picking work, especially in the Citrusdal, Ceres and Piketberg areas. The pay is negligible but accommodation is free.

If you have formal childcare and first-aid qualifications, Supersitters (☎ 439 4985) might be able to find you baby-sitting work. In this conservative society there might not be much demand for male sitters.

Getting There & Away

AIR

Cape Town has an increasingly busy international airport, and if you have the choice, arriving here is much nicer than arriving in Johannesburg.

A number of international airlines (including some that don't fly here yet) have offices and representatives in Cape Town. See the Cape Town Yellow Pages for the complete list.

> **Departure Tax**
> There's an airport departure tax of R18 for domestic flights, R39 to regional African countries and R60 for other international flights. The tax is usually included in the ticket price. ■

Airline Offices

Addresses of some international airlines, all located in the city centre (Map 8) are:

Air France
    Golden Acre Centre (☎ (021) 214760; fax 21 7061)
Air India
    20th floor, Trustbank Centre (☎ (021) 418 3558)
Air Mauritius
    11th floor, Strand Towers, 66 Strand St (☎ (021) 21 6294; fax 21 7321)
British Airways
    12th floor, BP Centre, Thibault Square (☎ (021) 25 2970)
KLM – Royal Dutch Airlines
    Main Tower, Standard Bank Centre (☎ (021) 21 1870)
Lufthansa
    Southern Life Centre, 8 Riebeeck St (☎ (021) 25 1490)
Malaysia Airlines
    Safmarine House, 22 Riebeeck St (☎ (021) 419 8010)
Namib Air
    Standard Bank Centre (☎ (021) 21 6685)
Qantas
    BP Centre (☎ (021) 25 2978)
SAA
    Southern Life Centre, 8 Riebeeck St (☎ (021) 403 1111)
Singapore Airlines
    14 Long St (☎ (021) 419 0495)
Swissair
    Southern Life Centre, 8 Riebeeck St (☎ (021) 21 4938)
Varig
    (☎ (021) 21 1850)

Domestic Flights

South African Airways (SAA) is a domestic as well as an international carrier. There are plenty of daily flights to most destinations. Fares aren't cheap but there are special deals on advance purchase tickets. Talk to your travel agent before you leave home. Once you're in South Africa there are a few discount options. Most SAA flights have a limited number of 15% discount seats, sold on a first-come, first-served basis. If you book and pay 10 days in advance there's a 30% discount, and one month in advance earns you 50% off (Apex fare). There are also big discounts on late-night flights (ask for 'slumber fares').

The free baggage allowance is 40/30/20kg in 1st/business/economy class. Excess baggage is charged at R11 per kg.

SAA flights can be booked at travel agents or by phoning ☎ (021) 403 1111. SAA flies between Cape Town and major centres, including Durban (R787), East London (R684), Jo'burg (R787), Kimberley (R661), Port Elizabeth (R513) and Upington (R627).

SA Airlink competes with SAA on a few major domestic routes and also has flights to smaller places not served by SAA. Make bookings at travel agents or phone toll free on ☎ 0800 114 799. Another smaller airline flying the main routes is SA Express (☎ (011) 978 5569). Comair (☎ 080 961 1196 toll free) is a reliable airline (associated with British Airways) with a reasonably large fleet and frequent flights.

There are also several regional airlines, such as National Airlines (☎ (021) 934 0350/1) which flies between Cape Town, Springbok, Kleinzee and Alexander Bay;

and Sun Air (☎ (011) 397 2244), which flies between Pilanesberg (Sun City) and Cape Town, Durban and Jo'burg.

Africa

Most regional African airlines now fly to/from South Africa, although most fly to/from Jo'burg rather than Cape Town. For example, Air Afrique flies to various West African countries, Air Gabon flies to Libreville (Gabon), with connections to West Africa and Europe, and Uganda Airlines flies to Harare (Zimbabwe) and Uganda. There are plenty of other regional airlines and SAA also has inter-Africa flights. Some European airlines stop in various African countries en route to South Africa.

As with other inter-African flights, the connections with South Africa's closest neighbours are also mainly via Jo'burg. The exception is Air Namibia, which has a flight between Cape Town and Windhoek for about R950.

Asia

Air India, Cathay Pacific, Malaysia Airlines, Singapore Airlines, Thai Airways and other Asian airlines now fly to South Africa – most to Jo'burg.

From South Africa, a cheap one-way fare to India costs from R1600 (Jo'burg to Mumbai). Air India has a twice-weekly service between Mumbai (Bombay) and Jo'burg and Durban. A cheap fare from Jo'burg to Kuala Lumpur (Malaysia) costs about R2250.

Australia

The return flight between Australia and Jo'burg is expensive, at around A$2278 for a standard mid-season economy fare. You should be able to find a discounted fare for around A$1800. Air Mauritius has a few direct flights from Perth to Mauritius with a stopover, then a direct flight to Jo'burg. It has other flights to South Africa via Mauritius originating in Singapore, Hong Kong and Mumbai.

Malaysia Airlines often has the cheapest flights from Sydney or Melbourne to Jo'burg and Cape Town. The hassle is that you fly via Kuala Lumpur, a long way out of the way. There are more-or-less direct connections but you might want to take advantage of their stopover deals in Malaysia.

The other alternative is to check out round the world (RTW) deals or a return ticket to Europe via southern Africa.

From South Africa, the South African Students' Travel Service (SASTS) has one way cheapies to Sydney from as low as R2500. The cheapest flight of all is from Jo'burg to Perth, from R2200.

Europe

Most of the major European airlines fly to Jo'burg, with many flights continuing on to Cape Town. An increasing number fly to Cape Town direct, including British Airways and Virgin Atlantic. There are also some charter flights.

Fares from the UK are quite competitive. It's worth shopping around, but you might be able to get a return flight for less than UK£500.

Although it is a long-haul flight, the journey from the UK is quite easy to handle (nothing like flying from the UK to Asia or Australia). The flight takes about 13½ hours, but as it is overnight and because South Africa is only two hours ahead of GMT, you won't arrive with your body clock too out of whack.

Some tickets include other African ports such as Cairo (Egypt), Nairobi (Kenya) and Harare (Zimbabwe). If you have plenty of time, you may find good-value RTW tickets that include Jo'burg. Return tickets to Australia via Jo'burg are also worth looking at.

For a cheap one way fare from South Africa to the UK, talk to SASTS (you don't need to be a student). It'll probably put you on a flight to New York, from where you catch another cheapie to Heathrow. Could be an interesting option and you might find a ticket for about R1900.

North America

SAA flies to/from New York and Miami, and by now there should be direct flights to/from

Washington DC. You should be able to find one-way/return fares from New York for US$1335/1750, and from Los Angeles for US$1926/2149. If you're coming from the west coast of the USA, it is worth looking at flights via Asia (eg Hong Kong or Singapore). It is also worth exploring the possibility of flying to London and buying a ticket from a bucket shop.

SASTS one-way fares from Cape Town include Vancouver, R3300; Toronto, R2700; and Los Angeles, R3300.

South America

SAA and Varig link Jo'burg and Cape Town with Rio de Janeiro and São Paulo. Currently, Malaysia Airlines offers good deals on flights to Buenos Aires. SASTS might find you a one-way ticket from Jo'burg or Cape Town to Buenos Aires for about R1800.

BUS
Domestic Lines

All long-distance buses leave from the main Cape Town train station. There's a left luggage facility next to platform 24, open weekdays from 6 am to 5.45 pm, and on weekends to 2.30 pm. The main bus lines operating out of Cape Town are:

Translux (☎ (021) 405 3333; fax 405 2545)
  The national bus line running many major routes at major prices. The Translux office is on the Adderley St side of the main train station block and is open from 7.30 am to 6 pm Monday to Saturday and from 11.30 am to 5 pm on Sunday. Phone bookings are taken from 8 am to 5 pm on weekdays and to noon on Saturday.
Greyhound (☎ (021) 418 4312; fax 418 4315)
  The other national line runs fewer routes from Cape Town, at prices generally a little higher than Translux.
Intercape Mainliner (☎ (021) 386 4400; 24 hours)
  Intercape has some extremely useful services, including along the west and south coasts; a little cheaper than the other major companies.

Two other useful bus lines are Chilwans Bus Services (☎ (021) 54 2506 or 905 3910) and Namakwaland Busdiens (☎ (021) 25 4245). Chilwans runs a basic bus east from Cape

Town to Port Elizabeth, via some of the beachside towns along the Garden Route; Namakwaland Busdiens runs north to Springbok.

Transtate and City to City are poor relations of Translux whose futures are in doubt. Neither runs many services in Western Cape.

Domestic Routes

Major destinations from Cape Town include:

Johannesburg
  Translux, Greyhound and Intercape run to Jo'burg at least daily for about R320, via either Bloemfontein or Kimberley (about 17 hours). Intercape also runs to Jo'burg via Upington, for R280. You might have to change buses in Upington but it is usually a direct connection; if so Cape Town to Jo'burg takes about 19 hours.
Garden Route
  Translux runs at least daily to Port Elizabeth (11 hours, R125) via Swellendam (R65), Mossel Bay (R85), Oudtshoorn (R100 – not all services stop here), George (R100), Knysna (R105), Plettenberg Bay (R110) and Storms River (R125).
  Intercape runs the Garden Route twice daily at slightly lower fares. Even cheaper is the weekly Chilwans Intercity (☎ (021) 934 4786) bus to Port Elizabeth (R100). It departs from the upper deck of the main train station on Friday and returns on Sunday.
  If you plan to visit several Garden Route towns, check out the options on the Garden Route Hopper (☎ (041) 55 4000) and the Baz Bus (☎ (021) 439 2323) – most hostels take bookings.
The Mountain Route
  Like the Garden Route, the Mountain Route takes you east from Cape Town, but inland for the first half of the trip. If you can find a daylight service, this route is more scenic than the Garden Route. Translux runs to Port Elizabeth (R140) three times a week via Robertson (R115), Montagu (R100) and Oudtshoorn (R100).
  Munnik Coaches (☎ (021) 637 1850) departs from the upper deck at the main train station and runs to Montagu thrice weekly for R35.
Eastern Cape
  City to City (a Translux subsidiary) runs daily from Cape Town to Umtata (19 hours, R115) via Worcester, Beaufort West and Graaff-Reinet. It's a useful route (although slow), but unfortunately much of the journey is at night. Transtate (a poor cousin of City to City) runs to Umtata once a week, along much the same route as City to City. It's a slower but cheaper trip.

Durban
Translux services to Port Elizabeth connect with a service to Durban via East London and Umtata. The total trip takes about 24 hours and costs over R300 – consider finding a discount air ticket. A slightly faster Translux service runs to Durban via Bloemfontein.

West Coast
Intercape runs to Upington (R150) via Citrusdal (R80) and Clanwilliam (R90). City to City (book through Translux) runs to Upington for R240.

Neighbouring Countries
From Upington you can get an Intercape bus to Windhoek (Namibia) for R200. Intercape also has a direct service between Cape Town and Windhoek (R325), running via Springbok (R170). With the exception of Intercape's Namibia service, no buses run direct to neighbouring countries. Jo'burg is the hub for bus travel in the region.

MINIBUS TAXI

Long-distance minibus taxis cover most of the country with an informal network of routes. Although they have traditionally been used by blacks only, an increasing number of non-blacks (mainly foreign backpackers) are now using them because they are a cheap and efficient way of getting around. The driving can occasionally be hair-raising, but it is mostly OK, especially compared with similar transport in other African countries.

As their clientele is largely black, minibus taxis will often travel via townships and will usually depart very early in the morning or in the early evening to cater to commuting workers and shoppers.

In Cape Town, most long-distance minibus taxis start picking up passengers in a distant township, especially Langa and Nyanga (Map 1), and will go to the main train station if they need more people, so your choices can be limited. Some townships aren't off-limits to outsiders, but they aren't great places to be wandering around in the early hours of the morning carrying a pack.

Do not go into a township without accurate local knowledge and preferably with a reliable local guide. Langa is currently relatively safe (but these things change), and long-distance minibus taxis leave from the Langa shopping centre early in the morning.

A local area minibus taxi from the main train station to Langa costs about R2.50. A taxi to Jo'burg costs about R170, but the trip is long, uncomfortable and potentially dangerous because of driver fatigue. Between a few people, hiring a car would be cheaper.

Minibus taxis also go into neighbouring countries, mainly from towns close to the borders. None travel direct from Cape Town.

Door-to-Door Minibus Taxi

Atkins Transport (☎ (021) 951 2045; it's best to call between 8 and 9 pm) runs a daily door-to-door minibus from Cape Town to Springbok for R90. Standard minibus taxis from Cape Town to Springbok cost about R75.

Abader's Long Distance Minibus (☎ (021) 418 1346) service departs from platform 24 at the main train station at 8 pm on a nightly run along the Garden Route to Plettenberg Bay (R80). Stops and fares for Cape Town/Plettenberg Bay include Swellendam, R45/55; Mossel Bay, R60/25; George, R65/15; and Knysna, R70/10. The trip takes eight hours or so and lands you in most towns in the early hours of the morning, so it's inconvenient and unscenic. The return trip departs from Plett at 8.30 am so you do get to see some of the country.

TRAIN

Several long-distance trains run to/from Cape Town, although the local Metro service is the best way to get to the wineries area (see under Train in the Getting Around chapter). All trains leave from the main Cape Town train station, where the booking office (☎ (021) 405 3871) is open from 7.30 am to 4 pm on weekdays and to 11 am on Saturday.

There's a left luggage facility next to platform 24, open from 7 am to noon and 12.30 to 6.50 pm Monday to Thursday, 6 am to noon and 12.30 to 6 pm on Friday, 7 to 11 am on Saturday and 7 am to 1 pm on Sunday. The charge is R5 per item per 24 hours.

Trans Karoo to Johannesburg

The daily *Trans Karoo* is competitive in price, but much slower than the bus (about 25 hours instead of 17). Still, this is an interesting train journey. First/2nd/3rd class fares are R326/ 220/137 (more for a sleeper).

Trans Oranje to Durban

It's possible to travel between Cape Town and Durban on the weekly *Trans Oranje*. This would be rather an eccentric decision, because although the price is competitive at R425/ 286/179 for 1st/2nd/3rd class, it takes an awfully long time – over 36 hours. The train runs via Bloemfontein, about 20 hours and costs R258/174/108 from Cape Town.

Southern Cross to Port Elizabeth

Although the weekly trip on the *Southern Cross* takes about 24 hours, it's an interesting route – stops include Huguenot (Paarl), Robertson, Ashton (near Montagu), Swellendam, George and Oudtshoorn. First/2nd/3rd class fares from Cape Town include Swellendam, R52/38/21; George, R86/ 62/35; Oudtshoorn, R96/69/39; and Port Elizabeth, R159/114/65.

Blue Train

Already a luxurious way to see the country, the *Blue Train* has recently undergone a major upgrading. See the New Blue Train boxed text between pages 32 and 33.

CAR & MOTORCYCLE

The main road routes to Cape Town are the N1 from Jo'burg, the N7 from Springbok (and Namibia) and the N2 from the Garden Route and Durban. If speed is your aim, stick to these highways. However, there are often alternative routes on smaller roads, passing through some interesting country and sleepy towns. Lonely Planet's *South Africa, Lesotho & Swaziland travel atlas* will help.

HITCHING

Hitching is never entirely safe in any country in the world, and we don't recommend it. Travellers who decide to hitch should understand that they are taking a small but potentially serious risk. People who do choose to hitch will be safer if they travel in pairs and let someone know where they are planning to go.

Hitching around Cape Town is generally easy. Those planning to hitch longer distances should either start in the city centre or catch public transport to one of the outlying towns – the idea is to miss the surrounding suburbs and townships (especially the Cape Flats, where safety can be a real issue).

In the city centre, make a sign and start at the foreshore near the entry to the Victoria & Alfred Waterfront where the N1 (to Jo'burg), the N7 (to Windhoek) and the N2 (to the Garden Route) all converge. Otherwise, if you're hitching east on the N2, catch a train to Somerset West. If you're heading to Jo'burg on the N1, catch a train to the Monte Vista train station (just south of the N1); not all trains stop here, so check the timetable.

Lift Net (☎ (021) 785 3802 or 088 128 3727 AH) connects drivers with passengers. It's a lot more expensive than hitching but cheaper than most other forms of transport. From Cape Town you'll pay R160 to Jo'burg, R60 to George, R120 to Bloemfontein, R190 to Durban and R190 to Windhoek (Namibia). You need to give at least 24 hours notice. Office hours are from 9 am to 5 pm from Monday to Friday and to 1 pm on weekends.

Hostel noticeboards often have offers of lifts.

TRAVEL AGENTS

Most hotels and hostels offer tour booking services (although not always a full range of options) and many have good deals on car hire. Some hostels offer services which rival those of a travel agency, and they are usually better informed about budget options than mainstream travel agencies.

You should at least check out what's on offer at the Africa Travel Centre (Map 8) (☎ (021) 23 5555; fax 23 0065) at The Backpack hostel, 74 New Church St. It books all sorts of travel and activities, including day trips, kloofing, hire cars and extended truck tours of Africa. The rates are good. As the centre has been in business for some time, it has vetted many of the operators – and there are some cowboys out there. Check out the Africa Travel Centre's Web site (www.kingsley.co.za\millennia\bp@atc.htm) for information on the hostel and on tours and activities. Other hostels also make bookings.

SASTS has offices at universities around the country. You don't have to be a student to use its services. It offers all the regular services plus student and youth cards, youth hostel membership, and special fares and flights during vacations. Staff also know about cheap tours through Africa. There's a branch (☎ (021) 685 1808) at the University of Cape Town (Map 7), Upper Campus, Leslie building concourse.

Rennies Travel has a comprehensive network of agencies throughout South Africa, and Cape Town is no exception. It's the agent for Thomas Cook travellers cheques and handles international and domestic bookings. It will also arrange visas for a moderate charge. See the Money section in the Facts for the Visitor chapter for some locations and phone numbers.

A reader has recommended Worldwide Travel (☎ (021) 419 3840), 12th floor, 2 Long St, as a good place to buy international air tickets. A handy travel agency for straight business is Intercape Travel & Tours (☎ (021) 419 8888), in the main train station. Visa Services (☎ (021) 21 7826), 4th floor, Strand Towers, 66 Strand St, arranges visas.

Gay esCape (Map 8) (☎ (021) 23 9001; fax 23 5907; email gayesc@cis.co.za), 2nd floor, 7 Castle St, is a gay-oriented travel agency which books tours and accommodation across the country. It's also a good source of information on other things, such as good restaurants and venues in and around Cape Town. Check out the Web site at www.icafe.co.za/gayes.

WARNING
Prices for international travel are volatile, routes are introduced and cancelled, schedules change, rules are amended, special deals come and go. Airlines and governments seem to take a perverse pleasure in making price structures and regulations as complex as possible, so you should check directly with the airline or travel agent to make sure you understand how a fare (and the ticket you buy) works.

You should get opinions, quotes and advice from as many airlines and travel agents as possible before you part with your hard-earned cash. The travel industry is highly competitive and there are many hidden benefits to be unearthed. The information in this chapter should be treated as a guide only, not as a substitute for your own careful research.

Getting Around

THE AIRPORT

The airport (Map 1) – formerly known as the DF Malan airport but now officially the Cape Town international airport – is small but copes well with the limited number of international flights. Chances are you'll be able to park within an easy walk of the terminal. Don't park in the drop-off zones – the authorities are keen on towing away vehicles. The airport is 20km east of the city centre, which is about a 20 to 25 minute drive depending on the current roadworks on the N2. People returning rental cars to the airport should note that there is no petrol station at the airport, so refuel before you get there.

Intercape's Airport Shuttle (☎ (021) 934 5455/6) links the main train station (outside platform 24) and the airport. The shuttle has a counter in the domestic terminal. The scheduled service costs R30; coming from the airport, the shuttle can usually drop you off where you want if it's reasonably close to the city centre for another R5. If you want to be picked up for a trip outside the regular schedule it will cost about R60 or R120 for the whole vehicle.

Taxis are expensive; expect to pay nearly R150.

A traveller who couldn't find a taxi after he arrived in the city centre from the airport reports finding someone to carry his bag to the hotel. He recommends negotiating the fee – we'd recommend having pretty good insurance!

BUS

Cape Town has a reasonably effective bus network (although many buses are ramshackle) centred on the Grand Parade terminal (Map 8) on the Castle St side of Grand Parade.

You can get almost anywhere in the city for less than R3. Only buses service the Atlantic coast; trains service the suburbs to the east of Table Mountain. People travelling short distances generally wait at a bus stop and take either a bus or a minibus taxi, whichever arrives first.

Main City Routes
Strand St is the main through road in the city centre, running north-west to become **High Level Rd**, which skirts the mountain and runs along the upper edge of Sea Point. **Riebeeck St**, parallel to Strand St, is less important in the city centre but becomes Main Rd, the main road in Green Point and Sea Point; it leads south (as Victoria Rd) through Clifton and Camps Bay, and on to the other Atlantic Coast suburbs.

Heading east, Strand St passes the Castle, joining the freeway to the southern suburbs (at the back of Table Mountain) and False Bay. The freeway splits into the **N1** (to Paarl, and eventually, Jo'burg) and the **N2** (to Swellendam and eventually, Durban). Alternatively, if you avoid joining the freeway you can continue on the **M4** through to other inner suburbs such as Observatory.

Running at right angles to Strand St is **Adderley St**, the city centre's main street. Heading south it narrows down to become **Government Rd** and runs past parliament; heading north it runs past the main train station as **Heerengracht**, the main boulevard in the section of the city built on land reclaimed from the sea. Until the reclamation, Strand St used to be on the shore.

Long St, parallel to Adderley St, is narrow but old and interesting, with many places to eat and drink.

Buitengracht St, also parallel to Adderley St, is a busy road dividing the city centre from Bo-Kaap, the 'Cape Malay' (Cape Muslim) quarter. As **New Church St**, it runs south through the inner suburbs until, as **Kloof Nek Rd** (the M62), it climbs steeply over Kloof Nek, the pass between Lion's Head and Table Mountain, to wind down the back of Camps Bay. ■

There's a helpful information kiosk at the Grand Parade terminal. It's open from 7.45 am to 5.45 pm Monday to Friday and from 8 am to 1 pm on weekends. There are two inquiry numbers, ☎ 934 0540 or 0801 21 2111 (toll free).

A bus to Sea Point costs R1.40, to Camps Bay R2.60 and to Hout Bay R5.30. If you are using a particular bus regularly, it's worth buying clipcards, which give you 10 trips at a discount price.

The Beachcomber Bus runs a useful circular route (with buses in both directions) stopping at the main train station (Adderley St side), the lower cable station, Camps Bay and the Waterfront. The trip takes about 40 minutes and each leg costs R3 or you can get a day ticket for R12.

TRAIN

Metro commuter trains are a good way to get around. All lines run to/from the main train station. The Metro information office (☎ (021) 405 2991) is in the main train station near the old locomotive opposite platform 23. It's open from 6 am to 6.45 pm Monday to Saturday and 7 am to 5 pm on Sunday.

Metro trains have 1st and 3rd class carriages. It's reasonably safe to travel in 3rd class (but check the current situation) though don't do it during peak hours (crowds offer scope for pickpockets), on weekends (lack of crowds offer scope for muggers) or when carrying a lot of gear. We've had the odd report of people having problems in both 1st and 3rd class.

Metro trains run some way out of Cape Town, to Strand St (on the east side of False Bay) and into the winelands to Stellenbosch and Paarl.

Probably the most important line for visitors is the Simonstad/Simon's Town line. It runs through Observatory and then around the back of the mountain through upper-income white suburbs such as Rosebank, down to Muizenberg and along the False Bay coast.

Biggsy's (☎ (021) 405 3870) is a privately run bar and dining car attached to some services running between Cape Town and Simon's Town. You need a 1st class ticket and about R4 to enter.

Some 1st/3rd class fares are: Muizenberg, R5/2.20; Paarl, R10/4.40; Simon's Town, R6.80/2.90; Stellenbosch, R8.70/3.80; and Observatory, R2.20/1.50.

CAR & MOTORCYCLE

With an excellent road and freeway system carrying surprisingly little traffic, driving in Cape Town is a pleasure. Signs on freeways and highways alternate between Afrikaans and English. You'll soon learn that, for example, Linkerbaan isn't the name of a town – it means left lane.

Petrol costs around R1.80 a litre.

Rental

Major international companies such as Avis (Map 8) (☎ 0800 021 111 toll free), 123 Strand St, and Budget (Map 8) (☎ 0800 016 622 toll free), 63A Strand St, are represented.

The larger local companies, such as Imperial (Map 8) (☎ 0800 118 898 toll free), on the corner of Loop and Strand Sts; and Tempest (Map 8) (☎ 0800 031 666 toll free), on the corner of Buitengracht and Wale Sts, offer comparable service to the majors at slightly lower rates.

The smaller, cheaper local companies come and go – at the time of writing two of the more prominent were Alisa (Map 8) (☎ 0800 21515 toll free), 139 Buitengracht, and Panther (☎ (021) 511 6196; fax 511 7802). You'll find plenty of brochures for other cheaper outfits at the Tourist Rendezvous and at hostels – read the small print! Their businesses are booming because of the increasing numbers of budget travellers to hit Cape Town, and there can be some good deals. There are so many companies and factors involved in deciding what's best for you (eg do you really need 400 free km a day if you're just tootling around Cape Town and the Winelands; can you drop the car in Jo'burg?) that you really need to gather as many brochures as you can, sit down with a beer and do some sums.

At the time of writing, some smaller companies were offering deals of around R800 per week with unlimited km. The majors are much more expensive if you hire in South Africa, but if you pre-book with an international company before you leave home the rates can be more comparable to (although still dearer than) the small local companies.

Le Cap Motorcycle Hire (Map 8) (☎ (021) 23 0823; fax 23 5566), 3 Carisbrook St, hires bikes and also runs longer tours. If you're looking for cheap transport you'd be better off hiring a car, but it's very tempting to explore the area by bike – warm weather, good roads and spectacular scenery. You need to be over 23 and have held a motorbike licence for two years to rent one of the Kawasaki KLR650s. The daily rate is R150 plus R15 helmet hire and R0.60 per km. There are deals for longer rentals which include free km.

Le Cap also rents 100cc scooters for R100 per day, including a helmet and 100 free km. You need to be 18 and have a motorbike licence. Another outfit plans to rent 50cc

Buying a Used Car

Jo'burg is the best place to buy cheap cars in South Africa, but Cape Town is the nicest. The process is inevitably time consuming and Cape Town is a much more enjoyable place to waste a week or two. Prices tend to be a bit higher so it's not a bad place to sell, but as the market is smaller you might wait longer. Cars that have spent their lives around Cape Town are more likely to be rusty than those kept inland, but as one dealer told me, 'What's wrong with rust? It just means that the car is cheaper'.

The main congregation (or is 'pack' a better word?) of used car dealers is on Voortrekker Rd between Maitland and Bellville. Voortrekker is the R102 and runs west from Salt River, south of, and pretty much parallel to, the N1.

Some dealers might agree to a buy-back deal, such as John Wayne at Wayne Motors (☎ (021) 45 2222; fax 45 2617), 13 Roeland St. He'll guarantee a buy-back price but he reckons that you have a fair chance of getting more cash by selling the car privately. He doesn't deal in rock-bottom cars, though.

Dealers have to make a profit so you'll pay less if you buy privately. The *Cape Times* has ads every day, but the big day is Thursday. The *Weekend Argus* also has a good selection. Whoever you're buying from, make sure that the details correspond accurately with the ownership (registration) papers and that there is a *current* licence disk on the windscreen. Check the owner's name against their identity document and the engine and chassis numbers. Consider getting the car tested by the Automobile Association (AA).

It is hard to find decent-quality used cars at low prices, although a glut of cheap new models on the market might see used-car prices fall. You will be lucky to find a reliable vehicle for under R8000. Of course, if nothing serious goes wrong, you will hopefully get most of your money back when you sell.

In the meantime, however, you'll have a lot of money tied up. Insurance for third party damages and theft is a very good idea. Unfortunately, it is surprisingly difficult to find an insurance company to take your money if you don't have a permanent address and/or a local bank account. If this concerns you, start shopping around early so you can figure out a way to meet their conditions – before you get the car. You'll need to budget around R250 a month. We would be interested to hear of any companies that are helpful to travellers.

Insurance companies will take cash if you buy a year's worth of insurance, but if you just want a month or so you must have a bank account. You might be able to negotiate paying a year's worth with a pro-rata refund when you sell the car, but get an agreement in writing, not just a vague promise.

Cheap cars will often be sold without a roadworthy certificate. A certificate is required when you register the change of ownership and pay tax for a license disk. Roadworthies used to be difficult to get but now some private garages are allowed to issue them, and some will overlook minor faults. A roadworthiness certificate costs R120.

Present yourself along with the roadworthy, a current licence disk, an accurate registration certificate, a completed change of ownership card (signed by the seller), a clear photocopy of your ID (passport) along with the original and your wallet to the City Treasurer's Department, Motor Vehicle Registration Division (☎ (021) 210 2385/6/7/8/9) in the Civic Centre (Map 8), Cash Hall, on the foreshore. It's open from 8 am to 2 pm from Monday to Friday and distributes blank change-of-ownership forms. Ring ahead to check how much cash you'll need, but it will be under R200. ■

mopeds, but they might have trouble on the steep hills.

Road Rules

South Africans drive on the left-hand side of the road and the road rules are broadly the same as anywhere else.

One important local variant is the 'four-way stop', which can occur even on major roads. If you're used to a system where drivers on major roads always have priority over drivers on smaller roads, you'll need to stay alert.

When you arrive at a four-way stop, you must stop. If there are other vehicles at the intersection, those which arrived before you cross first. Before you proceed, make sure that it *is* a four-way stop – if it is, you can safely cross in front of approaching cars. If you've mistaken an ordinary stop sign for a four-way stop, the approaching cars won't be slowing down ...

Speed Limits The speed limit on rural roads is 100km/h (about 60mph), and 120km/h (75mph) on most freeways and highways. Some dangerous sections of rural roads have a limit of less than 100km/h. The usual limit in towns is 60km/h (about 35mph). If you stick to the highway speed limit you'll feel lonely – most white traffic travels much faster, and most black traffic much slower.

The traffic police force is a separate organisation to the main police force and is not treated with a great deal of respect – hence the appalling accident rate.

Driving Hazards

South Africa has a horrific road fatality rate, mostly caused by dangerous driving.

Other Drivers On highways, fast cars coming up behind you will expect you to move over into the emergency lane to let them pass.

The problem is that there might be pedestrians or a slow-moving vehicle already in the emergency lane. Don't move over unless it's safe. It is becoming common for an overtaking car to rely on *oncoming* traffic to move into the emergency lane. This is sheer lunacy and you must remain constantly alert. Drivers on little-used rural roads often speed and tend to assume that there is no other traffic. Be careful of oncoming cars at blind corners on country roads.

Drink-driving has not been treated as a problem until recently. It is a major hazard – be careful.

Dirt Roads You don't have to get very far off the beaten track to find yourself on dirt roads. Most are regularly graded and reasonably smooth, and it's often possible to travel at high speed. Don't!

If you're travelling along a dirt road at 100km/h and you come to a corner, you won't go around that corner, you'll sail off into the fynbos. If you put on the brakes to slow down you'll probably spin or roll. If you swerve sharply to avoid a pothole you'll go into an exciting four-wheel drift then find out what happens when your car meets a telephone pole. Worst of all, if another car approaches and you have to move to the edge of the road, you'll lose control and collide head-on.

On dirt roads that are dry, flat, straight, traffic-free and wide enough to allow for unexpected slewing as you hit potholes and drifted sand, you could; with practice, drive at about 80km/h. Otherwise, treat dirt like ice.

Animals & Pedestrians Slow down and watch out for people and animals on rural roads. Standard white advice is that if you hit an animal in a black area, don't stop – drive to the nearest police station and report it there. This might be paranoia or arrogance, but then again it might not. If the animal you hit is a cow or a horse, leaving the scene might not be an option.

Weather Dense mist can reduce visibility to a few metres on roads over mountain passes.

Crime Car theft and theft from cars is a big problem. Take precautions. Car jacking, rife in Jo'burg, is almost unknown in Cape Town. That might change, so stay alert and keep windows wound up and all doors locked when driving at night. ■

Highway Etiquette

On freeways, a faster car will expect you to move into the emergency lane to let it pass. If you do, it will probably say 'thank you' by flashing its hazard lights. The excessively polite reply 'you're welcome' by flashing their high-beam lights. ■

TAXI

As always, taxis are expensive but worth considering late at night or if you are in a group. There is a taxi rank at the Adderley St end of the Grand Parade (Map 8) in the city, or phone Star Taxis (☎ (021) 419 7777), Marine Taxi (☎ (021) 434 0434) or Sea Point Taxis (☎ (021) 434 4444).

There are often taxis in Greenmarket Square (Map 8), near the Holiday Inn, outside the Cape Sun Hotel (Map 8) on Strand St, and on Adderley St between Church and Longmarket Sts. A taxi from the main train station to Sea Point could cost R30; to Tamboerskloof it will be around R15. For a cheaper alternative see the Rikki's section in this chapter.

MINIBUS TAXI

Minibus taxis cover most of the city with an informal network of routes. If there's a bus stop on the road, there's a good chance that minibus taxis also use that route. They are a

Minibus Taxi Etiquette

*   People with lots of luggage sit in the first row behind the driver.
*   Pay the fare with coins, not notes. Pass money forward (your fare and those of people around you) when the taxi is full. Give it to one of the front-seat passengers, not the driver. If you're sitting in the front seat, you might have to collect the fares and make change.
*   If you sit on the folding seat by the sliding side door, it's your job to open and close the door when other people get out. You'll have to get out of the taxi each time.
*   Say 'Thank you!' (not 'Stop!' etc) when you want to get out. ■

cheap (about the same as buses) and efficient way of getting around.

Their main terminus is on the upper deck of the main train station, accessible from a walkway in the Golden Acre Centre (Map 8) or from stairways on Strand St. It's well organised and finding the right rank is easy. Coming into the city from Sea Point, minibus taxis run via either Strand or Riebeeck Sts. There's no way of telling which route the vehicle will take except by asking the driver.

There has been a sporadic 'war' between rival taxi firms, so check the current situation. For further information, see the Minibus Taxis entry in the previous Getting There & Away chapter.

RIKKI'S

Rikki's tiny, open vans provide Asian-style transport in the City Bowl and nearby areas for low prices. Telephone Rikki's (☎ (021) 23 4888) or just hail one on the street – you can pay a shared rate of a few rand or more if you phone for the whole van. Rikki's runs from 7 am to 6 pm daily, except Sunday, and goes as far afield as Sea Point and Camps Bay. From the station out to Camps Bay a single-person trip will cost about R12; to Tamboerskloof it will be about R5. Rikki's also operates out of Simon's Town (☎ (021) 786 2136).

Although they are cheap and fun, Rikki's might not be the quickest, as there is usually a certain amount of meandering as other passengers are dropped off.

BICYCLE

The Cape Peninsula is a great place to explore by bike, but its hills and distances can be deceptively large – it's nearly 70km from the city centre to Cape Point. Unfortunately, you aren't supposed to take bikes on suburban trains.

Many hostels hire bikes and some of them are in reasonable condition. For a trouble-free bike contact Mike Hopkins Cycles (Map 8) (☎ (021) 23 2527), 133A Bree St (near the corner of Wale St), or Day Trippers (☎ (021) 461 4599 or 531 3274).

GETTING AROUND

Bikes on Flights

It's possible to bring your own bike by plane. Some airlines simply require you to cover the chain, remove the pedals and turn the handlebars sideways; others require bikes to be completely dismantled and packed in a box. Cardboard bike boxes are available for a small charge or for free from bike shops. Your bike is probably safer if it's not in a box, as it will probably be stowed upright or on top of the other luggage. My bike has flown 11 times, suffering a few scratches (in India) and one badly buckled wheel (at Heathrow).

Jon Murray

Apparently a bike-route map of Western Cape Province is in production.

WALKING

One of the nicest things about Cape Town is that the small size of the City Bowl (the city centre and the old inner city suburbs) area means that most everything is accessible on foot, much of it easily. For more energetic walking, see Activities in the Things to See & Do chapter.

ORGANISED TOURS

For a quick orientation on a fine day you can't beat Topless Tours (☎ (021) 448 2888), which runs a roofless double-decker bus. The two hour city tour (R30) runs between Dock Rd at the Waterfront and the Tourist Rendezvous about six times a day, less often (if at all) in winter. Longer tours are also available.

Major companies include Springbok Atlas Tours (☎ (021) 417 6545) and Hylton Ross (☎ (021) 438 1500), a big local company with an office on Quay Five at the Waterfront. As well as local tours it can arrange other tours around the country.

Several companies offer eco-oriented tours of the Cape and longer trips further afield. They include Greencape Tours (☎ (082) 891 5266 or (021) 797 0166). The maximum group size is seven people, and

with a consensus of customers, the itinerary can be changed.

One City Tours (☎ (021) 387 5351 or 387 5165) has an excellent three hour township tour for R75, plus other tours. The township tour is an absolute must.

Tana-Baru Tours (☎ (021) 24 0719; fax 23 5579) offers a two hour walk or drive through Bo-Kaap (the 'Malay' quarter). Shereen Habib lives in Bo-Kaap and is an excellent guide, as much for her knowledge of day-to-day life in this vibrant community as for her historical insights. Tours cost R45 and Shereen will take as few as one person. It's highly recommended. If you're going to take any tour of this area, make it this one, rather than a white-run bus tour that treats the area like a zoo.

Shereen's husband runs a Cape Flats tour, concentrating more on the coloured residential areas. We haven't tried it, but it should be good.

Court Helicopters (☎ (021) 25 2966/7) has short flights which depart from near the Waterfront and fly up to Lion's Head and Table Mountain, then swoop back down over the City Bowl. The flight lasts only 10 minutes but it is spectacular and exciting – well worth R990 for four people. Do whatever is necessary to sit in the front seat! There's also a sunset flight (covering the same route) for R210 per person (minimum two people). Another helicopter company is Civair (☎ (021) 419 5182).

See the Victoria & Alfred Waterfront section in the Things to See & Do chapter for information on boat cruises.

At least once a month there are steam train excursions to Simon's Town or Franschhoek for about R50. Contact Union Ltd Steam Rail Tours (☎ (021) 405 4391) at the Tourist Rendezvous.

More Adventurous Tours

Since backpacker travel to Cape Town began to boom, there has been a big increase in the number of tours catering to younger visitors. You certainly don't need to be a backpacker to go along, however, and these trips are more fun (and cheaper) than the more conventional tours.

One of the original outfits is Day Trippers (☎ (021) 461 4599 or 531 3274). It gets excellent feedback from travellers, and Steve really knows his stuff. Most trips take along mountain bikes, so you can do some riding if you want. Most tours cost aroundR120.

See the Activities section in the Things to See & Do chapter for some more activity-based tours.

Things to See & Do

HIGHLIGHTS

Just being in Cape Town's dramatic setting between the sea and Table Mountain (Map 2) is itself one of the highlights. The mountain's presence is always felt, but it changes colour throughout the day and in different weather conditions. Taking the cable car or walking to the top is essential.

The long string of beaches on the Atlantic coast (Map 1) and in False Bay (Map 1) are also highlights. Choose from ultra-trendy Clifton Beach, a deserted shore in the Cape of Good Hope National Park or one of the many others.

The sense of history and the echoes of Cape Town's complex past are also ever-present, in the old buildings in the City Bowl area and elsewhere, and in some fine museums.

The Victoria & Alfred Waterfront complex (Map 9) is a very modern alternative, although it too preserves the past, in a unique combination of working docks and very popular entertainment and eating places. From here you can take a tour to Robben Island (Map 1), the Alcatraz of South Africa.

You don't have to go far from Cape Town to visit the area's other world-famous attraction – the Cape Winelands, less than half an hour away by car. See the Excursions chapter for these and other out-of-town highlights.

Viewpoints

Cape Town has more than its fair share of places that show off its beauty. If you're lucky, the first unforgettable sight will be on arrival, should your plane come in low past Table Mountain.

There are views of the mountain from all over town, so there's no need to go looking for one. However, the most famous view is from the beach at Bloubergstrand (Map 1), north of the city. The mountain seen from a boat cruise on Table Bay is pretty special too, but for a view with a thrill, take one of the short helicopter flights on offer. Some of

these climb slowly up the back of the mountain then swoop low across the top and down into the City Bowl (Maps 5 & 8).

Once you've had your fill of views *of* Table Mountain, there are the views to be had *from* Table Mountain. Taking the cable car to the top and then following one of the trails will give you some extraordinary views. Queuing for a cable car or walking up is something that you might not have time to do twice, but there are some good views of the City Bowl and the sea from the road running past the lower cableway station. The road continues some way further on, and at the end there's a walking track.

There are good views from the Noon Gun

Street Names with a Past

Some streets in the city centre have been there for a long time. Castle (Kasteel) and Hout (meaning wood) Sts were two of the three original streets in Cape Town, although they were then called Heere and Oliphant Sts. Spin St was named during an unsuccessful attempt to begin a silk-weaving industry. Bree St advertises its width, and Plein St runs from Grand Parade or Grootplein. Parliament St was the first street to be paved.

You'll notice that a number of city centre streets have 'buiten' in their names. Buiten means 'near', so for example, Buitengracht St was near a canal.

Waterkant (waterfront) and Strand Sts were left high and dry after seafront land was reclaimed in the 1930s. Adderley St's original name was Heerengracht St (Gentlemen's Canal), after a canal in Amsterdam, and that name was given to Adderley St's continuation in the area of reclaimed land.

To see how apartheid bureaucrats named streets in townships, by contrast, have a look at the Cape Flats pages in a street directory.

After exhausting the usual lists of names of plants, animals and so on, the bureaucrats moved onto other things. You'll find pockets of streets with names such as Karate, Ludo, Scrabble and Korfball! Other names include Volvo, Chevrolet, Peugeot, Austin and – for you Australians – Holden. ■

---

area (Map 3) of Bo-Kaap. This is one of the few places offering a good view of the shipping activity in Cape Town's busy port.

Driving from the city to Camps Bay (Map 2) via Kloof Nek Rd (Map 5) (the continuation of New Church St, which is itself the continuation of Buitengracht St) you cross Kloof Nek (Map 2) (just past the cableway turn-off), with a breathtaking view of the beaches and the 12 Apostles (Map 2). Travelling south down the coast, the best views of lovely Hout Bay are from Chapman's Peak Drive (Map 1) (part of the M6). There are several places on this spectacular road where you can stop and admire the scenery. Further out of town, the coast road between Strand and Hermanus has superb views back across False Bay.

MUSEUMS & GALLERIES
Bo-Kaap Museum

The small but interesting Bo-Kaap Museum (Map 8) (☎ 24 3846), 71 Wale St, gives an insight into the lifestyle of a well-off Muslim family in Cape Town in the 19th century. The house itself was built in 1763. It's open

---

Bo-Kaap

The Waterkant area of Bo-Kaap (around Waterkant St on the north-eastern edge of Signal Hill) forms a distinct area. It is now occupied by yuppies and it's the centre of the gay scene. The prime real estate was quickly snapped up by whites after the apartheid regime began its forced removals of Muslims, dumping them on the Cape Flats. But after this first assault the residents of Bo-Kaap organised and fought back, winning the battle to stay in homes that their families had occupied for centuries.

The Waterkant area wasn't always socially desirable. Most Muslims came here as slaves or political prisoners, but there was a small proportion of common criminals who were given the choice between the guillotine (which was situated in the Waterkant) and serving time on Robben Island. Most chose the island and those who survived came back to live in the Waterkant. The stigma remained until quite recently. ■

District Six

District Six, just to the east of the city centre, was the suburb that, more than any other, gave Cape Town its cosmopolitan atmosphere and life. It was primarily a coloured ghetto, but people of every race lived there. It was a poor, overcrowded but vibrant community. The streets were alive with people, from children to traders, buskers to petty criminals. Jazz was its lifeblood and the district was home to many musicians, including the internationally known Dollar Brand (Abdullah Ibrahim). Being so close, it infected the whole city with its vitality.

This state of affairs naturally did not appeal to the National Party government so, in 1966, District Six was classified as a white area. The 50,000 people, some of whose families had been there for five generations, were evicted and dumped in bleak and soulless townships like Athlone, Mitchell's Plain and Atlantis. The bulldozers moved in and the coloured heart was ripped out of the city.

Today District Six is still largely an open wasteland and a depressing monument to the cruelty and stupidity of the apartheid government. Complex legal cases might see some of the former residents regaining their stolen land, but the old District Six is probably gone for good. ■

---

between 9.30 am and 4.30 pm from Tuesday to Saturday; entry is R1. Note that some residents of Bo-Kaap dislike the museum as they feel that it was imposed on them and does not reflect current realities in the community.

District Six Museum

On the corner of Buitenkant and Albertus Sts, this simple museum (Map 8) (☎ 461 8745) is as much for the people of the now-vanished District Six as it is about them.

The floor is covered with a large-scale map of District Six and former residents are encouraged to label their old homes and the features of their neighbourhood. After District Six was bulldozed, the government changed the street grid and the names of the few remaining roads. The vibrant community now exists only in the memories of those who lived there. There are a few other interesting displays, but the best reason to visit is to talk with the museum staff.

The museum is open daily, except Sunday,

Walking Tour

The following walk around the City Bowl could take the best part of a day, depending on the stops you make, although it is only about 6km.

The Castle, as the oldest surviving building in Cape Town, seems the most appropriate place to start a walking tour. Van Riebeeck's original mud-walled fort was a little to the west of the stone castle that replaced it (built between 1666 and 1679) and survives today. See the separate Castle of Good Hope section in this chapter.

Walk to the west across the **Grand Parade**, once a military parade ground, and now a bleak and windy car park. On Wednesday and Saturday mornings a section is kept clear for a flea market. Flower sellers congregate in a narrow mall near OK Bazaars, on the north-west side of the Parade.

The impressive old **Town Hall** on the southern side (1905) has been superseded by a much less attractive Civic Centre on the other side of the station.

Buses leave from the station side of the Parade, and minibus taxis compete for customers amid the friendly chaos on the Strand. At the Plein St end, an interesting bunch of permanent stalls form a colourful bazaar. Spices and takeaway food are sold – the samosas are cheap and excellent.

Circle around the post office and enter the **Golden Acre Centre** (1978) which was built on the site of the old train station, and dubbed 'the golden acre' by locals because of its valuable real estate. It has several levels of shops and is linked to more shops in the Strand Concourse (including Captour) that runs under the intersection of Adderley and Strand Sts. Black tiles on the floor indicate the waterline before land reclamation in the 1930s.

Exit onto Adderley St, named after a British parliamentarian and historically regarded as Cape Town's main street. Until 1849 it was named the Heerengracht, or Gentlemen's Canal, after a canal of the same name in distant Amsterdam.

Turn left along Adderley towards Table Mountain and continue until you reach the **Groote Kerk**, the mother church for the Dutch Reformed Church (Nederduitse Gereformeerde Kerk, or NG Kerk). The first church on the site was built in 1704, but the current building dates from 1841 (open 10.30 am to noon and 2 to 3 pm). A number of early personages have tombs inside.

The next building along is the **Cultural History Museum**, which was once the Dutch East India Company's slave lodge and brothel. The impressive façade was designed in 1811 and the building was later used as a debating chamber for the Cape Legislative Council (see the Museums & Galleries section in this chapter).

Follow the road as it turns right at the gardens (becoming Wale St) past the historically significant **St Georges Cathedral**, designed by Herbert Baker in 1897. This was Archbishop Desmond Tutu's cathedral. Turn right into St Georges St, which is now almost completely a pedestrian mall.

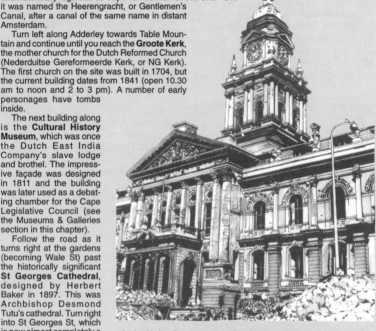

A mix of Italian Renaissance and British colonial architecture, the impressive Town Hall is home to the Municipal Library.

Turn left at Longmarket St and you come out on **Greenmarket Square**, one of the most interesting spots in the city. It was created as a farmers' market in 1710 and is now home to a flea market (open daily). The **Townhouse Museum** (1761) on the corner of Burg and Longmarket Sts was the original city watch house, and now houses the Michaelis Collection of 16th and 17th century Dutch and Flemish oil paintings (open 10 am to 5 pm every day, admission free). The building itself might be more interesting than the generally dour artworks, and there's a balcony overlooking bustling Greenmarket Square. Also note the magnificent Art Deco architecture of the building opposite, on the Shortmarket St side of the square.

Walk back towards Table Mountain along Burg St and turn right into Church St, which is lined with art and antique shops. The pedestrian section is a flea market specialising in antiques and bric-a-brac. Turn right down **Long St** which, along with Church St, retains a strong historical atmosphere, with elegant cast-iron decorated balconies and numerous old buildings. One of the oldest is the atmospheric **Sendinnestig Museum** (1802) at No 40, originally a missionary church (open Monday to Friday from 9.15 am to 4.15 pm). On the first Friday of the month the old gas lights are lit between 1 and 2 pm.

Continue until you reach Strand St. Turn right and a short distance on your right is **Koopmans de Wet House** (1701), a classic example of a Cape townhouse furnished with antiques. It's a quiet, self-satisfied house holding its own in the centre of a big city. The house is open from Tuesday to Saturday between 9.30 am and 4.30 pm; entrance is R2, free on Friday.

Backtrack along Strand St, passing on the right-hand side in the block before Buitengracht St the old **Lutheran Church**, which was converted from a warehouse in 1780, and the next-door parsonage **Martin Melck House**.

Cross Buitengracht St, and you enter the old **Cape Muslim Quarter** (sometimes erroneously referred to as the Malay Quarter, but more properly called Bo-Kaap), the historical residential suburb for the descendants of the Asian slaves and political prisoners imported by the Dutch. The steep streets, some of which are still cobbled, and 18th century flat-roofed houses and mosques are still home to a strong Muslim community. This group miraculously survived apartheid, but it is less certain it will survive unfettered capitalism. The cottages on the Waterkant edge of the Quarter have been bought by yuppies and while those streets might be neat and freshly painted, they are also lifeless (see the Bo-Kaap boxed text in this chapter).

Turn left down Rose St, which after a couple of hundred metres forms a T-intersection with Wale St. Here you will find a restored house, the **Bo-Kaap Museum**, which gives an insight into the lifestyle of a Malay family. It's open Tuesday to Saturday from 9.30 am to 4.30 pm; admission is R2 (see the Museums & Galleries section).

Walk down the hill, cross Buitengracht St and keep going until you reach Long St. Turn right into Long St and follow it until it becomes Orange St. The **Long St Baths** on the corner are still in operation. Turn left into Orange St, and left again into Grey's Pass, which takes you past the excellent **South African Museum**, open daily from 10 am to 5 pm. Entry costs R3 (free on Wednesday). It has some fascinating displays on indigenous black culture (see the Museums & Galleries section).

From here, you enter the top end of the impressive **Company's Gardens**, also known as the Botanical Gardens. This is the surviving six hectares of Jan Van Riebeeck's original 18 hectare vegetable garden, which was planted to provide fresh produce for the VOC's ships. As sources of supply were diversified, the garden was gradually changed to a superb pleasure garden with a magnificent collection of botanical species from South Africa and the world. The gardens are open from 9.30 am to 4 pm. The **Gardens Restaurant**, at the Adderley St end of the Gardens to the north of the oak-lined Government Ave, serves drinks and reasonably priced food and has inside and outside seating.

On the south side of Government Ave (Wale St end) are the **Houses of Parliament**. Opened in 1885, they have been enlarged several times. Double back towards the mountain and past **De Tuynhuys**, the president's office, which has been restored to its 1795 appearance.

Next on the left, on the south-eastern side of the gardens, is the **National Gallery** which has a permanent collection of important South African paintings and also holds temporary exhibitions. It's open daily from 10 am to 5 pm; from 1 pm on Monday (see the Museums & Galleries section).

Leave the gardens by Gallery Lane and turn left into St Johns (towards the bay), take the next left and then next right into Parliament St. This takes you through to **Church Square**, where the burghers would unhitch their wagons while they attended the Groote Kerk. Slaves were also auctioned under a tree in the square (the spot is now marked with a plaque).

Continue down Parliament St, keeping your eyes open for some of the many Art Deco details on the buildings. Turn right on Darling St and you're back at the Grand Parade where you started. Phew! ■

from 10 am to 4 pm. Admission is by donation. There are some interesting cards and books for sale, including an excellent book of District Six photos (paperback, R60).

Cultural History Museum

This museum (Map 8) (☎ 461 8280) at the mountain end of Adderley St is the former slave lodge of the Dutch East India Company (VOC), but it has gone through several incarnations since then – including Supreme Court and Legislative Assembly – and major physical alterations.

The museum originally aimed to give a cultural history of *Homo sapiens* from Egyptian, Greek and Roman times, but is now building collections on the early history of the Cape, including some VOC relics and postal stones. These stones marked caches of letters that were left by the crews of ships, in the hope that they would be picked up by the next ship heading in the right direction. They were engraved with the name of the ship and the names of those who sent the letters.

The museum is open Monday to Friday between 9.30 am and 4.30 pm; entry is R5.

Bertram House Museum

Bertram House (Map 8) (☎ 24 9381), on the corner of Orange St and Government Ave (the walkway through the Company's Gardens), is a Georgian house filled with antiques that once belonged to wealthy English-descended South Africans. It's interesting to compare the architecture and furnishing of this house with that of old Cape Dutch houses, such as Koopmans de Wet. The Georgian comes off second-best.

The museum is open Tuesday to Saturday from 9.30 am to 4.30 pm. Admission is R2.

Jewish Museum

The Jewish Museum (Map 8) (☎ 45 1546), 84 Hatfield St (next to the National Gallery), is in the oldest synagogue in South Africa. It contains items of Jewish historical and ceremonial significance. It's open from 11 am to 5 pm on Tuesday and Thursday in summer, with slightly longer hours the rest of the year. Entry is free.

Rust-en-Vreugd

This 18th century house (Map 8) (☎ 45 3628) at 78 Buitenkant St was once the home of the state prosecutor. It now houses part of the William Fehr Collection of paintings and furniture, and features important watercolours and engravings by renowned early South African artists like Baines. Shipwrecks in Table Bay seem to have excited the imaginations of several artists.

There's also a pleasant garden offering a quiet break from the city centre streets. The museum is open from 9 am to 4 pm on weekdays and on weekends over summer, and occasionally at other times. Admission is free.

South African Museum

The South African Museum (Map 8) (☎ 24 3330) at the mountain end of the Company's Gardens (also known as the Botanical Gardens) is the oldest and arguably the most interesting museum in South Africa. It has some startlingly lifelike displays of San communities (made from casts taken from living people in 1911) and interesting exhibits of other indigenous cultures. As an indirect testimony to Cape Town's importance as a stopping place for ships, the museum holds artefacts from the Pacific Islands left here by Captain Cook on his way home from his great voyages of discovery.

Despite some updating, it's a good, old-fashioned museum with cases and cases of stuffed animals (some, like the rotund platypus, overstuffed) and bloodthirsty dioramas of dinosaurs which must have inspired generations of young imaginations.

Don't miss the sociable weaver birds' nest, a veritable apartment block several metres across and capable of accommodating a sizeable colony.

The most interesting of the new displays is the whale room, where you can hear whale-speak while looking at models suspended high in the air.

There is a planetarium (☎ 24 3330) in the complex, which should help northerners unravel the mysteries of the southern hemisphere's night sky.

The museum is open daily from 10 am to 5 pm; entry is R3 (free on Wednesday). Planetarium shows are given at 1 pm on Tuesday and Thursday, at 2 and 3.30 pm on Saturday and Sunday, and at 8 pm on Tuesday and Wednesday. Admission is R6 (R7 for evening shows).

Townhouse Museum

The Townhouse Museum (Map 8) on Greenmarket Square is another old Cape Dutch building. It dates from 1761, although it has been considerably altered to suit its changing roles as headquarters of the Burgher Watch, the first city hall and, in 1916, Cape Town's first public art gallery.

Today it houses the Michaelis Collection of Dutch and Flemish paintings and etchings (all rather gloomy) from the 16th and 17th centuries.

Apart from the collection, it's worth visiting for the architecture and the views from the balcony overlooking bustling Greenmarket Square.

The museum is open from 10 am to 5 pm daily, and admission is free.

Western Cape Archives

Housed in a disused police station (one of the city's most notorious for apartheid-era abuses) at 72 Roeland St, the Archives (☎ 462 4050) hold some immensely important documents, some over 400 years old. There are also paintings. Admission is free and it's open on weekdays (until 7 pm on Thursday).

Rugby Museum

On Boundary Rd in Newlands, near the famous stadium (Map 7), this museum (☎ 686 4532) claims to be the largest rugby museum in the world, not surprising in the most fanatical rugby country in the world. It's open weekdays from 9.30 am to 4 pm.

National Gallery

This small but exquisite gallery (Map 8) (☎ 45 1628) in the Company's Gardens was always worth visiting for its architecture but now it also has some very interesting exhibitions, which begin to make amends for the artistic repression of the apartheid days.

There's a good shop with some interesting books and a pleasant café, with inexpensive snacks and light meals. The gallery is open from 10 am (from 1 pm on Monday) to 5 pm every day. Admission is free.

HOUSES OF PARLIAMENT

On the south side of Government Ave (Wale St end) are the Houses of Parliament (Map 8) (☎ 403 2911), which were opened in 1885 and enlarged several times since. During the parliamentary session (usually late January to June) gallery tickets are available; overseas tourists must present their passports. During the recess (usually July to January) there are free guided tours (☎ 403 2198) from Monday to Friday at 11 am and 2 pm. Go to the Old Parliament Building entrance on Parliament St.

CASTLE OF GOOD HOPE

Built near the site of van Riebeeck's original mud-walled fort, the Castle (Map 8) (as it's known) was constructed between 1666 and 1679 and is one of the oldest European structures in southern Africa. The impressive 10m-high walls have never had to repel an attack, but the Castle is nonetheless a striking symbol of the might of the VOC.

The Castle is still the headquarters of the Western Cape Military Command, but its tourist potential has been recognised and visitors are welcome. There's also a small shop selling drinks and cheap snacks.

Within the Castle are a couple of museums with collections of furniture and paintings. The paintings, mainly of Cape Town in the past, are fascinating.

There are guided tours hourly between 10 am and 3 pm, and taking one of these is the only way to see many of the sights. However, if you're visiting one of the excellent temporary exhibitions (lately they have focused on anti-apartheid themes) held in a hall in the Castle, you can do a little solo wandering. The Castle closes at 4 pm. Admission (from the Grand Parade side) costs R5.

LONG STREET

Long St (Map 8), narrow and overhung with balconied buildings, is undergoing a renaissance, with informal eating places, bars and backpacker accommodation appearing among the junk and antique shops. It's a lively area and forms the link between the city centre and City Bowl suburbs such as Tamboerskloof (Map 5). It was once the red light district and there are still a few massage parlours and the like (one, in a slightly bizarre melding of the old and new Long St, has a mural above it). Long St is also close to Bo-Kaap, the Muslim ('Malay') quarter, and the old Noor el Hamedia Mosque (1884) is on the corner of Dorp St.

Long Street Baths

The Turkish baths and heated pool (Map 8) (☎ 210 3302) at the mountain end of Long St, are something of an anachronism, but they have been restored and are very popular. The pool is open Monday to Friday from 7 am to 9 pm, to 8 pm on Saturday and from 8 am to 7 pm on Sunday. You have to get there at least an hour before closing time. Admission costs R6 (less if you just want a hot bath).

The Turkish baths are segregated. For men they are open from 9 am to 8.30 pm on Tuesday, Wednesday and Friday, and from 8 am to noon on Sunday. For women the hours are from 8.30 am to 8.30 pm on Monday and Thursday, and from 9 am to 6 pm on Saturday. A Turkish bath costs R35, a massage costs R25, and a bath and massage is R50.

SIGNAL HILL

Signal Hill (Map 3) (once also known as Lion's Rump, as it is attached by a 'spine' of hills to Lion's Head) separates Sea Point from the City Bowl. There are magnificent views from the 350m-high summit of Signal Hill, especially at night. Head up Kloof Nek Rd from the city and take the turn-off to the right at the top of the hill. At this intersection you also turn off for Clifton (also to the right) and the lower cableway station (left).

Signal Hill was the early settlement's lookout point, and it was from here that flags were hoisted when a ship was spotted, giving the citizens below time to prepare their goods for sale and dust off their tankards.

Noon Gun

At noon, every day except Sunday, a cannon is fired from the lower slopes of Signal Hill. You can hear it all over town. Traditionally this allowed the burghers in the town below to check their watches. You can walk up to the cannon through the Bo-Kaap area – take Longmarket St and keep going up until it ends. The Noon Gun Café (Map 3) is a good place to regather your senses after they've been frazzled by that big bang.

TABLE MOUNTAIN & CABLEWAY

The cableway (Map 5) is such an obvious, popular and clichéd attraction you might have difficulty convincing yourself that it is worth the trouble and expense. It is. The views from the top of Table Mountain are phenomenal, and there are some excellent walks on the summit. The mountain is home to more than 1400 species of flowering plants, which are particularly spectacular in spring. It's also home to rock dassies, curious rodent-like creatures, known as rock hyrax in East Africa, whose closest living relation is the elephant. They like to be fed.

If you do plan to walk, make sure you're properly equipped with warm and waterproof clothing. Table Mountain is over 1000m high and conditions can become treacherous quickly. There's a small restaurant and shop at the top, where you can post letters and send faxes.

Three marked walking routes taking from five minutes to half an hour wind around the top: the short tortoise walk, the mid-length rock dassie walk and the longer klipspringer walk.

Cableway

The cable cars don't operate when it's dangerously windy, and there's obviously not much point going up if you are simply going to be wrapped in the tablecloth. Ring in advance (☎ 24 5148 or 24 8409) to see if they're operating. When the winds reach

30km/h the cable cars stop taking people up, although they continue to bring them down. At 40km/h all services are stopped. Typically during the winter there will be five or six days each month when the cable cars cannot operate. Weather conditions permitting, they operate from 8 am to 9.30 pm in November, 7 am to 10.30 pm from December to mid-January, 8 am to 9.30 pm from mid-January to the end of April and from 8.30 am to 5.30 pm the rest of the year. The best visibility and conditions are likely to be first thing in the morning, or in the evening.

The cableway carried its 10 millionth passenger in 1994. It has never had a fatality. New cable cars were introduced in 1997, increasing capacity and cutting down on the three or four-hour queues. Unfortunately pre-booking was discontinued then, so you might still have to queue. A return ticket costs R45 and you can also buy a one-way ticket if you want to walk up or down.

To get to the lower cable station, catch the Kloof Nek bus from outside OK Bazaars (Map 8) on Adderley St to the Kloof Nek terminus and connect with the cableway bus. Buses operate about every half hour. A minibus taxi will cost R5 per person, while a regular metered taxi will be about R30 from central Cape Town. There are often taxis waiting at the cableway station, particularly late in the day. By car, take Kloof Nek Rd (Map 5) and turn off to the left (signposted).

Walking Up

Walking up (or down) Table Mountain is definitely possible – more than 300 routes have been identified. However, it is a high mountain and claims lives from time to time. It's safe enough if you are properly prepared with warm clothing and emergency food and water, and if you stick to the path. The trouble is, thick mists can make the paths invisible, and you'll just have to wait until they lift. You should always tell someone where you are going and you should never walk alone. Captour can put you in touch with a guide, and adventure activity outfits such as Day Trippers (see Organised Tours in the Getting Around chapter) can give

advice. Climbing the mountain is such a popular pastime that there's a good chance that you'll meet someone who will invite you along.

None of the routes are easy, but the beautiful Platteklip Gorge walk on the City Bowl side is at least straightforward.

Unless you're fit, try walking down before you attempt the walk up. It took me about 2½ hours from the upper cable station to the lower, taking it fairly easy. If you walk to/from the Kirstenbosch Botanic Gardens, you are in shade for a lot of the way.

Shirley Brossy's *Walking Guide to Table Mountain* (paper, R30) details 34 walks. Mike Lundy's *Best Walks in the Cape Peninsula* (paper, R40) is also useful. Serious climbers could contact the Mountain Club of South Africa (☎ 45 3412), 97 Hatfield St. Guided walks are available and Captour has details.

continued on page 80

MIKE REED

One of Table Mountain's do-it-yourself cableways.

Cape Floral Kingdom

If asked about the world's richest floral habitat, most of us would probably say it's the fantastically riotous Amazon rainforest – and we'd be wrong. The world's richest concentration of plant life is the Cape floral kingdom, which has more than three times as many species per square kilometre as South America.

The world's richest floral kingdom is also the smallest – and the most threatened. While it is home to nearly 8000 plant species, many of which exist only there, the habitat of many is incredibly small, sometimes no larger than a suburban backyard. As a result, a species can be destroyed almost as easily as you might mow the lawn.

The sheer variety of fynbos is astonishing, especially given the size of the area – a floral kingdom is usually continent-sized (eg Australia), not something you can leisurely traverse in a day or two. In part this is the result of ecological isolation, as South Africa's mountain ranges harbour mini-universes of biodiversity. But at least as impressive as the numbers is the colour; the profusion of hues could drive a would-be Post-Impressionist back to the banks of the Seine.

The Cape floral kingdom extends from Cape Point east to Port Elizabeth (or Grahamstown, depending on how the flora is defined) and north to the Oliphants River. The tiny Table Mountain and Cape Peninsula protected areas contain more plant species than all of Britain.

Fynbos

The most common vegetation in the Cape floral kingdom is fynbos (literally fine bush, from the Dutch). Fynbos somehow thrives in the area's nitrogen-poor soil – it's supposed that the fine, leathery leaves of the plants improve the odds of survival by discouraging predators.

Three main plant families comprise the fynbos: Proteaceae (proteas), Ericaceae (heaths) and Restionaceae (reeds). (An area with more than 5% restios cover is considered a fynbos area.) The family with the largest number of species is actually Asteraceae (daisies) – there are nearly 1000 species, of which nearly two-thirds are endemic to the area. Orchids (family Orchidaceae) are also found throughout the region, mainly in marshlands

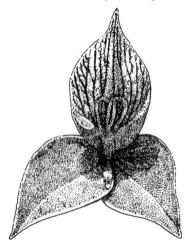

The beautiful red disa has flowers 10cm across, supported by scarlet or carmine sepals. The plant is about 60cm high. You can find them scattered around Table Mountain and in many local nature reserves and national parks.

and grasslands. Blue disa and red disa (*Disa uniflora*) are especially worth watching for. In addition, many species of Iridaceae not only thrive in the fynbos, they have also taken root in gardens around the world, eg freesia, iris, watsonia and gladiolus.

While many flowering natives have been domesticated elsewhere, there is nothing quite like the plants of the fynbos itself – the proteas in particular can be breathtaking. The South African floral industry is beginning to take off, with new hybrids appearing at overseas exhibitions and fynbos reeds touted as alternative ornamental grasses. Look for more and better flower markets as the industry grows, but be aware that the fynbos remains an extremely fragile floral realm.

The same may be said for research into the medicinal uses of fynbos (Buchu brandy and Rooibos tea, both distilled from fynbos, have been used as *boereraat* – home remedies): the more the value of the plants, the argument goes, the more danger of exploitation exists.

Proteas (Proteaceae)

Proteus, the metamorphising sea god, lent his name to these extraordinary flowers. A flower head appears singular but is actually multiple – brightly coloured overlapping scales (bracts) form the protea's deep cup, which contains myriad filament-thin flowers. Each flower has four (often fluffy) petals, three of which are joined and one free.

Proteas are undoubtedly the main attraction of a walk among the fynbos. Often taller than the surrounding vegetation, their stunning flowers stand out across the veld and on the Cape's many walking trails.

The king protea (*Protea cynaroides*), easily recognised by its huge, flat blossom (pale pink surrounded by dark pink or red 'petals'), is the national flower of South Africa.

Not all proteas have deep cupped flowers, eg red and yellow bottlebrush (*Mimetes hirtus*), which blooms from May to October, has longer, streaming flowers attractive to sunbirds and sugarbirds.

Pincushions Called luisiebosie in Afrikaans, *Leucospermum calligerun* has a green flower. Vaalkreupelhout (*Leucospermum conocarpodendron*), commonly known as grey tree pincushion, is a large pincushion flower which blooms from August to January. Its 'hairy' leaves (whose tips are dotted red) trap moisture and its bark (once used in leather tanning) protects it against fire.

South Africa's national flower, the king protea, has also lent its name to the national cricket team. The many varieties of protea are in high demand at flower shows around the world.

Erica obliqua, *with its distinctive pink flowers, is one of over 500 ericoid species in the floral kingdom.*

Conebushes

These leucadendrons (literally white trees) lack the deep, cup-shaped flower common to many proteas. Seeds of these plants are spread by wind once the bushes die from fire, or by ants. The silver tree (*Leucadendron argenteum*) is a striking example; writing in the 1930s, the Australian botanist John Hutchinson noted that the ancient silver trees at Kirstenbosch 'are seen at their best in a gentle breeze, when the silvery sheen of the leaves is displayed to great advantage'.

Daystar Another exception to the general description of proteas is *Diastella divaricata*, a low shrub with tiny pink flowers that resemble stars.

Ericas (Ericaceae)

The leaves of the Cape's heath plants give the fynbos its defining character. The Cape floral kingdom contains over 100 erica species. Many of the brilliant ericas can be spotted from the name alone, eg the blood red heath (*Erica cruenta*) and the amber heath (*Erica curviflora*).

Heathers Rooihaartjie (red african heather, *Erica cerinthoides*) flowers all year and its pink, orange and red blooms speckle the area's mountains. Pink heather (*Erica laeta*) is noteworthy for its lovely, tiny bell flowers.

Daisies (Asteraceae)

A daisy on the Cape may be a tree, shrub or bush. Everlasting (*Helichrysum vestitum*), which flowers from October to January, is recognisable by the etymology of its name: from the Greek helos (sun) and chrysos (gold). Leaves of gousblom (*Gazania krebsiana* and *Gazania maritima*) are dark green on top and white underneath; this daisy blooms in spring and is common near the sea.

Blombos Blombos (*Metalasia muricata*) is plentiful, and while the small greyish-green leaves of this tall shrub resemble those of an erica, its structure – and its tiny white flower heads – identifies it as a daisy. Tea is made from its leaves.

Reeds (Restionaceae)

With their dry, brownish leaves, Cape reeds fill the role usually occupied by grasses. Most restios (the Latin restis means rope) thrive in the wetter areas of the kingdom. Dekriet (genus *Thamnochortus*) has long been used to thatch houses. The veld is burned for regeneration of the reeds.

The Kingdom's Future

The fynbos is part of a delicate ecosystem which has thrived amid periodic climatic changes and fires; however, human activity has raised the stakes enormously, and now threatens the very existence of the Cape floral kingdom.

Lightning fires are one thing – some fynbos species actually require periodic fires for regeneration – but out of season and too frequent burning are another. Land clearing and commercial deforestation, twin pillars of 'development', are further dangers.

So far, some 26 fynbos species have become extinct; plants in danger of the same fate are mostly concentrated in the Cape Flats townships (which is not currently part of the World Bank's 'save the fynbos' project – see World Bank Project following).

Alien Plants

The main threat to fynbos comes from introduced flora. Some were brought

over from Australia in the 19th century, eg rock hakea (*Hakea gibbosa*), rooikrans (*Acacia cyclops*), black wattle (*Acacia mearnsii*) and Port Jackson wattle (*Acacia saligna*). Introduced to the Cape early this century, Sydney golden wattle (*Acacia longifolia*) has also become a pest. Probably the worst offender is *Hakea sericea* (locally called silky hakea), imported as a hedge plant in the 1830s and now declared a noxious weed in South Africa.

Australian plants were often imported for special purposes (eg the bark of the black wattle was used in leather-making and Port Jackson wattle served to bind soil), but the results have been devastating to local flora. These introduced species require more water than native plants do, but thrive without natural enemies; water sources dry up and fynbos are choked out of certain areas as a result.

The importation of plants was once common among the British-influenced realms (though not limited to them), when ecology was largely a branch of empire-building. But the trade wasn't one-way: boneseed (*Chrysanthemoides monolifera*) is a South African evergreen shrub which has choked out native plants in several areas of Australia.

World Bank Project

Table Mountain has been a Natural and Historic Monument since 1951, but if the World Bank has its way, a new 30,000 hectare national park will stretch from Table Mountain to the Cape Peninsula. To promote itself as a kinder, gentler 'development' organisation, the Bank is supporting the Cape Floral Kingdom project, brokering a no-strings-attached grant from the Global Environmental Facility – most of which goes towards creating a single management authority over the area's flora. The project also allocates money to support local conservation activites, which include creating an extensive database to model solutions to the dangers from alien plants.

The World Bank hopes that increased tourism to the area (and offshoots like Rooibos tea sales – see the Rooibos Tea boxed text in the Excursions chapter) will more than offset the initial investment. More awareness, and more people tramping through the bush, is a double-edged sword – rare species may come to the attention of 'plant poachers' and tourism means more activity among the fragile fynbos, but inaction means eventual death for the ecosystem. And, while the cause is a worthy one, some may wonder if and when the Bank's newly enlightened approach will be applied to, say, the development of township infrastructure.

What You Can Do

In addition to seeing the unique beauty of the fynbos for yourself (and leaving the area as undisturbed as possible), you can become more informed by contacting Cape Nature Conservation (Map 8) (☎ 483 4227) or by visiting the University of the Western Cape's Web site at www.botany.uwc.ac. za/fynbos/index.htm.

Russ Kerr

continued from page 75

VICTORIA & ALFRED WATERFRONT

The Victoria & Alfred Waterfront (Map 9) is pitched at tourists but it's atmospheric, interesting and packed with restaurants, bars, music venues and interesting shops.

The development seems to have given the whole city a boost, and is tremendously popular, day and night. There is an information centre (☎ 418 2369), in the middle of the complex, where you can get free maps of the Waterfront. It's open daily but not in the evenings. There's also an information kiosk in the Victoria Wharf mall that stays open until 9 pm in summer.

Despite all the development, it remains a working harbour and that is the source of the Waterfront's charm. Most of the redevelopment has been undertaken around the historic Alfred and Victoria Basins (constructed from 1860). Although these wharfs are too small for modern container vessels and tankers, the Victoria Basin is still used by tugs, harbour vessels of various kinds and fishing boats. There is still a smell of diesel and salt and the bustle of real boats and people doing real work.

The National Sea Rescue Institute (NSRI) has a rescue boat stationed next to Quay 4. When you see some of the waves that can be whipped up it's pretty brave to go out in such a small craft. On a slipway next to the NSRI you'll often see one of the small working craft that does battle with the seas.

Large modern shipping uses the adjacent Duncan and Ben Schoeman docks. These were constructed from the mid-1930s and the sand excavated was used to reclaim the foreshore area north-east of the Strand. The Castle used to be virtually on the shorefront, and the old high water line actually passes through the Golden Acre Centre.

The Waterfront is *the* place to go for nightlife. There is strict security and although it is safe to walk around, there are plenty of merry men, so women on their own should be a little cautious. The restaurateurs along Main Rd in Sea Point are reeling – a big proportion of their trade has been stolen. See the Places to Eat and Entertainment chapters for information on the Waterfront's numerous restaurants and bars, although if you just go for a wander you'll find something that appeals.

Make sure that you see the Cape fur seals, which are usually found on and near Berties Landing. Berties Landing is across a narrow channel from the Old Port Captain's building at Pier Head and is reached with a quick trip on the *Penny Ferry* (which now costs a couple of rand). If the ferry isn't too busy it will often make a detour to have a look at some seals.

There is a downside to the Waterfront, and many visitors quickly tire of it. The big shopping malls and the residential developments around the newly re-flooded Alfred Basin mean that it's becoming a self-contained upmarket suburb. It's also an antiseptic, security-conscious and decidedly white suburb. Transport logistics and economics can present almost as many barriers to non-whites as the old laws.

Cruises

A trip into Table Bay should not be missed. Few people nowadays have the privilege of reaching the Tavern of the Seas by passenger ship, but something of the feeling can be captured by taking a harbour cruise. The view of Table Mountain hasn't changed. Many cruises are on offer – for a range of options see Waterfront Charters (Map 9) (☎ 25 3804), Old Port Captain's building, where a half-hour cruise costs just R8. Full tours start at R20.

Aquarium

The aquarium (Map 9) is well worth a visit. It features denizens of the deep from both the cold and warm oceans which border the Cape Peninsula, including great white sharks, which congregate in False Bay. There are touch-tanks for the kids and the astounding kelp forest, which is alone worth the R22 admission.

Maritime Museum

This small museum (Map 9) is a bit of a poor relation at the glitzy Waterfront, but it's a pleasant place and worth a look.

Getting There & Away

Shuttle buses run from Adderley St in front of the Tourist Rendezvous, then up Strand St, with a stop near the Cape Sun Hotel, to the centre of the Waterfront. They also run along Beach Rd in Sea Point. They depart half hourly from early to late and cost R1.20.

If you're driving, there are free parking spaces, which are often full, but there's usually space in the inexpensive car park beneath the Victoria Wharf complex.

ROBBEN ISLAND

Robben Island (Map 1), not far off the mainland but quite far enough to prevent escapes, was the high-security prison for Cape Town and later the whole country. Illustrious prisoners of the early years included political prisoners from the Dutch East Indies; until recently it held many of the ANC's top leaders, including Nelson Mandela. The prison was recently decommissioned and the island is now open for tours.

Nelson Mandela

Nelson Mandela, the son of the third wife of a Xhosa chief, was born on 18 July 1918 in the small village of Mveso on the Mbashe River. When he was very young the family moved to Qunu, south of Umtata. He attended school in the Transkei before going to Jo'burg where, after a few false starts, he undertook legal studies and set up a law practice with Oliver Tambo. He shunned the opportunities offered to educated blacks and adopted a more militant stance, aspiring to help in the liberation of his people.

In 1944 he helped form the Youth League of the African National Congress (ANC) with Walter Sisulu and Oliver Tambo. Its aim was to end the racist policies of the white South African government. He met Nomzamo Winnifred Madikizela ('Winnie') and, after receiving a divorce from his first wife, Evelyn, married her. (They officially separated in 1991 after decades of separation while Nelson was in prison. They were recently divorced and Mr Mandela these days keeps company with Graca Machel, widow of the Mozambiquan leader.)

In 1964, after establishing the ANC's military wing, Mandela was captured and sentenced to life imprisonment on the infamous Robben Island prison near Cape Town. In the early 1970s conditions were relaxed enough on Robben Island to allow Mandela to write his now famous prison notebooks and teach courses in politics.

After the ANC was declared a legal organisation, Mandela was released from prison in 1990. In 1991 he was elected president of the ANC and began the long negotiations which were to end minority rule. He shared the 1993 Nobel Peace Prize with FW de Klerk and, in the first free elections the following year, was elected president of South Africa.

On 2 May 1994, in the presence of Coretta Scott King, wife of the late Martin Luther King Jr, he said to his people:

You have shown such a calm, patient determination to reclaim this country as your own and now the joy that we can loudly proclaim from the rooftops – Free at last! Free at last! I stand before you humbled by your courage, with a heart full of love for all of you. I regard it as the highest honour to lead the ANC at this moment in our history. I am your servant ... this is the time to heal the old wounds and build a new South Africa.

President Mandela is walking one of the thinnest tightropes imaginable. The freeing of the people from 20 generations of repression would, in any other post-colonial country, have resulted in an entirely understandable (and perhaps psychologically necessary) chaos of sudden change and revenge. Mandela, however, must ensure that as many whites as possible stay in the country and that their businesses remain lucrative. The ANC is a genuinely nonracial organisation and Mandela seems sincere in his desire to create a truly nonracial South Africa, but for the many, many thousands who suffered physically, mentally and economically under apartheid, this must be a bitter pill. ∎

'Madiba' has been true to his words: 'The struggle is my life'.

Robben Island ('robben' means 'seals') is possibly the most important historical site in South Africa. It was here, in what was dubbed the ANC university, that the leaders of the black resistance movement spent years directing the struggle and teaching younger comrades who came and went on shorter sentences. It was here that Mandela began his covert contact with the apartheid government which was to lead to negotiations and, ultimately, liberation.

Because the island was a prison (and later also a leper colony) since almost the beginning of white settlement, its ecology has been far less degraded than that of the mainland, just across the water. Penguin and several species of antelope are among the wildlife to be seen.

Tours to the island began in 1997 and got off to a shaky start, with people starting to queue at 4 am to be one of the 300 allowed on the island. Things have settled down a little, but the tours are still immensely popular. Guides are former guards and political prisoners, so the historical content is exceptional.

Tickets are sold on No1 Jetty at the Waterfront (☎ 419 1300) between 8 am and 5 pm and cost R80 (R25 for children). There are three daily 3½ hour tours, at 9 and 11 am and 1.15 pm. You have to arrive half an hour before departure.

SOUTHERN SUBURBS

Expensive and leafy white suburbs cling to the eastern slopes of Table Mountain. Visiting areas such as Mowbray and Rosebank (Map 6), Rondebosch, Claremont and Newlands (Map 7) present a complete contrast to the more gritty life on the other side of the mountain in the City Bowl, and an almost unimaginable contrast to life in the townships and squatter camps on the Cape Flats, which these suburbs overlook. The view is better looking across the flats to the mountain ranges around Stellenbosch and, on a clear day, to the succeeding ranges that eventually rise up into the great southern African plateau.

Getting There & Away

Following are transport options for the southern suburbs.

Train Trains on the Simon's Town railway line run through these suburbs, although you'll do a lot of walking to get from the train stations to most of the attractions. The exceptions are the rugby/cricket grounds (Map 7) (Newlands train station) and Cavendish Square (Map 7) (Claremont train station).

Car & Motorcycle To get here by car, take the Eastern Boulevard (the N2) from the city centre or De Waal Drive (the M3) from Orange St in Gardens/Oranjezicht. These freeways merge near the Groote Schuur Hospital (Map 6) in Observatory, then run around Devil's Peak. The M3 sheers off to the right soon after (it can be a dangerous manoeuvre getting into the right lanes!) and then runs parallel to the east side of the mountain.

If you were to follow the M3 you'd arrive in Muizenberg, on False Bay, but to visit the attractions of the Southern Suburbs, you'll have to keep a sharp eye out for the exits.

Just after the open paddocks on Devil's Peak (where you might see zebras), you'll pass the old **Mostert's Mill** (Map 6) on the left. Just past the old windmill, also on the left, is the exit for the **University of Cape Town** (Map 7). To get there, turn right at the T-intersection after you've taken the exit; to get to the **Baxter Theatre** (Map 7) and the **Newlands rugby/cricket grounds**, turn left at the T-intersection and travel along Woolsack Ave.

The Baxter Theatre is on the corner of Woolsack Ave and Main Rd (the M4). Main Rd continues south past Newlands, a Holiday Inn and several large shopping centres, to the suburb of Claremont, where the **Cavendish Square** centre is *the* place to shop.

The exit for the **Rhodes Memorial** (Map 6) is at the Princess Anne Interchange on the M3. The turn-off (on the right) to the **Kirstenbosch Botanic Gardens** (Map 7) is at the intersection of Union (the M3) and

Rhodes Aves (the M63). Stay on the M3 for an exit (on the left) for Claremont.

University of Cape Town (UCT)

For the nonacademic there is no real reason to visit UCT (Map 7), but it is an impressive place to walk around. Unlike most universities it presents a fairly cohesive architectural front, with ivy-covered neoclassical façades, and a fine set of stone steps leading up to the temple-like Jameson building. Check out Smuts and Farrer halls halfway up the steps.

The student centre is in the Leslie Social Sciences building (turn left at the curving road near the top of the steps). There's a cafeteria and a South African Students' Travel Service (SASTS) office, but few other facilities.

Visitors can usually get parking permits – call at the information office on the entry road, near the bottom of the steps.

Rhodes Memorial

In 1895 Cecil Rhodes purchased the eastern slopes of Table Mountain as part of a plan to preserve a relatively untouched section, and bequeathed the property to the nation on his death in 1906. An impressive granite memorial (Map 6) to Rhodes was constructed, commanding a view of the Cape Flats and the mountain ranges beyond – and by implication, right into the heart of Africa. Despite the classical proportions of the memorial and the eight large bronze lions, the bust of Rhodes looks somewhat bored and testy.

There's a pleasant tearoom in an old stone cottage nearby.

The memorial is a popular place from which to see the sun rise on New Year's Day. On one memorable occasion, the new year dawned on a New Age gathering being harassed by chanting anti-Satanists.

Kirstenbosch Botanic Gardens

The Kirstenbosch Botanic Gardens (Map 7) (☎ 762 1166) on Rhodes Ave, Constantia, are among the most beautiful gardens in the world, and are a must see for any visitor to Cape Town. They have an incomparable site

on the eastern side of Table Mountain, right at the foot of the final steep escarpment overlooking False Bay and the Cape Flats. The 36 hectare landscaped section seems to merge almost imperceptibly with the 492 hectares of fynbos that cloaks the mountain slopes.

Portions of the hedge that Jan van Riebeeck planted in 1660 to isolate his settlement from the Khoisan can still be seen.

Although there are some magnificent oaks, Moreton Bay fig trees and camphor trees, the gardens are devoted almost exclusively to indigenous plants. About 9000 of southern Africa's 22,000 plant species are grown in the gardens. They are predominantly from the winter rainfall region, but there are also large numbers of hardy species from other parts of the country, including Namaqualand. There is always something flowering, but the gardens are at their best between mid-August and mid-October. A new conservatory is atmosphere-controlled and displays plant communities from a variety of terrains, the most interesting of which is the Namaqualand/Kalahari section, with baobabs, 'quiver' trees and others.

The gardens have been thoughtfully laid out and include a Fragrance Garden that has been raised so you can sample the scents of the plants more easily, a Braille Trail, a *koppie* (rock outcrop) that has been planted with pelargoniums, and sections featuring cycads, aloes, euphorbias, ericas and, of course, proteas. There are several signposted circular walks that explore the forest and fynbos that surround the cultivated section.

The gardens are now growing 'muti' plants, to be used by *sangoma* (traditional healers) in traditional medicine to help conserve the supply in the wild.

The information office is open daily from 8 am to 4.45 pm, and staff can provide maps and advice on various walks. There is also a shop where you can buy a wide range of indigenous plants and some excellent books on South African flora.

The restaurant is open daily for breakfast. It's not formal or flash but it is good value. You can get something cheap and filling like

Cecil Rhodes: Empire Builder

Cecil John Rhodes (1853-1902), the sickly son of an English vicar, was sent to South Africa in 1870 to improve his health. After working on his brother's farm in Natal, Rhodes left for the new diamond fields near Kimberley in 1871. By 1887 he had founded the De Beers Company and could afford to buy Barney Barnato's Kimberley Mine for £5 million. By 1891 De Beers owned 90% of the world's diamonds and Rhodes also had a stake in the fabulous reef of gold discovered on the Witwatersrand (near Jo'burg).

Rhodes was not satisfied with merely acquiring personal wealth and power. He personified the idea of 'empire' and dreamed of 'painting the map red', building a railway from the Cape to Cairo (running through British territory all the way) and even had far-fetched ideas of bringing the USA back under British rule.

The times were right for such dreams, and Rhodes was a favourite of Queen Victoria and of the voters (both Boer and British) in the Cape. In 1890 he was elected prime minister of the Cape Colony.

To paint Africa red, Rhodes pushed north to establish mines and develop trade. Although he despised missionaries for being too soft on the natives, he used them as stalking horses in his wrangling and chicanery to open up new areas.

He was successful in establishing British control in Bechuanaland (later Botswana) and the area that was to become Rhodesia (later Zimbabwe), but the gold mines there proved to be less productive than those on the Witwatersrand.

The Transvaal Republic in general and Paul Kruger in particular had been causing Rhodes difficulty for some time. Both Kruger and Rhodes were fiercely independent idealists with very different ideals, and there was no love lost between them.

It irked Rhodes that Kruger's pastoralist republic should be sitting on the richest reef of gold in the world, and the republic was also directly in the path of British expansion.

The miners on the Witwatersrand were mainly non-Boers, who were denied any say in the politics of the republic. This caused increasing resentment, and in late 1895 one Dr Leander Star Jameson led an expedition into the Witwatersrand with the intention of sparking an uprising among the foreigners.

The Jameson raid was a fiasco. All the participants were killed or captured, and Jameson was jailed.

The British government was extremely embarrassed when it became apparent that Rhodes had prior knowledge of the raid and probably encouraged it. He was forced to resign as prime minister and the British government took control of Rhodesia and Bechuanaland, his personal fiefdoms.

Rhodes' health deteriorated after these disasters. His empire-building days were over, but one more stock episode from the Victorian omnibus awaited: an honourable chap becomes entangled in the schemes of a glamorous and ruthless woman, in this case the Princess Randziwill. She was later jailed for her swindles.

After his death in 1906, Rhodes' reputation was largely rehabilitated by his will, which devoted most of his fortune to the Rhodes Scholarship, which still sends winners to Oxford University. ∎

Considered a visionary by admirers, Cecil Rhodes once publicly declared, 'The native is to be treated as a child and denied the franchise'.

a salad or sausages and vegetables for R15, or a steak for around R25.

The gardens are open year-round from 8 am, closing at 7 pm from September to March, and 6 pm from April to August; entry is R5. There are guided walks on Tuesday and Saturday from 11 am for approximately 1½ hours.

Getting There & Away If you're driving, see the main Getting There & Away entry at the beginning of the Southern Suburbs section in this chapter for directions.

It is possible to catch buses from Mowbray station on the Simon's Town railway line, but there aren't many buses running. Phone

Golden Arrow (☎ 080 121 2111) for an up-to-date timetable. A minibus taxi running from the main train station to Wynberg might take you within walking distance of the gardens, but check the route carefully.

You can also walk uphill to the upper station of the Table Mountain cableway. This could be done in three hours by someone of moderate fitness. Make sure you have a map (from the Kirstenbosch Botanic Gardens information office or the Table Mountain shop) and are prepared for any sudden changes in weather. The trails are all well marked, and steep in places, but the cableway station is not signposted from the gardens or vice versa.

Groot Constantia

Groot Constantia (Map 1) is the Cape's oldest and grandest vineyard and homestead – a superb example of Cape Dutch architecture. It embodies the gracious and refined lifestyle that wealthy Dutch created in their adopted country. Groot Constantia was built by one of the early governors, Simon van der Stel, in 1692. Not surprisingly, van der Stel could not bear to be parted from his creation; after his retirement he refused to return to Europe and stayed until he died in 1712.

In the 18th century, Constantia wines were exported around the world and were highly acclaimed. Today, the estate is owned by a syndicate, and fine wines are still produced. Unfortunately, it is a bit of a tourist trap, but it's worth visiting, especially if you don't have time to explore the Winelands around Stellenbosch – but if you've made the trip to Boschendal (see the Excursions chapter) you don't need to come here. Try to avoid visiting on a weekend; it can get very crowded.

The beautiful homestead has been carefully restored and appropriately furnished. The nearby wine museum traces the history of wine from the 6th century BC. Entry is R5, and the building is open from 10 am to 5 pm daily.

You can take a tour of the modern winemaking operation for R7; hourly in the high season, and at 11 am and 3 pm in the low season. Wines are on sale daily. Prices range

from R7 to R26 per bottle depending on the variety and vintage; the '89 Governor's reserve red bordeaux is its top wine. For R8 you can taste five wines – and you get to keep the glass. Tastings are free if you do the cellar tour, and are available between 10 am and 4.30 pm; the office sales stays open until 5 pm.

There are a number of places to eat (see the Places to Eat chapter) and for provisions, there's the excellent Old Cape Farm Stall on the corner of Constantia and Groot Constantia Rds.

Getting There & Away A visit to Groot Constantia could easily be combined with a visit to the brilliant Kirstenbosch Botanic Gardens. The easiest (if not the most direct) route to Groot Constantia is to turn right off the M3 onto Rhodes Ave (the M63), then continue south past Kirstenbosch until you reach Main Rd (the M41). Turn left and keep going until you come to signs directing you to Groot Constantia, down a road on the right.

Unfortunately, there is no public transport.

ATLANTIC COAST

The Atlantic coast of the Cape Peninsula has some of the most spectacular coastal scenery in the world. The combination of beaches and mountains is irresistible. The beaches include the trendiest on the Cape, and the emphasis is on sunbaking rather than swimming. Although it is possible to find shelter from the summer south-easterlies, the water comes straight from the Antarctic (courtesy of the Benguela current) and swimming is nothing if not exhilarating.

On the more popular beaches in the city area you might see the work of sand artists, who create huge and complex naive artworks in return for donations. They will take requests. Unfortunately, the council regards them as a nuisance and wants to make them pay a licence fee.

Buses and minibus taxis run around Victoria Rd from the city to Hout Bay, but after that, you're on your own. Hitching is reasonably good.

How to Pick the Best Beaches

There is a huge number of beaches within an easy drive of the City Bowl – some are an easy train ride or walk. For a complete description, look for *101 Beaches on and around the Cape Peninsula*, a paperback by Ross Torr & Andy Wood. You might have to hunt for it in second-hand bookshops.

As well as the usual factors in deciding which beach to visit – crowds, surf, facilities – Cape Town has a couple more. The water on the Atlantic coast is *cold* year-round, and while there are some beautiful beaches you won't want to spend long in the water. Also, the strong seasonal winds can make exposed beaches unpleasant. Luckily, while one side of the peninsula is being sandblasted, the other side is sheltered, though you can often find sheltered spots on either coast.

In summer, the prevailing wind is the south-easterly. The city beaches of Sea Point and Clifton are usually sheltered, as is Boulders on False Bay near Simon's Town. On the western side of False Bay, Gordon's Bay is also a good bet during a south-easterly. When the winter north-westerlies blow, head for Hout Bay or the northern end of Muizenberg beach, known as Surfers' Corner. Boulders, near Simon's Town, is also usually sheltered.

During summer, surfers flock to Blouberg, Kommetjie's Long Beach or Scarborough, and in winter Blouberg or Muizenberg.

The winds are usually lightest in the morning in summer, gaining strength rapidly in the afternoon. A southerly wind indicates good weather, while a northerly indicates bad weather.

Note that 4WD vehicles are allowed on some beaches, so beware of drunken idiots behind the wheel. ■

Bloubergstrand

Bloubergstrand (Map 1), 25km to the north of the city on Table Bay, was the site for the 1806 battle between British and Dutch forces that resulted in the second British occupation of the Cape. This is also the spot with the most dramatic (and photographed) view of Table Mountain – you know, the one with wildflowers and sand dunes in the foreground, surf and, across the bay, the cloud-capped mountain ramparts looming over the city.

This is a boom area for antiseptic new suburbs, but the village of Bloubergstrand itself is still quite small. There are a couple of small resorts where you can have a *braai* (barbecue) and buy snacks, and find some long, uncrowded, windy stretches of sand. The Beach Club (keep going through Bloubergstrand) is a pleasant spot with takeaway food available. Blue Peter has been recommended as a good spot for sundowners (drinks at sunset).

Beaches Blouberg, in addition to having that famous view of Cape Town and Table Mountain, offers the best surfing close to Cape Town. Swimming is also safe and windsurfing is popular. **Big Bay**, at the northern end, is the place for surf. South of Blouberg is **Table View**, with a long beach and good swimming. Nearby, **Milnerton** is another long beach, with a sheltered lagoon at the southern end, which is ideal for children. The water in the lagoon will probably be warmer than the sea.

Getting There & Away Unfortunately, you'll need a car. Take the R27 north from the N1.

The Docks

Definitely not beautiful but perhaps interesting, the Duncan and Ben Schoeman docks (Map 4) might make a rainy-day outing. The docks were constructed from the mid-1930s as part of the foreshore reclamation project.

The docks are very busy, and there's a healthy yacht-building industry. Cape Town yachts have a reputation for being tough enough for anything. You'll see plenty moored at the **Royal Cape Yacht Club** and in the nearby small craft harbour. The massive supertankers that call in at Cape Town because they are too big to use the Suez Canal are also too big to enter Table Bay, so they are serviced by helicopter. There are a couple of interesting places to eat tucked away in the docks – see the Places to Eat chapter. Yachties can probably talk their way into the dining room at the yacht club.

Getting There & Away To get here, drive towards the sea on Adderley and Heerengracht Sts. Go under the freeway and turn right onto Duncan St at the T-intersection. You have to go through the Customs checkpoint but it's rarely staffed.

Green Point & Mouille Point

The next outcrop of land west of the Waterfront is Green Point (Map 3), a largely undeveloped area of reclaimed land with a stadium, a golf course and a large Sunday market. As well as the actual point, Green Point is also the name of a suburb, similar in style and facilities to neighbouring Sea Point. Right on the coast from Green Point is Mouille Point (Map 3), an oddly isolated little residential area. The lighthouse houses a small **museum**. It used to house a booming foghorn that could be heard all over town.

The coast is too rocky for swimming, but Mouille Point is a good place to visit on a stormy day.

Sea Point

Separated from the City Bowl by Signal Hill, Sea Point (Map 3) is a bustling residential suburb with numerous multistorey apartment buildings and hotels fringing the coast. It's one of the most densely populated suburbs in Africa. Main and Regent Rds are lined with restaurants, cafés and shops.

Beach In addition to the long beach (dangerous because of the rocks), Sea Point offers a number of rock pools. At the northern end, **Graaff's Pool** is for men only (yep). Just south of here (but out of sight of all those male bodies) is **Milton's Pool**, which also has a stretch of beach. The **Sea Point Pavilion Pool**, at the end of Clarens St and next to the Hard Rock Café, is open from 8.30 am to dusk; entry is R4. The pool is huge but a sunny day will heat it up. If it's 12°C in the ocean the pool will be about 20°C.

A number of reefs produce good waves for surfing. **Solly's** and **Boat Bay**, near the Sea Point pavilion, have lefts and rights that work on a south-easterly wind. Further along the beach towards Mouille Point there are a number of left reefs.

Getting There & Away To get here, catch any Clifton, Bakoven or Camps Bay bus from the main bus station (R2.60) – or walk. There's a pedestrian promenade above the beach.

Clifton

Unless you are interested in real estate and have seriously deep pockets, the only reason to visit Clifton (Map 2) is for its beach. But that's a pretty good reason! There are actually four linked beaches accessible by steps from the main road. They're the trendiest, busiest beaches on the Cape, but although they have the advantage of being sheltered from the wind, the water is cold. Consequently, favoured activities are sunbaking, people watching, tennis and frisbee. It's *very* hard to remember you're in Africa.

There's a friendly and relaxed mood, although the occupants and atmosphere tend to vary with each beach. **Fourth Beach**, at the Camps Bay end, is the most accessible and popular, and there's a shop at the Fourth Beach car park (on the Ridge, off Victoria Rd). **First Beach** is definitely the place to be seen.

Getting There & Away There are frequent buses from OK Bazaars, Adderley St, and minibus taxis from Strand St. Buses cost R2.60; minibus taxis are a bit less. It's a pleasant 3km walk from Sea Point and another 1km or so to Camps Bay. In summer there's no point driving to Clifton as you won't be able to park.

Camps Bay

The only difference between Camps Bay (Map 2) and Clifton is that there are places to eat, drink and stay in Camps Bay. Otherwise, it's the beach you come for, one of the most beautiful in the world. The fact that it is within 15 minutes of the city centre makes it even more extraordinary. It is often windy, and it is certainly not as trendy as the beaches at Clifton, but it is more spectacular. The **Twelve Apostles** running south from Table Mountain tumble into the sea above the broad stretch of white sand.

It is amazing how relatively unspoilt and uncrowded it is. The only drawbacks are the wind and the temperature of the water. There are no lifesavers and there is strong surf, so take care. There is a rock pool or two.

The small batch of shops and restaurants include the trendy Blues and a St Elmo's Pizzeria. Accommodation possibilities range from the five star Bay Hotel to the Stan Halt Youth Hostel, a stiff 20 minute walk up the hill towards Kloof Nek. This walk does, however, run through **The Glen**, a beautiful spot described by an entrepreneur last century as having 'umbrageous Bowers and sequestered Dells'. Earlier this century The Glen was said to be haunted by the ghost of a Dr James Barry. The hostel was once the stables for the neighbouring **Roundhouse**, formerly a shooting lodge.

Getting There & Away There are frequent buses from OK Bazaars, Adderley St, and minibus taxis from the main train station. Buses cost R2.60, minibus taxis about the same. It's a 1km or so walk north to the more sheltered coves at Clifton.

Llandudno
Llandudno (Map 1) seems completely removed from Cape Town (although it's only 18km away), let alone Africa. It's a small, exclusive seaside village clinging to steep slopes above a sheltered beach. There are no shops. The remains of the tanker *Romelia*, wrecked in 1977, lie off Sunset Rocks.

There's surfing on the beach breaks (mostly rights), best at high tide with a small swell and south-easterly wind. Be warned that the water is cold, even for the Atlantic coast. Turn into Llandudno from the M6 (Victoria Rd).

Sandy Bay
Sandy Bay (Map 1) is an unofficial but famous nudist beach. Just mentioning the name anywhere in South Africa causes male guffaws. Unfortunately, this attitude can intrude onto the beach itself, and women are sometimes harassed.

Like many such beaches, there are no direct access roads. Turn into Llandudno from the main road and keep left to the Sunset Rocks parking area. It's a 20 minute walk to the south. There can be waves; best at low tide with a south-easterly wind.

Hout Bay
Hout Bay (Map 1) opens up behind the almost vertical Sentinel and the steep slopes of Chapman's Peak. Hout Bay has a beautiful beach, offering safe swimming and some surfing – except when the south-easterly is blowing. Inland from the kilometre of white sand, there is quite a large and fast-growing satellite town that retains something of its village atmosphere. The southern arm of the bay is still an important fishing port (snoek and crayfish) and processing centre.

The bay is beautiful, and by far the best views of it are from Chapman's Peak Drive. Perched on a rock in the bay near the end of Chapman's Peak Drive is a bronze leopard. It has been sitting there since 1963 and is a reminder of the wildlife which once roamed the area's forests – which have also vanished.

The information centre (☎ 790 4053) is in the Trading Post shop on the main road and is open daily (reduced hours in the low season).

Hout Bay Museum (☎ 790 3270), 4 St Andrews Rd, tells the story of Hout Bay. **World of Birds**, Valley Rd, is an eccentric aviary with 450 species of birds. Although caging birds is not an attractive idea, a real effort has been made to make the aviaries large and natural.

There are daily **cruises** from Hout Bay, with Circe Launches (☎ 790 1040). The one-hour trips (R25) run out to Duiker Island, with its colony of Cape fur seals. There's at least one trip daily all year, at 10.30 am, and many more in summer. You can't book.

You can hire a hobie cat (catamaran) on the beach (☎ 790 4511). There are a number of restaurants, including a wharfside complex, Mariner's Wharf.

Getting There & Away Buses to Hout Bay (R5.30) leave from outside OK Bazaars on Adderley St. There are several early in the morning before 9 am, few in the middle of the day and several between 2.15 and 5.30 pm; there aren't many on weekends. Minibus taxis also cover this route for about the same price.

Chapman's Peak Drive

This 10km drive is cut into the side of sheer mountain walls, between layers of brilliantly coloured sedimentary rock. There are great views over Chapman's Bay and back to the Sentinel and Hout Bay. It is one of the great scenic drives in the world and should not be missed. Some of the backpacker tour outfits (notably Day Trippers) take along bicycles when they go down to Cape Point, which means you can cycle Chapman's Peak Drive – fabulous!

Noordhoek

Thirty km south-west of Cape Town in the shadow of Chapman's Peak, Noordhoek (Map 1) has a 5km stretch of magnificent and uncrowded beach. Favoured by surfers and walkers, it tends to be windy, and dangerous for swimmers. The Hoek, as it is known to surfers, is an excellent right beach break at the northern end that can handle a large swell, only at low tide and best with south-easterly winds. There's a caravan park.

Long Beach

At the Kommetjie end of Chapman's Bay, Long Beach (Map 1) is another popular surf and windsurf beach, with an attractive caravan park. Swimming can be a bit too exciting among the dumpers and rips. There are several distinct beaches offering different breaks – ask one of the surfers. There are lefts and rights, best on south-easterly or south-westerly winds.

To get here, take the turn-off to Kommetjie (to the right off the M6) and turn right before the village. The nearest shop is in Kommetjie.

Kommetjie

Kommetjie (Map 1) is a smallish crayfishing village with a quiet country atmosphere. There's a pub (with bar lunches), a restau-rant, a couple of caravan parks, a few shops and not much more. It is, however, the focal point for surfing on the Cape, offering an assortment of reefs that hold a very big swell. Outer Kom is a left point break out from the lighthouse. Inner Kom is more protected, with smaller lefts and lots of kelp, only at high tide. They both work best on south-easterly or south-westerly winds.

FALSE BAY

False Bay (Map 1) lies to the south-east of the city. Although the beaches on the east side of the peninsula are not quite as spectac-ular as those on the Atlantic side, the water is often 5°C or more warmer, and can reach 20°C in summer. This makes swimming far more pleasant. Suburban development around the coast is considerably more intense, pre-sumably because of the railway which runs all the way through to Simon's Town.

On the east side of False Bay, Strand and Gordon's Bay are a cross between satellite suburbs and beach resorts. They have great views back to the Cape and are in the shadow of the spectacular Hottentots-Holland moun-tains. Further on, there's a superb road that rivals Chapman's Peak Drive – see the Coast Road to Hermanus section in the Excursions chapter.

During October and November, False Bay is a favoured haunt for whales and their calves – southern right, humpback and bryde (pronounced breedah) whales are the most commonly sighted. They often come quite close to the shore. Great white sharks also frequent the bay.

Muizenberg

Unless the sun is shining, Muizenberg (Map 1) can be pretty bleak, but when the sun's out, you can escape the fairly tacky waterfront for a broad white beach that shelves gently and is generally safer than most of the peninsula beaches. And there are all those colourful 19th century bathing boxes. Unfortunately, they are let by the season – you can't hire one for the day.

Muizenberg is at the beginning of a long beach that curves all the way around to

Gordon's Bay. Surfing is best a bit further around at **Cemetery Beach** – beware of the sewage outfall pipe! Heading east from here on the long beach are some other resort-style facilities at **Mnandi** and **Monwabisa**, built for residents of the nearby townships.

Heading south on the road between Muizenberg and Kalk Bay, you'll come to the **Labia Museum**. The Italian Count Labia was a wealthy patron of the arts and his plush house is worth a look. There's also a reasonable little café here. You can't park at the Labia Museum and you'll probably pass it before you think of looking for a parking space. About 100m further on (coming from the Muizenberg direction) there's a car park on the right; if you miss that go on over the hill, where there's parking on the left, across from the **Rhodes Cottage Museum**, in a collection of thatched, whitewashed old buildings.

Kalk Bay

Kalk Bay (or Kalkbaai) (Map 1) was named after the lime kilns that were operated in the 17th century to produce lime from seashells for painting buildings. In 1806 it became a whaling station, and it is still a busy fishing harbour, particularly during the snoek season which peaks during June and July, but can begin earlier. To the north of the harbour there's an excellent left reef break (best in west to north-west winds).

The Brass Bell on the bay side of the train station, with a terrace right beside the sea, is a favourite spot for seafood braais and live music. See the False Bay section in the Places to Eat chapter.

Clovelly & Fish Hoek

Both these resorts/suburbs have wide, safe beaches. Clovelly (Map 1) is flanked by sand dunes. Further around at **St James** there's a popular tidal pool which is always safe and usually protected from the wind.

Peers Cave, which can be reached by climbing the dunes behind 19th Ave, is named after the discoverer of the fossilised skeleton of a man who lived 15,000 years ago. From Kalk Bay south there are numerous grottoes and caves that have been occupied by humans. There's a caravan park right on the beach at **Fish Hoek** (Map 1).

Simon's Town (Simonstad)

Named after Simon van der Stel, an early governor, the town (Map 1) was the VOC's official winter anchorage from 1741 – it's sheltered from the winter north-easterlies that created havoc for ships in Table Bay. The British turned the harbour into a naval base in 1814 and it has remained one ever since.

There is an information bureau (☎ 786 3046) at the **Simon's Town Museum** (off the main road about 600m south of the train station), which traces the history of the town and port. It's in the old Governor's Residency (1777). Both are open from 9 am to 4 pm on weekdays, and from 10 am to 1 pm on Saturday; admission to the museum is R2. Next door is the **South African Navy Museum**, open daily from 10 am to 4 pm. No cameras are allowed.

Beaches Near the train station, **Long Beach** has safe swimming and good views. At the other end of town, **Seaforth Beach** is a safe and sheltered family spot. South of the town centre, turn off the main road (St George's St) into Seaforth Rd after the navy block. Take the second right on Kleintuin Rd. Day visitors are charged R4 entry.

A bit further on, **Boulders** is still within walking distance of Simon's Town. As the name suggests, it has a number of attractive coves among large boulders that offer shade and shelter. Boulders is also home to a growing colony of jackass penguin. Take the coast road south and turn left on Miller Rd. Day visitors are charged R4 entry.

Millers Point, a few km further on, offers a tiny beach and a popular saltwater pool. The proximity of the Black Marlin restaurant (with outdoor tables and views) makes this a good place for a day's outing. The south-easterlies can make things unpleasant.

Strand

Strand (Map 1) is quite a large satellite town, built along a nice stretch of gently shelving beach. It's very much a city by the surf, but some people like this combination. There are a number of trendy shops and a couple of restaurants at the new Strand Pavilion Hotel complex.

Gordon's Bay
Pretty much a southerly continuation of Strand's sprawl, Gordon's Bay (Map 1) is smaller and has camping accommodation close to the beach. The beach here is perhaps the best on False Bay.

From Gordon's Bay a spectacular road runs down the coast to **Hermanus**. See the Coast Road to Hermanus section in the Excursions chapter for more information.

Getting There & Away
False Bay is fairly easily accessible by public transport. From Monday to Friday there are trains between Fish Hoek and Cape Town which depart every half hour to 9 pm; every second one runs through to Simon's Town (hourly). On Saturday and Sunday nearly all trains run through to Simon's Town, and they're roughly hourly. Cape Town to Muizenberg is R5/2.20 in 1st/3rd class; to Simon's Town is R6.80/2.90. There are less frequent trains to/from Strand, leaving every couple of hours from Monday to Saturday and infrequently on Sunday; the journey takes a bit over an hour.

CAPE OF GOOD HOPE NATURE RESERVE
Francis Drake's chronicler said it all. This is a beautiful peninsula (Map 1). If the weather is good, or even if it isn't, it can absorb at least a day. In some ways, the coastline is not as dramatic here as that between Clifton and Kommetjie, but there is drama nonetheless. There are numerous walks, a number of beaches (there's 40km of coast within the reserve), a great cross-section of the Cape's unique flora as well as fauna – baboon, hard-to-spot eland, bontebok, rhebok, grysbok and abundant birdlife.

For food, there are a number of picnic places where you can braai; the Homestead Restaurant on the main road, which is mod-

---

Don't Feed the Baboons!
There are signs all over Cape Point warning you not to feed the baboons. This isn't just some mean-spirited official stricture designed to keep baboons from developing a taste for potato crisps and chocolate. One group told us about how they stopped and opened the car windows to take photos of baboons:

The next thing we knew, the baboons were in the car and we were out of the car. It took about half an hour before they were satisfied that they'd thoroughly trashed the interior, and we drove back to the rental agency in a car full of baboon shit. ∎

---

erately expensive; and a kiosk near Cape Point. A tramway takes you right up to the point from the kiosk, although there's no reason not to walk.

The reserve is open daily from 7 am to 6 pm. Maps and firewood are available at the gate. The entrance fee is R5 per person and R5 per surfboard.

Beaches
There are some excellent beaches, usually deserted. This can make them dangerous if you get into difficulties in the water, so take care. Remember, never swim after drinking alcohol. One of the best beaches for swimming or walking is **Platboom**. **Maclear Beach**, near the main car park, is good for walks or diving but is too rocky for enjoyable swimming. Further down towards Cape Point is beautiful **Diaz Beach**. Access is on foot from the car park.

On the False Bay side, the small but pretty **Buffels Bay** beach offers safe swimming. It closes at night.

Getting There & Away
The only public transport to the Cape peninsula is with Rikki's (which runs those Asian-style mini-mini open vans). Vans run from Simon's Town (accessible by train) and charge about R70 per hour.

Numerous tours include Cape Point on their itineraries. Day Trippers, and perhaps

The Flying Dutchman

The most popular version of the Flying Dutchman legend says that the ghost ship must haunt the Cape for eternity because its captain bet his soul that he could round the Cape in a storm. In the spooky equinoctial sea mists it doesn't seem too unlikely that the ancient square-rigger with its doomed crew might appear. In fact, the Flying Dutchman is 'sighted' near the Cape Peninsula more often than anywhere else in the world.

The Cape has a fearsome reputation for wrecking ships. Part of the reason is the fast-flowing current a few km offshore. Ships that avoid the current by sailing between it and the coast are at risk if one of the area's violent storms sweeps in. And there's a good chance it will – the Cape of Good Hope was originally called the Cape of Storms. Also, if the wind is blowing in the opposite direction to the current, freak waves can develop. If you add to this a panicky crew claiming to see a ghost ship flying before the wind, there's a good chance of coming to grief. ■

other backpacker-oriented companies, takes along mountain bikes so you can ride in the nature reserve and along Chapman's Peak Drive on the way to/from the Cape. They say that they haven't yet lost anyone over the edge. See the Getting Around chapter for more on Rikki's and tours.

Consider getting a group together and hiring a car for the day. If you plan to loop around the peninsula, start at Kirstenbosch Botanic Gardens and Groot Constantia, stock up on supplies at the Old Cape Farm Stall and head down through Muizenberg. If you tackle the drive clockwise, you'll be on the right side of the road to stop and take in the unforgettable views. The section along Chapman's Peak Drive and on to Llandudno and Clifton is one of the most spectacular marine drives in the world.

CAPE FLATS

For the majority of Cape Town's inhabitants, home is in one of the townships out on the vast, desolate Cape Flats (Map 1) – Guguletu (Our Pride), Langa (Sun), Nyanga (Moon), Philippi, Mitchell's Plain, Crossroads or

Khayelitsha (New Home). The first impression as one approaches is of an endless, grim, undifferentiated sprawl, punctuated by light towers that would seem more appropriate in a concentration camp. Black and coloured townships tend to be separated by a 'no-person's land', eg a highway, railway or strip of open land.

Cape Town's townships have played a major role in the struggle against apartheid. Given the history, the friendliness that is generally shown to white visitors is almost shocking.

Any outsider should try to get objective advice on the current situation within the townships. This isn't easy, however, since most whites would not dream of visiting and have no first-hand experience of doing so. Visiting without a companion who has local knowledge is foolish. If a trustworthy black or coloured friend is happy to escort you, however, you should have no problems, and tours have operated safely for years – see Organised Tours in the Getting Around chapter.

The Cape Flats dialect is locally called Kapie-taal (not to be confused with Tsotsi-taal, a patois of gangsters, lately fashionable among buppies). Here Afrikaans, English and Xhosa have mixed in a unique blend – like Afrikaans, perhaps one day Kapie-taal will become the mother tongue of non-whites. Cape Flats is called Vannie Toun in Kapie-taal.

ACTIVITIES

Outdoor activities are an important part of life for Cape Towners. It's not unusual to be overtaken by a grandmother and her grandchildren while you are wheezing your way up Table Mountain, and there are always joggers on the foreshore paths at Sea Point and elsewhere. There's plenty to do.

The boom in backpacker accommodation has seen a boom in organised adventure activities, and going along on one of these trips can be much more fun than doing it by yourself. See the Organised Tours section of the Getting Around chapter for information.

Abseiling

Abseiling off Table Mountain (or even

Chapman's Peak, depending on the weather) with Abseil Africa (☎ 25 4332; Web site www.millennia.co.za/abseilafrica) costs R90 (plus the cableway fare, if applicable). Head along to the desk at the Tourist Rendezvous at 11 am, daily. On Thursday and Saturday Abseil Africa also has day tours to 'Kamikazi Kanyon' (R190), which include hiking, *kloofing* (see Kloofing later in this section) and abseiling through a waterfall.

Canoeing

Several canoeing operators run short trips from Cape Town (as well as regular longer trips). Felix Unite (☎ 762 6935; fax 761 9259) is a major operator and has a desk at the Tourist Rendezvous.

Cycling

Mountain biking is a sport that's booming in South Africa, and trails are being developed in some of the parks and reserves. A bike is also a good way to get around Cape Town and the Winelands. See the Bicycle section in the Getting Around chapter for information on hiring bikes, and see the Cederberg Wilderness Area section of the Excursions chapter for another cycling option.

The Argus Tour from Cape Town to the peninsula, held in the second week of March, is the largest bicycle race in the world, with more than 20,000 entries. Some entrants are deadly serious, but many go along just for some fairly strenuous fun.

Diving

Cape Town has a wide variety of diving – the Agulhas and Benguela currents create a unique cross section of marine conditions. Diving can be enjoyed at any time of the year, but is best between June and November. Believe it or not, the water on the False Bay side of the peninsula is warmer then and visibility is greater. There are a number of excellent shore dives. Hard and soft corals, kelp beds, wrecks, caves and drop-offs, seals and a wide variety of fish are some of the attractions.

Life in the Townships

Most residents of Cape Town live in one of the Cape Flats townships. Although all the townships are depressing and inconveniently situated, not all present scenes of squalor and misery. Under the apartheid regime, the coloured population was given some preference over blacks, and there was a programme to provide a little decent housing in some of the black townships. It has been suggested that this was a way of dividing the non-white community and thus defusing its opposition to apartheid.

Most blacks live either in hostels or in shacks in the vast squatter camps. However, unlike the hostels in Jo'burg, which were cut off from the life of the surrounding township and became armed camps, hostels in Cape Town are integrated with the community. Some are owned by the city council, and others by large corporations such as Coca Cola.

Until the pass laws were abolished, hostels were for men only. The basic units, which were each home to 16 men, had one shower, one toilet and one small kitchen. Tiny bedrooms were home to three men. After the pass laws were abolished, most men brought their families to live with them (previously, if you didn't have a job outside the Homelands you were not allowed to leave). So now each unit is home to 16 *families*; each room sleeps three families. Some people have moved out of the hostels and built shacks, but the hostels remain the source of electricity, water and sanitation. Rent is R7.50 per month, but over the years many bed spaces (called 'squares' – your own square was your sole private area, the size of a single bed) have been sublet, and the most recent arrivals can pay up to R50 per month.

All the black townships except Khayelitsha have hostels. With a population of one million, Khayelitsha makes up for this by the huge proportion of squatters.

There are a few day hospitals in the townships, but for an illness requiring an overnight stay, residents have to travel into the city. A hospital is now being built at Khayelitsha.

If you're going to really understand Cape Town, it's essential that you visit the Cape Flats. They are still off-limits to visitors travelling on their own but there are some tours. Paula Gumede's One City Tours (☎ (021) 387 5351) is excellent and charges about R70. Other companies such as Day Trippers (see Organised Tours in the Getting Around chapter) also visit the townships. ■

There are several dive operators, such as Ocean Divers International (Map 3) (☎/fax 439 1803), Ritz Plaza, Main Rd, Sea Point. A certificate course costs around R750.

Cage Diving This increasingly popular activity involves descending in a cage and (hopefully) getting a close-up look at a fearsome great white shark. Cage diving costs from R600 and is offered by several operators. Compare their brochures at the Tourist Rendezvous. You'll pay considerably less if you go with an operator based in Mossel Bay.

Golf

Golf courses are dotted around Cape Town, and some are superb. Many welcome visitors (but you should book) – contact Captour at the Tourist Rendezvous for more information. Green fees are very reasonable, mostly under R100.

Kloofing

Table Mountain and other mountains in the area are full of *kloofs* (cliffs or gorges) and kloofing is a way of exploring them which involves climbing, walking, swimming and jumping. It's a lot of fun. Kloofing requires local knowledge, equipment and experienced guides, so it's best to go along with one of the adventure activities outfits. Several offer kloofing; Day Trippers (see the Organised Tours section of the Getting Around chapter) claims to have been the first. It offers kloofing between November and April and charges about R120.

Surfing

The Cape Peninsula has fantastic surfing possibilities – from gentle shorebreaks ideal for beginners to 3m-plus monsters for experts only. There are breaks that work on virtually any combination of wind, tide and swell direction.

In general, the best surf is along the Atlantic coast, and there is a string of breaks from Bloubergstrand through to the Cape of Good Hope. Most work best in south-easterly conditions. The water can be freezing (as low as

8°C) so a steamer wetsuit and booties are required.

With the exception of the excellent left reef at Kalk Bay, the waves at the False Bay beaches tend to be less demanding in terms of both size and water temperature (up to 20°C). Most work best in north-westerlies. There's a daily surf report on Radio Good Hope at 7.15 am.

Surprisingly there aren't all that many surf shops on the peninsula, but the Surf Centre (Map 8) (☎ 23 7853) is a decent shop at 70 Loop St (on the corner of Hout St) in the city centre, with a good stock of wetsuits and second-hand boards. It also rents boards and wetsuits.

Walking

There are some fantastic walks on the peninsula, including Lion's Head, Table Mountain and the Cape of Good Hope Reserve.

It is important to be properly equipped with warm clothing, a map and compass. There are numerous books, brochures and maps that give details. Shirley Brossy's *Walking Guide to Table Mountain* (paper, R30) is good, and Mike Lundy's *Best Walks in the Cape Peninsula* (paper, R40) covers the area well. Serious climbers could contact the Mountain Club of South Africa (☎ 45 3412), 97 Hatfield St. Guided walks are available and Captour has details.

Trails The following information was supplied by Noel and Dudley Gross. The Cape is covered with walking trails well worth exploring, and there are a number of guide books which cover them – the two books mentioned above are recommended. However, not all the trails listed in every brochure or book were actually completed, and others can be hard to follow (trails aren't always maintained or well signposted). These are areas around Cape Town where walking trails are especially reliable:

Cederberg Wilderness Area (north of Cape Town)
Cape of Good Hope Nature Reserve (south of Cape Town)
Kleinmond Nature Reserve (outside Kleinmond)

Vrolijkheid Nature Reserve (south of Robertson)
Marloth Nature Reserve (north of Swellendam)
De Hoop Nature Reserve (east of Cape Agulhas)

See the earlier Table Mountain & Cableway section in this chapter for information on walking up (or down) the mountain.

Water-Skiing

If you want to try water-skiing (or knee-boarding), or just have a fun day of falling over in the water, try Sunfish (☎ 083 26 17 542). Monika, a German water-ski champion, has a good boat and equipment and takes groups to Rietvlei Lake (Map 1) (near Bloubergstrand) for a braai on an island and as much high-speed action as you could want. It's recommended. It costs R160 (including transport and lunch) and you can book at most hostels. Monika also does ocean crayfishing trips for R160.

THINGS TO SEE & DO

Places to Stay

There is a huge range of accommodation and most people will find something that suits their pocket, but note that top-end hotel prices have soared way out of line with other costs in the country. If you have any difficulties, contact the Captour accommodation service (☎ 418 5214).

Cape Town is very crowded during school holidays, particularly around Christmas (mid-December to the end of January) and Easter – prices can double and many places are fully booked (see the When to Go section of the Facts for the Visitor chapter for more on pricing seasons). Now that Cape Town is gaining a reputation as one of the world's top cities to visit, it is necessary to book at all times of the year.

The rates at many places fluctuate according to demand, and it's always worthwhile asking about special deals. For longer stays rates are definitely negotiable.

B&B & GUESTHOUSE ORGANISATIONS
The Bed 'n' Breakfast organisation (☎ 683 3505; fax 683 5159) has a number of members around the Cape Peninsula. The accommodation is exceptionally good value. Most rooms are in large, luxurious suburban houses (often with swimming pools) and all have private bathrooms; self-catering flats and cottages are also available. The only problem is that Bed 'n' Breakfast prefers advance bookings (at least a day or so) and most houses are difficult to get to without private transport. Prices start around R70/100 per person in the low/high seasons. You can pay a lot more than this.

For consistently excellent places to stay covering a wide range of budgets, travel with the booklets produced by the Portfolio Collection: *The Bed & Breakfast Collection* (with singles/doubles from about R100/120 to R450/600), *The Retreats Collection* (guesthouses and lodges), averaging around R200/300 and up and *The Country Places Collection* (guesthouses, hotels and game

lodges, from R300/500 and way up). Contact Portfolio Collection in Johannesburg at Shop 5E, Mutual Square, Oxford Rd, Rosebank, 2196; by mail at PO Box 52350, Saxonwold 2123; by phone on ☎ (011) 880 3414; or by fax on (011) 788 4802. The booklets are recommended.

There's also the South African Farm Holiday Association (☎ (021) 96 8621), 'Farm & Country Holiday', Head Office, PO Box 247, Durbanville, Cape Town 7550.

SELF-CATERING ORGANISATIONS
A number of agencies specialise in arranging fully furnished houses and flats, including Cape Holiday Homes (☎ 419 0430), 31 Heerengracht St, PO Box 2044, Cape Town 8000; and Private Places (☎ 52 1200; fax 551 1487), 102 South Point Centre, Loxton Rd, Milnerton 7441.

PLACES TO STAY – BOTTOM END
Camping
There are no particularly central caravan parks, so if you do intend to camp, a car is virtually a prerequisite. The exception is *Zandvlei Caravan Park* (Map 1) (☎ 788 5215), The Row, Muizenberg, which is within walking distance (about 2km) of the Muizenberg station (on the Simon's Town line) and the beach (about 1km). Walk east around the civic centre and pavilion, turn right onto Atlantic Beach Rd, which doglegs and crosses the mouth of the Zandvlei lagoon, and take the first left after the bridge down Axminster Rd, which becomes The Row. For two people the tariff ranges from R25 to R50 in December and early January.

Fish Hoek Beach Caravan Park (☎ 782 5503), Victoria Rd, Fish Hoek, is also accessible by train but doesn't allow tents. Van sites cost from R30, rising to R66.

The caravan parks at Kommetjie and Noordhoek allow tents but you need a car to get there. A bit closer to town, but still handy for Atlantic surf beaches, *Chapman's Peak*

SUSAN STORM

SUSAN STORM

Top: Housing in the Cape Flats township is the product of sheer determination and local ingenuity.
Bottom: Postmodern Victoriana? Muizenburg's bathing huts bring a bit of Brighton to the Cape.

Top: Lime-washed cottages near windswept Cape Agulhas mark the area where the British troop carrier *Arniston* ran aground in 1815.
Middle: Vineyards thrive in the shadow of the spectacular Hottentots-Holland mountains.
Bottom: At Clifton, Lion's Head shelters four of the world's best – and trendiest – beaches.

Caravan Park (☎ 789 1225), Dassenheuwel Ave, Noordhoek, is in a beautiful setting. Rates are about R30 for two people, rising to R50 from mid-December to mid-January.

Millers Point Caravan Park (☎ 786 1142), about 5km from Simon's Town, on the Cape Point side, is on a small private beach and has just 12 sites. It doesn't always accept tents.

Hostels

In the past few years, the number of hostels in Cape Town has increased by about 400% and there's no reason to suppose that this boom is dying down. Competition between hostels is fierce and you can expect most places to offer free pick-ups, discounts at local businesses and a range of excursions.

Costs Hostel prices have remained remarkably stable for years. A dorm bed that once cost R20 might cost R35 now, but when you convert that it's still around US$8. We haven't given prices for individual hostels here because the prices can be flexible at many of them. You'll pay around R35 for a dorm and between R90 and around R110 for a double at an average hostel.

It's likely that there will be a shortage of backpacker beds in summer for the next few years, so expect prices to rise when everything is full.

Which Hostel? Just about any hostel is a good hostel if you like the people staying there. If you have the suspicion that you've landed in some sort of tacky backpackers' version of the Costa de Sol, full of boozy xenophobes, just try another hostel – there are some distinct personalities.

Some hostels tout at the airport, which can be annoying after a long flight.

We haven't included every hostel here – there are just too many. Listed below is a selection of good hostels (old favourites, newer favourites and the inexplicably popular), but just because a hostel isn't listed doesn't mean that it isn't good.

Unless otherwise indicated, you can assume that the hostels mentioned here have private rooms as well as dorms but you can't assume that any will be vacant when you arrive. Book ahead.

City Bowl *The Backpack* hostel (Map 8) (☎ 23 4530; fax 23 0065; email backpack@ gem.co.za), 74 New Church St (the top of Buitengracht St), was the first non-IYH hostel in Cape Town and one of the first in South Africa (yep, five years ago you could count the number of hostels in the country on one hand). It is arguably still the best hostel in town, as Lee and Toni are constantly making improvements and innovations. The latest, apart from the never-ending upgrading, is private safes. There's a good bar/café and a pool. It's about a 15 minute walk from the main train station, or you can catch the Kloof Nek bus from Adderley St, outside OK Bazaars. See the Travel Agents section in the Getting There & Away chapter for information on the helpful Africa Travel Centre at the hostel.

A few doors up at 82 New Church St is friendly *Zebra Crossing* (Map 8) (☎/fax 22 1265), which is smaller, quieter and more personal – and slightly cheaper. There's a good piano and a good atmosphere. It's one of our favourites.

Hostels have been mushrooming in Long St. The first was *Long St Backpackers* (Map 8) (☎ 23 0615), at No 209. It is in a block of 14 small flats, with four beds and a bathroom in each – this is one hostel where you don't have to queue for a shower. Standards have risen lately and it's a pleasant place.

The *Overseas Visitors' Club* (Map 8) (☎ 24 6800; fax 23 4870; email hross@ovc. co.za), 236 Long St (near the corner of Buiten St), has dorm beds only. It's a nice old building, with high-quality facilities and a pub-like bar, but it doesn't really have a backpacking atmosphere – although some might consider this a bonus. It sometimes closes in winter. *Cat & Moose* (Map 8) (☎ 23 5456; fax 23 8210) is a new place near the Long St Baths, and it's a comfortable warren of rooms in an historic building. Russian is also spoken here.

Oak Lodge (Map 5) (☎ 45 6182; fax 45 6308; email oaklodge@lantic.co.za) is at 21

Breda St, Gardens. What can we say? You'll love it or hate it. The hostel was once a commune but the astute communards saw that they'd have more fun (and make some money) if they turned it into a backpacker hostel. They have done a good job, and it's one of the most interesting hostels in town. I haven't actually stayed there but every time I visit I end up spending the night on a couch. There's a big bar (with murals), a good kitchen and smoking and non-smoking dorms. It has a Web site at www.lantic.co.za/oaklodge.

Ashanti Lodge (Map 5) (☎ 23 8721; fax 23 8790; email ashanti@iafrica.com), 11 Hof St, Gardens (a block from Orange St), is in a big old house which was once a guesthouse, so the facilities are good (including a decent pool and a big bar) and the rooms are comfortable. This place has definite potential. *Cloudbreak* (Map 5) (☎/fax 461 6892; email cloudbrk@gem.co.za) is a friendly little place at 219 Buitenkant St, Oranjezicht.

Sea Point & Around *Waterfront Lodge* (Map 9) (☎ 439 1404; fax 439 4875), at 6 Braemar Rd, Green Point, is close to the Waterfront and not too far from the city. It's a large, relaxed and friendly place with very good facilities, including a large garden and two pools. Jeff is one of the better hosts in town.

Hip Hop Travellers Stop (Map 3) (☎ 439 2104), 11 Vesperdene Rd, Green Point, describes itself as being on the Waterfront. It isn't, but it is one of the closest hostels to the Waterfront. The hostel also describes itself as lively, and it is that. The free beer on check-in gets you started. Hip Hop is in a pleasant old house and has a pool and a garden where you can camp.

The Bunkhouse (Map 3) (☎ 434 5695), 23 Antrim Rd, Three Anchor Bay, is pretty well equidistant from the Waterfront, Sea Point and the city – although it's a bit of a walk to get to any of them. At the far end of Sea Point is *The Globe Trotter* (Map 3) (☎ 434 1539), 17 Queens Rd.

The people who have the Stumble Inn hostel in Stellenbosch and the hostel and fine guesthouse at Boulders Beach (Simon's Town) have opened a new place, called *One on Main* (Map 3) (☎ 439 9471/2/5; email stumble@iafrica.com). It's at 1 Main Rd (corner of Boundary St) in Green Point. We haven't seen it yet, but they know what they are doing and it should be good.

Camps Bay *Stan Halt Youth Hostel* (Map 2) (☎ 438 9037), at The Glen, is near the Round House Restaurant, which is better signposted than the hostel. In fact, the hostel buildings were once the stables for the Round House, which was built as a hunting lodge. The hostel, a pleasant national monument, has a beautiful position, surrounded by trees, with a great view. You pay for this, however, with a steep 15 minute walk to the nearest shops and restaurants in Camps Bay. Dorm beds (only) cost less here than in most other hostels and even less if you are an International Youth Hostel (IYH) member (also called Hostelling International). This would be a good place to spend a few days recuperating from an overdose of nightlife. Take the Kloof Nek bus from outside OK Bazaars in Adderley St to the top of Kloof Nek, then take the road to the right. It's a longish but picturesque walk. Like all other IYH hostels in South Africa, this one has 24 hour access and there are no chores – it's the same deal as any backpacker place, in fact.

Observatory This suburb, a favourite with students, is a long way from the city centre and the Waterfront – by Cape Town standards, anyway. It's only a few minutes to the city by car or train, and it is a nice neighbourhood with some good music venues and places to eat – a good place to hang out for a while. A minibus taxi from town costs R1.50 (get off at Chippies for the hostel), and a train costs R2.20/1.50 in 1st/3rd class (don't take luggage in 3rd class and don't travel at rush hour).

Green Elephant (Map 6) (☎/fax 448 6359), 57 Milton Rd (on the corner of Lytton St), is a two storey house in a walled garden. It's run by experienced travellers and it seems to be one of the more maniacally happy hostels in town. And how many other hostels can boast a tree-climbing dog?

False Bay *Abe Bailey Youth Hostel* (Map 1) (☎ 788 2301), on the corner of Maynard and Westbury Rds, Muizenberg, is a quiet IYH hostel with dorms and doubles. It's a short walk to the beach and it's near Valsbai station on the Simon's Town railway line. Also accessible by train is *Harbourside Backpackers* (☎ 788 2943; fax 788 6452), 136 Main Rd, Kalk Bay, in a pub across from the beach and close to Kalk Bay train station. It's a little rough and ready but the rooms are nice, with mezzanine beds and sea views. It's also a little cheaper than many places.

Further around at Boulders Beach, Simon's Town, *Boulders Beach Backpackers* (☎ 786 1758) is right on the beach and is a pleasant enough place in a great location. If you want a bit of a splurge, stay at the excellent guesthouse next door, where there's a good restaurant (see under Simon's Town in the Places to Stay – Middle section). Both the hostel and the guesthouse are run by the people who have the very popular Stumble Inn in Stellenbosch. The hostel is about 2km south of Simon's Town train station. A Rikki between the station and the hostel costs about R1.50.

Guesthouses

City Bowl *Ambleside Guesthouse* (Map 5) (☎ 45 2503; fax 45 3814), 11 Forest Rd, Oranjezicht, has comfortable single/double and family rooms, and a fully equipped guest kitchen. Doubles start at R85 per person, more with private bathroom. The Ambleside offers inexpensive guided walks on the mountain.

Travellers Inn (Map 8) (☎ 24 9272; fax 74 9278), 208 Long St, is in one of the old wrought-iron decorated buildings and was once the British Guesthouse; that name is still on the door. It has been taken over by an enthusiastic new management and is undergoing a much-needed refurbishment. Singles (they really are singles) cost R90/120 in the low/high seasons and doubles are R120/160, including a make-it-yourself breakfast.

The Lodge (Map 3) (☎ 21 1106), 49 Napier St, used to be one of the nicer little hostels but the owners have wisely decided to avoid that cut-throat game and to concentrate on running The Lodge as a very pleasant, inexpensive guesthouse. It's well located in the newly 'yuppified' edge of the old Cape Muslim quarter, not far from the city and the Waterfront. Rooms cost around R100, rising as high as R200 in the high season.

Sea Point *St John's Lodge* (Map 3) (☎ 439 9028), 9 St John's Rd, on the corner of Main Rd, Sea Point, is both a hostel and a guesthouse, with the usual hostel facilities such as kitchens and good information. It's an attractive old building with wide verandahs and you're sure to meet other travellers here. The rooms are fairly small and basic but the place is friendly and good value from R45/90 a single/double. You'll pay nearly twice that in the high season. The lodge has its own security patrol covering the surrounding streets, so it's pretty secure.

PLACES TO STAY – MIDDLE
B&Bs & Guesthouses

There are many mid-range B&Bs and guesthouses – the following is just a small sample.

City Bowl *Belmont House* (Map 5) (☎ 461 5417), 10 Belmont Ave, Oranjezicht, is a small but comfortable guesthouse overlooking the City Bowl, charging from R100/170 a single/double to R120/190 in the high season. There are kitchen facilities and staff say that they'll give you a discount if you're carrying this book.

Sea Point *Ashby Manor Guesthouse* (Map 3) (☎ 434 1879; fax 439 3572), 242 High Level Rd, is a rambling old Victorian house, on the slopes of Signal Hill above Sea Point. All rooms have a fridge and hand basin and there is a kitchen. Singles/doubles go for about R90 per person, more in high season. There's also a two bedroom flat, from R280.

Villa Rosa (Map 3) (☎ 434 2768), 277 High Level Rd (on the corner of Arthur's

Rd), Sea Point, is a nice old house, restored into a quality guesthouse. Well equipped rooms start at R180/290 a single/double, rising to R220/380 in peak season. *Olaf's Guest House* (Map 3) (☎/fax 439 8943), 24 Wisbeach Rd, also has high-quality accommodation, starting at R320 a double. German is spoken here.

Simon's Town Right across from beautiful Boulders Beach, with its penguin colony, *Boulders Beach Guesthouse* (☎ 786 1758; fax 786 1825; email stumble@iafrica.com), is a good new place with an excellent café and restaurant. Singles/doubles with en suite cost R210/300 (R245/340 with sea view) and there are two self-catering units, each with two bedrooms, at R450.

Hotels

Many of the mid-range hotels were built in the 1960s and are beginning to show their age. Some weren't especially appealing in the first place, with small rooms, low ceilings and tacky furnishings. If this bothers you, B&Bs and guesthouses are a definite alternative. However, practically all the hotels are very clean and perfectly reasonable places to stay.

City Bowl There's a member of the *Formule 1* chain (Map 8) (☎ 418 4664) in the city centre between Jan Smuts St and Martin Hammerschlag Way offering basic but comfortable rooms for R114 for up to three people.

Tudor Hotel (Map 8) (☎ 24 1335), on Greenmarket Square, is a cosy little hotel (30 rooms) with a great position right in the middle of town, but away from main roads. It could do with renovation but it's OK. Parking is available nearby (at a price). Singles/doubles start at R150/200, including breakfast.

Metropole Hotel (Map 8) (☎ 23 6363), 38 Long St, is an attractive old-style hotel, with a dark, wood panel interior. Its prices are very reasonable considering the degree of comfort offered. In the low season, smallish standard rooms are R170/205, luxury rooms are R230/270 and there are more expensive

suites. *Cape Gardens Lodge* (☎ 23 1260), on Queen Victoria St, opposite the South African Museum, is well located and fair value, although the rooms are small. Standard rooms start at R210/280, rising to R265/350 around Christmas.

The two star *Pleinpark Travel Lodge* (Map 8) (☎ 45 7563), on the corner of Corporation and Barrack Sts, is a conveniently located hotel with reasonable prices. Rates start at around R240 a double, including breakfast. In the same league is the high-rise *Cape Town Inn* (Map 8) (☎ 23 5116), on the corner of Strand and Bree Sts. Further out of the centre, but still within walking distance, *Cape Swiss Hotel* (Map 5) (☎ 23 8190), on the corner of Kloof and Camp Sts, Gardens, is another characterless but decent hotel. Rates start at around R220 a double, higher in peak season.

Close to the city and the Waterfront, *City Lodge* (Map 4) (☎ 419 9450; fax 419 0460), on the corner of Dock Rd and Alfred St, is a big new place, something like an upmarket motel. Room rates start at R260/310 a single/double.

Waterfront Area The *Breakwater Lodge* (Map 9) (☎ 406 1911; fax 406 1070), Portswood Rd, should be one of the best places to stay, as it's in a restored jail right next to the Waterfront and the prices aren't bad. However, it's not only a restored jail, it's also a restored tertiary institution and the rooms are very small. Some people like it, although the rates seem high for what you get – R239 per room.

Atlantic Coast In Hout Bay, *Chapman's Peak Hotel* (☎ 790 1036) has rooms from R270 in mid-season. The rooms aren't flash but it's a pleasantly relaxed place. *The Beach House Hotel* (☎ 790 4228), Royal Ave, charges R220 a double, including breakfast. No children under 14 are allowed.

False Bay *Lord Nelson Inn* (☎ 786 1386), 58 St George's St, Simon's Town, is a small, old-style pub. On the main street of Simon's Town overlooking the harbour, it's accessible by train. Singles/doubles start at R240/290, 15% more in the high season. Although this is a pleasant, refurbished place, it isn't great value, and the more expensive rooms overlooking the sea (which is largely obscured by a shed in the naval dockyards) get traffic noise.

Self-Catering
There are a number of agencies that specialise in arranging fully furnished houses and flats, including Cape Holiday Homes (☎ 419 0430), 31 Heerengracht St, PO Box 2044, Cape Town 8000, and Private Places (☎ 52 1200; fax 551 1487), 102 South Point Centre, Loxton Rd, Milnerton 7441.

City Bowl *Diplomat Holiday Flats* (Map 8) (☎ 25 2037, 2341), right in the city on Tulbagh Square, is one of those rare places where the quality of the accommodation is higher than the quality of the foyer would suggest. It's old fashioned but clean and in good condition. The rooms are large and the two-room flats have an enormous lounge. There is a huge array of rates and seasons, but basically the rate for two people in a single bedroom flat is R170; for three/four people in a two bedroom flat it's R290/360. Add about 30% from December to mid-January.

Gardens Centre Holiday Flats (Map 5) (☎ 461 5827) is the distinctive multistorey building on Mill St, Oranjezicht. The single-bedroom flats are above an excellent small shopping mall and, although the flats only go up to the 5th floor, the views are still good. Rates vary widely according to the season, starting around R240 for two people and rising by about 15% at peak times.

Atlantic Coast *Lions Head Lodge* (Map 3) (☎ 434 4163), 319 Main Rd (on the corner of Conifer Rd), Sea Point, has rooms and self-catering apartments. The nightly rate is from R230/350 a single/double. If you stay longer than a day or so, the rates fall.

The Hout Bay information centre can tell you about self-catering cottages and apart-

ments in that area. Something reasonable will cost from about R150 for two people.

A good spot if you have a car, *Flora Bay Bungalows* (☎ 790 1650), Chapman's Peak Drive, Hout Bay, has magnificent ocean views. One-room 'oceanettes' cost from R140 to R220 per night depending on the season; two-bedroom units cost between R240 and R360.

False Bay *Oatlands* (☎ 786 1410), Seaforth Beach Front, Simon's Town, is a member of the Club Caravelle chain and has self-catering rondavels for R190 a double in mid-season. Next door, the *Blue Lantern* (☎ 786 2113) has serviced chalets for a little less.

PLACES TO STAY – TOP END
Guesthouses
There are some outstanding top-end guesthouses, such as *Villa Belmonte* (Map 5) (☎ 462 1576; fax 462 1579), 33 Belmont Ave, Oranjezicht. It's an ornate Italianate villa with excellent facilities, charging from around R380/560 for a single/double. *Underberg Guesthouse* (Map 5) (☎ 26 2262) on the corner of Carstens St and Tamboerskloof Rd is a very nice place – restored Victorian but not too fussy. Rooms start at R230/350, including breakfast. Nearby at 10A Tamboerskloof Rd, *Table Mountain Lodge* (Map 5) (☎ 23 0042; fax 23 4983) is another restored house with B&B from R284/308. Not far away at 93 New Church St, *Leeuwenvoet House* (Map 5) (☎ 21 24 1133; fax 24 0495) is another quality guesthouse, with rooms from R285/330, including a huge breakfast.

Hotels
City Bowl The good four star *Townhouse Hotel* (Map 8) (☎ 45 7050; fax 45 3891), 60 Corporation St (on the corner of Mostert St), charges from just R260/360 for singles/doubles with only a slight rise in summer. Rooms with numbers ending in six have views of the mountain. *Mijloff Manor Hotel* (Map 5) (☎ 26 1476), 5 Military Rd, Tamboerskloof, was once an attractive small

hotel in a converted mansion – now it has grown into a reasonable but quite large hotel, with a lot of new rooms. Rooms start at R250 and rise steeply.

There are a few members of the Holiday Inn Garden Court chain (with minimal service), including:

Greenmarket Square (Map 8)
> On Greenmarket Square (☎ 23 2040; fax 23 3664), R270/290

St George's Mall (Map 8)
> On the corner of Riebeeck St and St George's Mall (☎ 419 0808; fax 419 7010), R290/340

De Waal (Map 5)
> Mill St, Gardens (☎ 45 1311; fax 461 6648), R280/310

There are a couple of Protea hotels in the city centre: the four star *Capetonian Protea* (Map 8) (☎ 21 1150; fax 25 2215), Pier Place, Heerengracht St, with rooms for around R500; and the slightly cheaper *Tulbagh Protea Hotel* (Map 8) (☎ 21 5140; fax 21 4648) on Tulbagh Square.

Victoria & Alfred Waterfront The excellent four star *Victoria & Alfred Hotel* (Map 9) (☎ 419 6677; fax 419 8955) has rooms from R590/900. On the Green Point side of the Waterfront, the *Portswood Square Hotel* (☎ 418 3281; fax 419 7570), Portswood Rd, is a new four star hotel. Rates start at R420/545. The rooms aren't especially large but it's a pleasant place.

Atlantic Coast West of the city centre towards Green Point, *Victoria Junction Hotel* (Map 3) (☎ 418 1234; fax 418 5678), on the corner of Somerset/Main and Ebenezer Rds, is a big new member of the Protea chain in a stylishly recycled building. Rooms cost R625/750 all year.

The Place on the Bay (Map 2) (☎ 438 7069; fax 438 2692), on the corner of Victoria Rd and The Fairway in Camps Bay, is a large complex of modern, very comfortable self-catering apartments. The two-bedroom apartments have a double and two single beds, plus a couch in the downstairs lounge that sleeps an adult or two children. Low season rates start at R200 per person for a studio apartment and R650 for a two bedroom suite. In the high season you'll pay from R1000 for a studio and from R2000 for a suite. The penthouse comes with a chef and a butler and costs much, much more.

In Kommetjie, *Kommetjie Inn* (☎ 783 4230) is a refurbished seaside hotel with rooms starting at around R250/330, more in summer.

Southern Suburbs There are some good places to stay in the leafy white residential suburbs at the back of Table Mountain, although you're some way from the city and the beaches, and you'll need your own transport. One of the nicest is *Alphen* (☎ 794 5011; fax 794 5710), on Alphen Drive, Constantia, a quality hotel in a beautiful Cape Dutch manor that has been declared a national monument. The building is shaded by old oak trees and is in 16 acres of parkland. There's a swimming pool, restaurant and bar, and access to sports facilities. Prices are reasonable for what you get: around R600 a double in a standard room, R1000 in a luxury room.

Five-Star Hotels
Staying at *Mount Nelson Hotel* (Map 5) (☎ 23 1000), 76 Orange St, Oranjezicht, is like stepping back in time to the great days of the British Empire. Dating from 1899, the hotel is set in seven acres of parkland, a short walk through the Company's Gardens to the city. Part of the Venice Simplon Orient Express group, the rooms are full of character. Mid-season rates start around R800/1100. Unfortunately, the exterior is painted in a pink and grey colour scheme that makes it look like an underfunded institution.

In complete contrast, *Cape Sun Hotel* (Map 8) (☎ 23 8844), Strand St, is a large, modern (if a little faded), multistorey hotel in the middle of the city. It has a swimming pool, fitness centre and several restaurants. Rates are similar to those at the Mount Nelson.

Cape Town's newest five star hotel is *Table Bay Hotel* (Map 9) (☎ 406 5000; fax

406 5686) on Quay Six at the Waterfront. It's very impressive and the staff are excellent. Standard rooms start at R1350, luxury rooms at R1690 and suites at R2375. Prices rise by about 10% between December and April.

If you want to be close to a beautiful beach, consider the *The Bay Hotel* (☎ 438 4444), a luxurious hotel across the road from the Camps Bay beach. Singles/doubles start at R465/600 in the low season and R800 a double (only) in the high season. For a sea view you'll pay at least R620/900 or R1360 in the high season.

Places to Eat

Cape Town could easily claim to be the gastronomic capital of Africa. Unlike the rest of South Africa there's a cosmopolitan café/restaurant culture. Whites go out to eat. Why they do here, and not elsewhere, is a mystery – perhaps it's harder to find live-in cooks, or perhaps the city's history as the Tavern of the Seas has simply created a more dynamic urban culture.

There is a tremendous variety of cuisines in Cape Town and you can spend a lot of money, or a little, on food. The quality of the ingredients is high. Fruit and vegetables are excellent, and most are locally grown. The seafood is also top quality, and the local wines are sensational. Although you have to go looking for it, the traditional Cape cuisine – a curious cross between Dutch/European and Indonesian/Malay – is worth searching for.

FOOD

South African cuisine was once a case of 'what sort of meat do you want?', and portions were ridiculously large. If you wanted a smaller steak you had to order a 'ladies' steak. Spices were viewed with deep suspicion and 'rich and creamy' were the highest compliments you could pay. (Not really surprising in a nation of cattle herders with an overlay of British culture.)

That's still the case in much of the country but in the big cities, especially Cape Town, the wonderfully fresh and inexpensive local produce is being used more imaginatively in some restaurants. Australian/Californian-style food is becoming popular. But don't worry – if you want to gorge yourself on an excellent steak covered with a rich and creamy sauce (for about R35) there are plenty of opportunities to do so. You can also get rich and creamy minestrone, rich and creamy chow mein ...

DRINKS

Firstly, it's OK to drink the water. There are plenty of good local fruit juices (the Ceres brand is produced a mountain range or two inland from Cape Town) and international soft-drink brands are sold everywhere.

The huge South African Breweries (SAB) produces several brands of lager beer, very similar to Australian beers. Castle and Black Label are the most popular. Be warned that the alcohol content is around 5%, about the same as in Australia or Canada but significantly stronger than in the UK or the USA. SAB has a licensing agreement to sell its version of Hofbrau, the German brew. Beer aficionados drink Windhoek, a lager brewed in Namibia to strict standards of purity.

The wines of the Cape region are justifiably famous (see the Cape Wineries section in the Excursions chapter) and they are also inexpensive. Nearly all restaurants have long wine lists. Wine is rarely sold by the glass but if you want to try a few wines without drinking a few bottles, most places have a decent range of wine available in small bottles (smaller than a half bottle).

Brandy-making has a long history at the Cape and brandy and Coke is a popular poison. If you prefer your brandy unsullied, try a bottle of Oude Molen. It's not the most expensive of the 14-year-olds but it's one of the best.

SELF-CATERING

If you are preparing your own food, check the *Woolworths* supermarkets (there's one on Main Rd, Sea Point, and another in the city centre). They're a bit pricey, but they have a wide range of high-quality foods, including fresh fruit and vegetables and some excellent frozen and semi-prepared meals.

Atlas Trading Company (Map 8) in Bo-Kaap (Wale St, across and down from Bo-Kaap Museum) services the Cape Muslim community. As this community cooks the most adventurous food in town, you should check out this shop.

For processed meat, *Morris's Boerewors*

(Map 8) on Long St near the corner of Buiten St is legendary.

WHERE TO EAT

The short answer is – anywhere. New cafés and restaurants are opening all the time and it's a rare neighbourhood that doesn't have a few.

The main restaurant zone was once Main Rd in Sea Point and there are still many good places there, but since the opening of the Waterfront complex Sea Point has lost its status as the city's kitchen. The Waterfront has an extensive range of eateries catering to all budgets and most tastes. The city centre is crowded with places to eat and Long St is fast turning into a strip of trendy cafés and restaurants, more adventurous than you'll find at the Waterfront. Gardens, Oranjezicht and Tamboerskloof also offer interesting choices and there's an outpost of café culture in Observatory.

CITY CENTRE
Restaurants

If you're looking for a pleasant and stylish place to have lunch in the city centre, try *Squares* (Map 8), a bright, good-value restaurant in Stuttaford's Town Square, overlooking St George's Mall. A good meal will set you back about R40, but there are plenty of snacks for less. At the *Tudor Hotel* (Map 8) on Greenmarket Square pub meals are well under R30, with daily specials around R15. *Ploughman's Pub* (Map 8) on Church Square isn't anything special but it's OK for a beer and a lunchtime meal such as bangers and mash.

Spur (Map 8) family steakhouse on Strand St near the corner of Loop St serves standard dishes at standard prices – around R30 for a steak. It would come in handy for refuelling after a night at the nearby clubs except for the fact that it closes just when the action is getting under way, at 1 am on Friday and Saturday, midnight from Monday to Thursday and 11 pm on Sunday. It's open for breakfast, though, so you could still end your night there if you've had a particularly good time.

Nino's (Map 8) (☎ 24 7466), on Greenmarket Square, looks as though it's aiming to attract tourists from the Holiday Inn across the street, but it's actually a good, Italian-run restaurant and pizzeria. As is the case with most South African Italian restaurants, Nino's dishes are not quite the same as the originals; but unlike most, Nino's has *extra* spices and adventurous ingredients. Try the veal pizzaiola (R30) or, for something lighter but still good, a chicken salad (R18). Nino also serves Italian wines. It's open from 8 am to 6 pm on Monday and Tuesday, until 10.30 pm Wednesday to Friday and to 5 pm on Saturday.

Bonthuys (Map 8) (☎ 26 2368), at 121 Castle St, combines neo-industrial decor with 'fresh out of private school' staff and some very imaginative food. Main courses cost R35 to R60, pricey but excellent, with dishes like fillet of ostrich with calvado apples, lamb and freshwater crayfish at the upper end of that bracket. It also serves great desserts.

Kaapse Tafel Restaurant (Map 8) (☎ 23 1651), 90 Queen Victoria St, is a pleasant little place that serves a variety of traditional Cape dishes. There are starters such as Cape pickled fish (R12.50) and seafood bobotie (R15). Main courses (mostly R25 to R30) include Malay chicken biryani, bobotie, waterblommetjie bredie and springbok goulash.

Within the Metropole Hotel, 38 Long St, is the *Commonwealth Restaurant* (Map 8), which serves pub-style meals at reasonable prices. On Sunday there is a three course roast lunch for less than R30.

Yellow Pepper (Map 8), 138 Long St (near Dorp St), has a casual atmosphere and inexpensive, fairly interesting food, with main courses under R15. Try the spicy peasant sausage stew. Yellow Pepper is open during the day (not Sunday) and from 7.30 pm on Friday and Saturday. A little further up Long St, on the corner of Pepper St, *Mama Africa* (Map 8) is a very stylish bar and restaurant with interesting decor and a slightly African menu. You'll be offered a choice of rice or pap with your meal. Starters such as roasted beef marrow bone or mussels cost from R15; main courses include steak (even ostrich steak) and Malay-influenced dishes such as bobotie, and cost around R25 to R35. There's live African music on Friday and Saturday nights.

On the rim of the City Bowl, relaxed *Café Manhattan* (Map 3) is on the corner of Dixon and Waterkant Sts. It's a neighbourhood bar and restaurant which has been renovated without losing its casual appeal. The food is inexpensive and good, and vegetarians are catered for. It's open from noon until late on weekdays and from late afternoon on weekends.

There are some interesting possibilities hidden away in the docks (east of the main Waterfront area). To get there (you'll need transport) head towards the sea on Adderley St, then go along Heerengracht St, under the freeway and turn right onto Duncan St at the T-intersection.

Just past the Royal Cape Yacht Club (Map 4), turn left onto Vanguard Rd (the first left-turn lane after the yacht club) and you'll come to the Chinese Seamen's Club. Here there's a genuine Chinese restaurant, *Jewell Tavern*. It's open daily for lunch and from 5 pm for dinner. The large menu features seafood. Many dishes cost around R20, although some are R40. Unaccompanied women aren't allowed into the Seamen's Club but if they don't suspect you of being there on business you'll probably get in. If you park out the front, beware of the very deep gutter.

The next turn-off from the main road is Goliath Rd, which takes you to *Panama Jack's*, a dockside bar and restaurant with atmosphere and good food. It's open daily, but not for lunch on Saturday and Monday. Lobster bisque or mussel chowder costs R15, starters such as calamari are around R22 and main courses start at R38.

Cafés & Snacks

There is quite a range of takeaway places in the city centre. A good place to start if you're peckish is the so-called *Fruit and Vegetable Market* (Map 8) at the Adderley St end of Grand Parade. There's an inexpensive bakery and a number of stalls that sell Indian food, including excellent samosas. Plenty of street vendors sell boerewors (literally farm sausage) rolls, the local equivalent of the hot dog. The quality of the sausages varies, so shop around.

World of Coffee (Map 8) on Adderley St, near Darling St, offers a chair and caffeine when you need to recuperate. Another possibility is *Mark's Coffee Shop* (Map 8) (☎ 24 8516), 105 St George's Mall (on the corner of Church St), the oldest coffee shop in Cape Town. It serves good coffee and reasonably priced light meals. *Brazilian Coffee Shop* (Map 8) near the corner of Long and Waterkant Sts sells good coffee for R4.50.

If it isn't too busy, *Cycles* (Map 8) is a pleasant terrace outside the Holiday Inn, overlooking Greenmarket Square. There's a large menu and prices aren't too bad. Across from Cycles, in the Art-Deco Namaqua building on the corner of Burg St, *Le Petit Paris* (Map 8) is a pleasant, trendy café, good for a coffee and a snack during the day. *Mr Pickwicks Deli* (Map 8), 158 Long St, is a licensed, deli-style café that stays open very late for good snacks and meals. Try the footlong rolls. It's just the place to recuperate in a civilised atmosphere after a night out at the clubs.

Off Moroka Café Africaine (Map 8), 120 Adderley St, near Church St, is a pleasant place to sample some fairly genuine African food and listen to tapes of African music. It's open daily, except Sunday, for breakfast and lunch. Breakfast starts at R12, soup is R9 and salads cost between R10 and R15. There are also sandwiches and pancakes.

Sooz Baguette Bar (Map 8), 150 Long St, has inexpensive snacks and meals, and is about the only place in the city (other than hotel dining rooms) to get breakfast on a Sunday morning. Not far away is *Backpacker Bob's* (Map 8), a bar and café serving fuel such as bangers and mash (R12.50), and lamb chops (R15).

Gardens Restaurant (Map 8) in the Company's Gardens is licensed and has quite a large menu. There are snacks as well as standards such as omelettes (R15), salads (from R12), chicken dishes from R20 and steaks from R25. It's open for breakfast.

Wellington Dried Fruit (Map 8) is a Cape Town institution. It's a long, narrow shop on Darling St, near Plein St, that sells a huge range of dried and glacé fruit, deli items, tinned foods and *lots* of lollies (sweets or candy). It's well worth a visit even if you don't want to buy anything.

Just up from the city centre in the Cape Muslim Quarter, is *Karima's Café* (Map 8) on the corner of Rose and Longmarket Sts, a takeaway outlet selling Cape Muslim snacks. Karima herself is friendly and very knowledgeable about the area.

GARDENS & TAMBOERSKLOOF

This area is becoming populated with places to eat. A night out could involve a beer in the *Stag's Head Hotel* (Map 8) on Hope St (rowdy) or *Perseverance Tavern* (Map 8) on Buitenkant St (civilised), dinner at *Maria's Greek Restaurant* (Map 8) or *Rozenhof* (Map 8) and Irish coffees at *Roxy's Coffee Bar* (Map 8).

Restaurants

Perseverance Tavern (Map 8) (☎ 461 2440), 83 Buitenkant St (across from Rust-en-Vreugd, an historic 18th century house), is a pub that was built in 1808 and licensed in 1836. It's a bit of a rabbit warren inside, with bar areas and plain wooden tables. In addition to beer (some draught) and an excellent range of wines, it serves good pub food from a blackboard menu. There's a relaxed atmosphere, and you'll find generous meals from R20 to R30. On Friday nights it can be too crowded to move.

Dunkley Square (Map 8) (between Dunkley, Wandel, Barnet and Vrede Sts) has a number of places, most with outdoor tables. On a warm night this is a nice place to linger over a meal.

Maria's Greek Restaurant (Map 8) (☎ 45 2096) is a small taverna with plastic tablecloths, naive-style murals and good-value food (although some dishes still subscribe to the 'more is better' school of South African cuisine). There are starters such as tara-

masalata (R10.50), Greek salad (R12.50) and mezze platter (R41). Main courses include roast lamb (R35) and spanikopita (R21). Maria's is open from 7 to 11.30 pm daily. Next door is *Dunkley Inn* (Map 8) and across from the square is *Bistrot la Boheme* (Map 8), a trendy place with a fairly standard menu.

Rustica (Map 8) (☎ 23 5474, booking advised), on Buitengracht St, is an excellent Italian restaurant. Most main courses cost between R20 and R30. Not far away, in the recycled Longkloof Studios building off Kloof St (near the corner of Rheede St) is one of the trendiest places in town, the big *Café Bar Deli* (Map 8). It's open from 8.30 am daily, except Sunday, until 1 am (midnight for meals), and it's usually packed. Surprisingly, given the hip crowd and industrial decor, the food is not only excellent, with an emphasis on fresh and healthy dishes, but it's also very good value. Breakfast is very good – a fresh fruit platter and bottomless coffee will set you back R15, and is just the thing to get you going after a long night. Tapas are around R6, bruschetta starts from R14, pasta from R20, salads R16 and larger meals around R30. The enormous Bar Deli platter is just R24.50. It's highly recommended.

Just down the street, but a world away in atmosphere, *Rozenhof* (Map 8) (☎ 24 1968), 18 Kloof St, is one of the best restaurants in town. Its small but interesting seasonal menus are big on quality but not too bad on prices. Starters and salads are around R20 and most main courses cost around R40. There is parking for patrons, something of a rarity in Cape Town. Across the road, *The Blue Plate* (Map 8) is another good upmarket restaurant.

Sukothai (Map 8) (☎ 23 4725), 50 Orange St, at the corner of Dorman St, is a good Thai restaurant. It's open for lunch on weekdays and for dinner most nights. The menu includes the less complicated Thai standards. On Kloof St, on the corner of Upper Union St, *The Happy Wok* (Map 5) is an offshoot of Sukothai and sells similarly good meals and takeaways at much lower prices, around R10 for starters and R22 for main courses. The emphasis here is more on Chinese than Thai cooking.

Cafés & Snacks

Mario's Coffee Shop (Map 8), on Rheede St, not far from several hostels, is shabby but it has excellent and very cheap meals. It's open from 8 am to 4 pm. A big breakfast is R12 – a ridiculously big breakfast is R18 and a mixed grill is R20. There are also burgers and inexpensive pasta dishes. Not far away, on the corner of Kloof St and Park Rd, *KD's Bar & Bistro* (Map 8) is very popular with impoverished students and backpackers.

Roxy's Coffee Bar (Map 8) (☎ 461 4092), on Dunkley Square, is self-consciously bohemian and serves good coffee (including a long list of alcoholic coffees, from R8) and light meals from under R20. It's open from noon to 2 am on weekdays and from 7 pm on Saturday. *Café Paradiso* (Map 5), on Kloof St on the corner of Malan St, is a fashionable, but informal, upmarket café. It's a bit pricey and we're not as infatuated as many locals are, but the outdoor tables are a nice place to sip a drink and watch Kloof St go by.

Friends Health Store on Kloof St (on the corner of Camp St), Gardens, sells health food and products and has a pleasant snack and juice bar.

Labia Cinema café, 60 Orange St, is a popular place for coffee and cake. The grand old *Mount Nelson Hotel* (Map 5) offers high tea on the terrace, with lots of cakes, lots of waiters and a grand piano. Expect to pay about R40.

VICTORIA & ALFRED WATERFRONT

New restaurants and nightspots are mushrooming in the area and the Waterfront information centre (Map 9) has a sizeable booklet listing them all. As well as the franchised places such as *St Elmo's* (pizza and pasta) and *Spur* (mainly meat), there are some interesting places to eat, although most are aimed squarely at tourists. An exception is the group of smaller places in the King's Warehouse, next to the Red Shed Craft Workshop (Map 9). You can buy from various stalls and eat at common tables.

Ari's, the Sea Point institution for Middle Eastern dishes, has a branch here. *Seafood Grill* has starters such as lobster bisque for R25 and main courses from R40.

Musselcracker Restaurant, upstairs in the Victoria Wharf complex (Map 9), has a seafood buffet at lunch (from noon) and dinner (booking advisable) for R66. There's also the relaxed *Musselcracker Oyster Bar*, a good place for a drink and some seafood. Oysters are R35 a dozen, R18 for half a dozen.

Green Dolphin (☎ 21 7471), beneath the Victoria & Alfred Hotel (Map 9), is a popular restaurant with excellent live jazz, nightly from 8 pm. If there's an international act in town it will probably play here. There's a cover charge of R10 (R6 if you don't have a view of the stage). The jazz is probably more important than the food, but the meals aren't bad, with starters around R20 and mains around R40.

One of the cheap and cheerful options is *Ferryman's Tavern*, adjoining Mitchell's Waterfront Brewery (Map 9). The emphasis is on an interesting variety of freshly brewed beers and good-value pub meals. To give you an idea, a calamari starter is R15, fish and chips costs R17 and steaks are under R30.

For fish and chips overlooking the water, head for *Fisherman's Choice* where you can take away or eat in. Calamari rolls are R10, fish (or prawns) and chips costs R24 (less for kids) and seafood boxes are R28.

Caffe San Marco (☎ 418 5434), on the ground floor of the Victoria Wharf complex, is the offspring of the San Marco restaurant in Sea Point. Here you can sample San Marco's famed Italian cooking, but at lower prices. Pizzas and pasta start around R18 and other meals start at R25. Excellent tiramisu costs R8.

There are many other restaurants – it's a matter of walking around and seeing what appeals. There are a couple of places on Bertie's Landing (Map 9), across a 20m channel from the main Victoria & Alfred complex – take the ferry (R2) from near the Old Port Captain's building, otherwise it's quite a long walk around the basin.

SEA POINT

There are dozens of places to eat along Main and Regent Rds, between the suburbs of Three Anchor Bay and Queens. The following suggestions start at the Three Anchor Bay end.

There are surprisingly few Indian restaurants in Cape Town. One worth considering is *Little Bombay* (Map 3) (☎ 439 9041), 245 Main Rd. It's a Hindu-run 'pure-veg' restaurant and the meals are good value, eg full thalis with a starter cost R32 and mini thalis are R22. The spices have been toned down for South African palates but you'll get the real thing if you ask. It's open daily for lunch and dinner.

L'Orient (Map 3) (☎ 439 6572), 50 Main Rd (near the corner of Marine Rd), is a good restaurant serving Malaysian and Indonesian dishes. Try the spicy prawn soup for flavours you might have been missing in South Africa. Main courses cost between R35 and R60. It's open for dinner daily, except Monday.

Café Erté (Map 3), on Main Rd near the corner of Frere St, is a relaxed (despite the stark black-and-deco paint job) and gay-friendly bar and café open from 11 am to 5 am. You can have snacks such as burgers for R15. For larger meals of modern cuisine with lots of fresh ingredients, two people can probably eat and drink for under R70.

San Marco (Map 3) (☎ 49 2758), 92 Main Rd (on the corner of St James Rd), is a long established and excellent formal Italian restaurant, with some of the few professional waiters in town (who let it go to their heads, sometimes). Prices match the quality. You might find a starter under R25, a pasta under R35 and a main course under R45, but why not forget about the bill and enjoy some great food. San Marco is open daily, except Tuesday, for dinner, plus lunch on Sunday. The gelateria in front of the restaurant has delicious takeaway gelati and other ice cream.

Peasants (Map 3), just off Main Rd on Wisbeach Rd, is a pizza and pasta place with food that's a little better than the franchises offer. Pastas and pizzas cost around R30 (try the seafood pizza). *Ari's Souvlaki* (Map 3) (☎ 439 6683), 150 Main Rd (on the corner of Oliver Rd), is a popular Sea Point institution famous for its felafels and souvlaki. A schwarma is R15. The food is good, although, as is usual in this country, a little blander than the original.

Across the road, between Albany and Bellevue Sts, is a bunch of places, including another Middle Eastern place, *Ardi's* (Map 3) and a *Steers* (Map 3), both of which are open 24 hours.

Currently extremely popular (booking is essential) is *Mr Chan's* (Map 3) (☎ 439 2239) at 178A Main Rd. The food is Chinese and it is authentic.

For kerbside tables and good snacks (and a good deli inside) go to *Reise's Deli* (Map 3) on Main Rd near Arthur's Rd. It's open daily from 8.30 am to 7 pm. Nearby on St John's Rd, beneath St John's Lodge, *The Wooden Shoe* (Map 3) (☎ 439 4435) is the oldest surviving steakhouse in Cape Town, if not South Africa. It's tiny but it's very good and specialises in Austrian dishes. Prices are reasonable.

For biltong, which can be vacuum-packed for export (but no matter how it's packed you can't take it home to Australia or the USA), try *Joubert & Monty's Meat Boutique* (Map 3), 53 Regent St, near the corner of Clarens St. Next door is *New York Deli* (Map 3), where bagels are the speciality.

CAMPS BAY

Camps Bay (Map 2) is a pleasant destination for an evening drink and a meal, especially if the south-easterly isn't howling. A stroll along the beach, followed by a beer at one of the pavement tables and dinner is a genuine pleasure.

For those on a budget there's a *St Elmo's*, but for cool Californian style, there's the acclaimed *Blues* (☎ 438 2040), upstairs in The Promenade centre, Victoria Rd, overlooking the beach. The crowd here tends to be relatively young and informal, but smart – this is a place to be seen. The menu is interesting and prices are surprisingly reasonable – from R35. Booking is recommended in the evening, and during the day on summer weekends.

La Med (☎ 438 5600) is another casual but upmarket place. It's at the Glen Country Club, and often has live music. There's probably no better place to be at sunset in summer.

OBSERVATORY

Observatory is an inner-city suburb to the east of the city centre and Devil's Peak. It's near the University of Cape Town and is favoured by student-types, although yuppies are starting to appreciate the suburb's advantages.

The main batch of restaurants (all on Map 6) is only a short walk from the Observatory train station (on the Simon's Town line), 10 minutes and R2.20/1.50 in 1st/3rd class from the main train station. There are frequent trains until 10 pm Monday to Saturday, until 8 pm on Sunday. From the station, walk west (towards the mountain) along Trill Rd until it intersects with Lower Main Rd. Turn right and walk through to the intersection with Station Rd – most places are around here. Turn left on Station for Heidelberg Hotel, which has a popular student bar.

All the following places are on Lower Main Rd. Just south of Trill Rd is *Stews R Us*, with good-value and filling meals. On the other side of Lower Main Rd on the corner of Trill is *Elaine's* (☎ 47 2616), a good Indian/Asian restaurant with curries for around R30. On the opposite corner is *Zulu Warrior Café* and a few doors up from here is *Die Blou Okapi*, a student-type café with good, cheap food. Breakfast (served all day) is just R10 and there are pittas from R4.50. It's open until 2 am daily. Just next door is its antithesis, the trendy *Observatory Café*, which is also a bar. A little along from here is *Pancho's Mexican Restaurant*, with good value food (most dishes under R25) and a cheerful atmosphere. Across the road from Pancho's is *Seasons*, a vegetarian restaurant – the meal we had there was bland, if healthy.

Fiddlewoods Restaurant (☎ 448 6687), 40 Trill Rd (near the corner of Lower Main Rd), serves modern, delicious and healthy food. Many dishes are vegetarian and start at less than R20. Next door, set back from Trill Rd, is *Café Ganesh*, which is trendy but cool. *The Planet* on Station Rd opposite Heidelberg Hotel is a bar and restaurant with budget specials.

Africa Café (☎ 47 9553), 213 Lower Main Rd (on the corner of Bishop Rd), serves African dishes from across the continent. There's an all-you-can-eat communal feast for R59 per person. It's open for dinner nightly, except Sunday.

Not in Observatory but on the way there, at 297 Albert Rd in Woodstock, *The Palace* (☎ 47 9540) *is* palatial and its clients are mainly wealthier members of the Muslim community. It's run by Boete Achmad, who has been a big name in Cape Town catering for nearly 50 years. Curries start around R30, rising to about R70 for prawn curry, and steaks are around R40. There are also set menus. It's pricey but a nice change from standard restaurants.

HOUT BAY

Hout Bay, formerly a fishing village, is at the northern end of Chapman's Peak Drive. It still supports a number of fish factories and is a popular destination, especially on weekends. *Snoekies*, at the far end of Hout Bay harbour, has a fresh-fish shop; *The Laughing Lobster* close by serves fried fish and piping-hot chips. Both places are open seven days a week from 8.30 am to 5.30 pm. *Fish on the Rocks*, in the same area, is basically a takeaway outlet for workers at the fish factories, but it does very good fish and chips at reasonable prices.

Mariner's Wharf (☎ 790 1100) is a harbour-front complex with a restaurant and open-air bistro, both specialising in seafood. It is a tourist trap but a lot of work has gone into it and it's quite pleasant. The nautical antiques *are* antiques, not reproductions. *Mariner's Wharf Grill* has less expensive dishes, such as fish pie and salad (R25), but most fish dishes are pricey. There's a fish market in the complex, so you could buy and cook your own.

FALSE BAY
Kalk Bay

Brass Bell (☎ 788 5455), Kalk Bay train station, is right between the railway line and the sea, with magnificent views over False Bay. Besides its main à la carte restaurant, Brass Bell has two bars and an open-air patio. It isn't cheap but it is worth it.

There's live music every Saturday afternoon which drifts on into the night, and on some evenings (check the papers). Brass Bell used to be a legendary rock venue, but these days it's much more laid-back. If you want to see music at Brass Bell but don't care to pay the meal prices, there are a number of good places across the road, such as *Cafe Matisse*, with snacks and pizzas.

Boulders Beach

Penguin Point Café is a pleasant café with sea views from the deck, and it's a very good restaurant. There are snacks such as spicy kedgeree (R19), starters such as calamari (R16 and prepared much more imaginatively than in most restaurants) and dishes such as pasta (R28).

SOUTHERN SUBURBS

Forries (the Foresters' Arms) (Map 7) in Newlands is a big, mock-Tudor pub with a convivial atmosphere and good pub meals. Steak costs around R30, bangers and mash under R20 and a generous serving of roast is R25. In the same area, on the corner of Kildare Lane and Main St (not Main Rd), *Barristers* (Map 7) is another snug, English-style pub, with a slightly more adventurous menu at similar prices. (See the Entertainment chapter for more on these pubs.)

There are plenty of cafés in shopping centres, such as *La Scala* in Cavendish Square (Map 7), Claremont.

Groot Constantia

Groot Constantia (Map 1) is the oldest and grandest of the Cape's wine estates. The buildings date from 1685 and have been beautifully restored. It's a bit of a tourist trap, but nevertheless worth visiting, especially if you don't have time to explore the Winelands around Stellenbosch. See the earlier Groot Constantia section in the Things to See & Do chapter.

Tavern, beside the modern cellars near the main homestead, has a pleasant outdoor eating area, although it is expensive. You'll pay about four times more for a bottle of wine here than it costs in the nearby cellar. *Jonkerhuis* looks as if it's expensive, but it's actually good value. It's in an old, restored estate house, a short walk from the main homestead. Teas and light lunches are served daily from 10 am to 5 pm. There are some great cakes and pastries, and at lunch there are some traditional dishes such as bobotie and rice (R35) and chicken pie (R35) as well as standard and lighter dishes.

Kirstenbosch Botanic Gardens

The restaurant at *Kirstenbosch Botanic Gardens* (Map 7) (☎ 797 7614) is good value. It is open daily for breakfast, tea and lunch; there are indoor and outdoor eating areas. It's not formal or flash but you can get something cheap and filling like bangers and mash (R15), a vegetable platter (R17) or a steak (from R20). On Sunday there's a roast lunch for about R25. It's open from 9 am to 5 pm Monday to Friday, and from 8.30 am to 5 pm on weekends.

Entertainment

Cape Town is returning to its roots – the old Tavern of the Seas has dusted itself down and is back in the business of beguiling doubloons from visiting foreigners. If you're staying at a top-end place your doubloons will already be flowing fairly rapidly, but even if you're paying a pittance for a hostel bunk there are still plenty of wallet-emptying temptations. Although there aren't many stand-out entertainment venues, the city has such a good atmosphere (especially in summer) that many people put in some very long nights drifting from bar to club to bar to club ...

As well as the more commercial venues there's a range of informal places which come and go. Some started out as private parties that were just too good to stop.

You can't do without the entertainment guide in the *Weekly Mail & Guardian*. The *Cape Times* newspaper has an entertainment section on Friday. *Going Out in the Cape* is a monthly booklet listing most mainstream events; it's sold at various information offices for R3.

For any entertainment booking, contact Computicket (☎ 21 4715), a computerised booking agency that has *every* seat for *every* theatre, cinema and sports venue on its system. You can be shown the available seats and get your ticket on the spot. There are outlets in the Golden Acre Centre, in the Gardens Centre, at the Waterfront, in Sea Point's Adelphi Centre and many other places. In addition to the entertainment sphere, Computicket also accepts classified advertising for major newspapers and bookings for various bus lines.

When in doubt, the place to go is the Waterfront, which is easily accessible and has a number of entertainment possibilities all within walking distance of each other.

To see how the majority of Cape Towners enjoy themselves, take a tour of clubs in the townships. These are a little hard to come by, unfortunately, as operators go in and out of business quickly. Ask at Captour for those currently running.

CINEMAS

See the local press for a rundown of cinemas and films.

The best cinema for 'mainstream alternative' films is *Labia Cinema* (Map 8) (☎ 24 5927), named after Count Labia, a patron of the arts, at 68 Orange St, Gardens. Admission is a very reasonable R12. Similar fare is offered at *Baxter Theatre* (Map 6) (☎ 689 1069), on the corner of Main and Woolsack

A Fistful of Rand?

It's a sign of South Africa's new status on the global scene: if you're getting tired of films where Vancouver or Toronto stands in for New York or LA, Hollywood has an answer – try Cape Town.

The city, or at least the scenery around it, has been discovered by the image merchants. While the big business of looking good has also taken note of the area's charms (Elite and Boss, two major modelling agencies, have opened offices in Cape Town), it's the movie and TV market that is attracting the attention.

Film investors like the weak currency, cheap (and largely non-union) labour, blue skies and exotic ersatz locations (they say the Cape can double for any place from Arizona or Bordeaux to Scotland or Greece – even, in a pinch, for Africa). The number of foreign feature films, documentaries, TV series and commercials shot around Cape Town is rapidly growing, bringing about R100 million into the country each year. A Cape Film and Video Foundation has been formed to encourage the poorly funded local film industry, and to see that blacks share in the benefits, including industry training and unionisation.

One Man One Vote, an end-of-apartheid film starring Sidney Poitier and Michael Caine, was filmed in Cape Town (logically enough). Look for shoot-'em-ups amid the fynbos in future blockbusters.

For a taste of Hollywood dreams (with fries), try the new Planet Hollywood at the Waterfront.

Russ Kerr

Rds, Rondebosch. There are *Nu-Metro* cinemas at the Waterfront and on Adderley St for commercial fare.

In the flashy BMW Pavilion (Map 9) at the Waterfront, *Imax* cinema offers Imax-format films (shown on a giant square screen). There are hourly shows from 11 am to 11 pm.

BARS & CLUBS

Wednesday, Friday and Saturday are the biggest nights in the clubs. In the city centre, the blocks around Bree, Loop, Long Sts and, say, Waterkant are incredibly lively all night long on summer weekends. The actual entertainment rarely matches the level of activity (most clubs play techno to expensively dressed young suburbanites and visiting Vaalies), but it's a good buzz. Cover charges are around R10.

Clubs in this area come and go quite rapidly, but some seem to survive, such as *Café Comic Strip* (Map 8) on Loop St, which is pretty standard, with lots of bouncers and lots of young whites from the outer suburbs. Around here you'll find plenty of other places, such as the *Havana Bar* (Map 8), the *Crew Bar* (Map 8) and *Carlos O'Brien's* (Map 8). A reader recommends *The Rockin' Shamrock* (Map 8) (Loop St), 'but only if you like dancing on the tables and the bar'. Entry is free.

For less clean-cut entertainment, try Riebeeck St around Loop and Bree Sts, where there are strip shows and the like.

The strip clubs might not be very savoury but they are culturally interesting. This is where you're likely to meet up-country Afrikaner men who are in the big city for a spree. Amidst the smashing of all sorts of racial and sexual taboos you can almost see their Calvinist upbringing beginning to crumble. It's like something out of William Faulkner.

Jon Murray

Currently the place to be seen is *Hemingways* (Map 8), an upmarket nightclub in the impressive old Martin Melck House on Strand St between Bree and Buitengracht Sts. Admission is a hefty R30 but a foreign accent (especially a US one) combined with model looks might get you in free. It's that sort of place.

Shebeen on Bree (Map 8) serves beer in 750mL bottles and drinks in tin cups – and the bar is lined with young whites sitting around waiting for something to happen. Apparently that something includes good township jazz, but there wasn't much happening when we dropped by. If you want to see a real shebeen, take a township tour or get yourself an invitation from someone who knows what they are doing.

Fireman's Arms (Map 3), on the corner of Buitengracht and Mechau Sts (near Somerset Rd) is one of the few old pubs left in town and it dates from 1906. There's a cheerful bar and a lounge where you can buy cheap meals.

The Purple Turtle (Map 8), right around the corner from Greenmarket Square on Shortmarket St, has a relaxed and student-pub-like atmosphere. There are meals and bands, although it seems to be a place where people meet before going on to the clubs. *Funktion*, nearby on the corner of Loop and Shortmarket Sts, plays Drum & Bass, House and Trip-Hop.

The crowd at *The Lounge* (Map 8), upstairs at 194 Long St, tends to the alternative, and it's a small, relaxed place. It's in the narrow section of Long St with all the iron-lace balconies, and with own balcony is a great place for a drink on a hot night. *District Six Café* (Map 8), on the corner of Sir Lowry Rd and Darling St, is similar but more down-to-earth – it's a dim but friendly place that describes itself as a 1990s pub. It's open from 8 pm to 4 am from Monday to Thursday and until 6 am on Friday and Saturday. Upstairs there's *Gel*, with a couple of levels of dance floors. Behind the café is *The Magic Lush Room*, playing Jungle, Trip-Hop and Trance.

A grungy neighbourhood bar with a reputation among fastidious Cape Towners as catering to 'bergies' (bums, tramps, derros) is *The Whistle Stop* (Map 8) – it's actually not bad. It's about the only bar in the city area where you'll drink with ordinary people of all colours in anything like an ordinary bar atmosphere and it has a good juke box. There are also simple but good meals, from hot chips (fries) to kassler chops for R13. The Whistle Stop is at the top end of Long St, near the Long St Baths, and is open until 4 am daily.

The Firkin Brew Pub Company (Map 8) is a pub brewery on Kloof St near the corner of Beckham St, Gardens. It has some interesting beers and inexpensive food, but not much atmosphere.

Stag's Head Hotel (Map 8) (☎ 45 4918), 71 Hope St, Gardens, is a very popular, very grungy pub. It's also one of the very few English/Australian-style downmarket pubs in South Africa. The ground floor bar has a motley assortment of locals staring morosely into their beers and the ground floor lounge (in the rear) has a younger crowd, but the real action happens upstairs, with plenty of pool tables, pinball machines and loud music (sometimes live).

At the Waterfront (Map 9), the *Hard Rock Cafe* is always crowded and *Cantina Tequila* is currently very popular with visitors. *Quay 4 Bar* is also popular. There are plenty of other places.

Blue Rock on Main Rd, Sea Point, is a smallish, coolish bar specialising in cocktails (complete with juggling barpeople) and hoping to attract an 'unpretentious yuppie' crowd. It plays good music, sometimes live, and stays open very late.

Away from the city centre but not too far to go by Rikki or taxi, *The Shed* (Map 5), De Villiers St, Gardens, is a bar and a pool hall. It attracts an interesting crowd and the décor is good. *The Fringe* (Map 8), 46 Canterbury St, Gardens, is a relaxed and unpretentious place where people actually dance to enjoy themselves. The night we called by it was full of happy young lesbians. Thursday is reggae night.

Heidelberg Hotel (Map 6), Station St (near the corner of Lower Main Rd), Observatory, is another classic – the clientele is dominated by students and the name of the game is drinking beer. What else are hotels for? Nearby on Lower Main Rd is *Rolling Stones* (Map 6), a large, upstairs pool hall with a long balcony that's a nice place to

have a drink. As with everywhere else in Cape Town, the tables are not full-size (we'd be pleased to hear if you have found a full-size table) but it's a good spot. Opening hours are noon to 3 am, daily.

For a *bar/cafeteria* which has zero design qualities but à friendly atmosphere, go upstairs from the main train station's Strand St entrance (Map 8). The clientele is exclusively non-white.

One of the few remaining old-style pubs is the *Kimberley Hotel* (Map 8), on the corner of Roeland and Buitenkant Sts. For something completely different try *Forries* (Map 7) (The Forester's Arms) in the leafy suburb of Newlands, on the corner of Newlands Ave and Manson Close. Another pleasant middle-class watering hole is *Barristers* (Map 7), nearby on the corner of Kildare Rd and Main St (not Main Rd).

Cape Town Women's Cafe

We discovered this on the Internet – appropriate, given that there is no fixed venue and it's a monthly *event*, not a café as such. The Cape Town Women's Cafe calls itself a women-only version of the boys' night out, a chance to redress the imbalance in men and women's social options. It's got rave reviews, and is apparently a lot of fun.

The first 'café' was held at Manenburg's Jazz Cafe. To find out when and where it may be held while you're in town, send an email to cafe@gem.co.za or visit the Web site at http://members.gem.co.za/cafe.

Elvis Snack & Dance

This place wouldn't warrant a heading all to itself or even an entry in this book, except that it's about the only example of genuine eccentricity you'll come across in this country. It's a tiny (and probably unlicensed) bar adjoining a tiny barber shop (just R13 for a haircut), run by Michael, a devoted fan of Elvis. He'll sing you a song if you ask nicely and buy a beer at an inflated price. Elvis Snack & Dance (Map 3) is on Main Rd in Sea Point, to the city side of the San Marco restaurant, and sometimes stays open very late.

THEATRE

Baxter Theatre (Map 6) (☎ 685 7880), Woolsack Rd, Rosebank, and *Little Theatre* (Map 8) (☎ 24 2340), Orange St, are venues for non-mainstream productions. The Long St Theatre (Map 8) (☎ 418 3496), corner of Waterkant and Long Sts, is a long-running venue presenting alternative music and theatre. Some of its *raison d'être* disappeared with the end of apartheid but it's still worth a look.

The various theatres in the large *Nico complex* (Map 8) (formerly Nico Malan, but now shortened to avoid the apartheid-era connotations of the Malan name) on the foreshore have ballet, opera and more mainstream theatre – at prices way below what you would pay in Europe. After an evening performance you'll have to phone for a taxi as there is no rank and walking isn't very safe in this area after dark.

LIVE MUSIC

Several music venues have already been covered in the earlier Places to Eat chapter. *Green Dolphin* (☎ 21 7471) is a top class jazz venue at the Waterfront, and *Brass Bell* at Kalk Bay train station has live bands on Wednesday and Saturday nights, and Saturday and Sunday afternoons.

Classical Music

The Cape Town Symphony Orchestra used to give regular concerts in the *Town Hall* (Map 8), but the orchestra has lost its funding and the future looks grim. The *Nico complex* (Map 8) also has concerts (see the earlier Theatre section).

Bands

There is occasionally live music at *Quay 4 Bar* at the Waterfront. There is nearly always something on at *The Pumphouse* (☎ 25 4437) also at the Waterfront. It's a great venue – formerly a pumphouse for the dry docks nearby – but it's fairly small and can be ridiculously crowded.

One of the best venues is, unfortunately, a long way from the city. *River Club* (Map 6) (☎ 790 5839), near the corner of Station Rd and Liesbeek Parkway, Observatory, often hosts big-name bands with a cover charge of around R10. There's another club on the premises called *The Water Room*.

The earlier Bars & Clubs section lists more places which might have bands. It's noteworthy that a recent South African tour by ZZ Top resulted in concerts in Cape Town selling out instantly, while they were cancelled for lack of interest in other cities.

Jazz

Jazz offered (and still offers) one of the few opportunities for black and white South Africans to interact as equals. Some excellent jazz is played in Cape Town and while there are few permanent venues, many places occasionally have jazz – check the papers for details. Cover charges range from R10 to R20, depending on the venue, performance and night of the week.

One of the best places for a drink, a snack and live jazz is *Manenberg's Jazz Cafe* (Map 8), upstairs on the corner of Adderley and Church Sts. It's a pleasant place with tables on the balcony and a relaxed, racially mixed clientele. There is live music seven nights a week and often through the day, with improvised jazz being a regular feature. There's a cover charge of R10 at night (more if there's a big act).

Café Blue Moon (Map 8) (☎ 24 5100), on the corner of Shortmarket and Long Sts, in the city centre, is a restaurant and bar which features jazz as part of a wider programme of live music.

Take Four Bistro (Map 8), located in the Longkloof Studios (near the corner of Park and Kloof Sts), has an eclectic mix of music, including some jazz on Friday and Saturday nights.

Dizzy Jazz (Map 2) (☎ 438 2686) is on the corner of The Drive and Camps Bay Drive, just off Victoria Rd in Camps Bay. It's open daily until very late, and has live jazz from Thursday to Sunday.

Township Jazz Visiting a township jazz club is an unforgettable experience, but you are strongly advised not to go alone. Companies

Musical Notes

In the city centre and surrounding white suburbs you'll have to search for anything other than mainstream, MTV fare. In the townships, the problem isn't lack of musical imagination but more a lack of infrastructure – venues, often informal, tend to come and go as fast as the word gets around. This is also true of township jazz tour outfits, which are about the only way you're likely to visit Cape Flats at night.

Some internationally known music has come out of Cape Flats: jazz musicians like Dollar Brand (Abdullah Ibrahim), Robbie Jansen, Basil Coetzee, Winston Mankunku and Ezra Ngcukana.

The African drum echoes far beyond the townships. Jungle, a frenetic, drum 'n' bass-heavy version of dub music, has found its way from the mixing boards of London to Cape Town dance clubs (don't say you weren't warned). The popularity of black music with white audiences also extends to live music – while blues music developed in the USA, its roots are African; the Blues Broers (pronounced 'brews', it's slang for Brother) are five Afrikaners who dress in black and play the blues.

The music of the Flats often reveals a distinctive Brazilian influence (for reasons that are unclear). And white pop music is becoming more global in style – some band names almost sound made in Japan, eg Stellenbosch's own Springbok Nude Girls.

Russ Kerr

Pianist Abdullah Ibrahim became famous in the 1960s as Dollar Brand, a *marabi* (African jazz) virtuoso.

such as One City Tours (☎ 387 5351/5165) are based in the townships and offer a well organised and safe visit. Captour may know of other tours currently running. Better-known clubs include *Club Ubuntu* (☎ 419 4732) in Guguletu and *Tiger's Club House* (☎ 694 1866) in Langa.

GAY SCENE

Although there's quite a healthy gay scene there aren't many exclusively gay venues. Most are close together in the Waterkant area. *The Bronx* (Map 3) is a small bar and cabaret venue on the corner of Somerset Rd and Napier St between the city and Green Point. When there's entertainment (usually on Saturday night) it starts around 10 pm. *Angels*, a few doors towards the city from The Bronx, is a mixed dance venue. *Café Manhattan* (Map 3) is a nearby bar and restaurant up on the corner of Waterkant and Dixon Sts. *Café Ertè* (see the Places to Eat chapter) on Main Rd in Sea Point is a gay-friendly place that stays open late for after-club recuperation.

Cape Town Queer Project is a massive party held at the River Club in mid-December.

See the Travel Agents section of the Getting There & Away chapter for details on Gay esCape, a gay-oriented travel agency which is a great source of information on good restaurants and venues in and around Cape Town.

SPECTATOR SPORT

South Africans are mad about sport and Cape Towners are no exception. International sanctions on sporting contacts during the apartheid era probably caused more heartache among whites than the economic sanctions did (see the It's Not How You Play, It's Who boxed text in this section).

The biggest change since the free elections is that all South Africans cheer for the national teams. In the past, barracking for the other side was one of the few legal protests that blacks and coloureds could make. And while it might have been legal, it certainly didn't do anything to make them popular!

National teams have been called the Springboks (Die Bokkies), although it is the rugby team that has the main claim to the name. The name was supposed to be dropped after the free elections (it was strongly associated with apartheid) but has since gained strong support from a cross-section of the community, thanks to the Springboks winning the 1995 rugby union World Cup.

Rugby

Rugby has been traditionally the Afrikaners' game, with its 'manly' virtues and barely controlled violence. However, since South Africa hosted (and won) the 1995 rugby union World Cup, the game is seen as a national one.

That's the theory, anyway. More than a few blacks have wondered why their strikes for increased pay and better working conditions have been called subversive, yet the Jo'burg Stock Exchange and many businesses shut down for the cup's opening game.

Important games are played at *Newlands Stadium* (Map 7), one of rugby's shrines.

It's Not How You Play, It's Who

In 1968 Basil D'Oliveira became entangled in events that mark the long beginning of the end of apartheid. 'Dolly' was one of the finest cricketers to come out of South Africa. The Cape Towner first made his mark in a match in 1951, scoring all but 8 of his side's 233 runs. He later became a club and then provincial captain, but by 1958 there was nowhere left for him to go in South African cricket. Basil D'Oliveira was coloured, and the national team was whites only. The only way to continue his career was to emigrate – by 1966 he was playing for England.

D'Oliveira was an injury replacement in the England side that was to tour South Africa in 1968-9, but the all-rounder never got a chance to play. The South African government insisted D'Oliveira contradicted its policy of 'non-mixed sport', and the English cancelled the tour.

England's motives are unclear (many suspected that D'Oliveira had been left off the original team so that the tour could go ahead). England had long been (along with Australia) a supporter of 'constructive engagement' with apartheid cricket, and a South African return tour in 1970 was only called off at the last second – and only after large public protests in England made security for the tour untenable.

'The D'Oliveira Affair' was one of a series of incidents. New Zealand rugby's decision to tour South Africa led to an African boycott of the 1976 Montreal Olympics; fears of similar problems in future Commonwealth Games led to vague but high-sounding declarations against 'Apartheid in Sport'. One of the more intriguing declarations was made by the National Party itself in 1977, when it announced that South Africa would practise 'normal sport' (thus unwittingly admitting that racial sport was anything but 'normal'). The results for South Africa were mixed – though banned from major competitions, some tours continued by various means, and inside the country nothing changed for non-white athletes off the sporting field.

With the end of apartheid South African sport has a new image, and new international support. Perhaps as a goodwill gesture to the new South Africa, its cricket team returned to international competition without undergoing Zimbabwe's 10 year probation period (during which Zimbabwe was expected to develop nonracial cricket at home).

Cricket has been called the best hope for nonracial sport in South Africa, lying somewhere between black-identified soccer and white Afrikaner rugby. There is a long, grassroots history of nonracial organisation, spurred largely by the coloured community – whose contributions, some say, are now being forgotten as the mainly white cricket administration attempts to 'bring the game to the townships'. Meanwhile, coloured fans still sit in the section of Newlands they were once confined to by law, but which was (not unlike the old Bay 13 at the MCG in Melbourne) the liveliest part of the grounds. Paul Adams, the coloured left-arm wrist-spin bowler from Cape Town's St Augustine club (which also produced Basil D'Oliveira), is a member of the national team.

D'Oliveira has remained a popular figure in his home town. He was at Newlands to watch South Africa defeat England in the fifth Test in January 1996. There was obvious irony in the occasion, especially when D'Oliveira, who remains a British citizen living in England, was toasted as 'one of the most famous people in South Africa's nonracial society'. Irony, however, is one of the milder legacies of apartheid.

Russ Kerr

Soccer

Soccer (football) has traditionally been played by blacks. The national soccer team, Bafana Bafana (a Xhosa term usually rendered as The Boys), won the 1996 Africa Nations Cup final, and has qualified for the 1998 World Cup. The Cape Town Spurs are a successful soccer team in the National Soccer League; their home ground is *Athlone Stadium*.

Cricket

South Africa's cricket team was the first of the national teams to be allowed back into international competition, in the 1992 World Cup. The euphoria which followed the team's success probably helped many whites to resign themselves to the political reform that was becoming inevitable.

In a bold move, the national team has been renamed the Proteas. But as with most political decisions in South Africa today, this one is a compromise – like Springboks, Proteas is a name not unsullied by apartheid (the 'coloured' rugby team was called Proteas during the era of 'normal' sport). See the earlier It's Not How You Play, It's Who boxed text.

Important games are played at Newlands, which vies with Australia's Adelaide Oval for the title of the world's prettiest cricket ground.

Shopping

WHERE TO SHOP
Shopping Centres
So far, Cape Town has avoided the fate of other South African cities, where the wealthier (mainly white) citizens shop at anonymous suburban malls, leaving the decaying city centre to the poorer (mainly non-white) citizens. The big, new shopping complexes at the Waterfront might be a sign that things are changing, unfortunately.

You'll find most things you need at shops in the city centre. OK Bazaars (Map 8) on Adderley St is a department store selling inexpensive merchandise; Woolworths (Map 8), across the road, is more upmarket.

Golden Acre Centre (Map 8), on the corner of Adderley and Strand Sts, contains numerous shops and is connected to St George's Mall by underground arcades. One arcade branches off to become the *Cape Sun Gallery*, an underground arcade which has some good shops and a coffee bar or two. There are entrances to the Sun Gallery on the north-east corner of St George's Mall and Strand St, and near the Allied Bank on St George's Mall, near the corner of Castle (Kasteel) St.

If you hunger for a suburban mall, try Cavendish Square (Map 7), off Protea Rd in Claremont, the most stylish shopping centre in Cape Town.

Markets
In addition to the specialised markets (see the following sections), there are markets in Greenmarket Square (Map 8) (daily) and at Green Point, by Green Point Stadium (Map 3) (Sunday). The market at Grand Parade (Map 8) (Wednesday and Saturday) doesn't sell much of interest to visitors but it is much livelier than the others, with people scrambling for bargains, mainly clothing.

Flower sellers congregate in a mall off Adderley St, next to OK Bazaars (Map 8). Unfortunately, it's a cramped and shaded location. Once, the flowers were picked on Table Mountain by the sellers.

Craft Shops
The Siyakatala stall, in the Red Shed craft market (Map 9) at the Waterfront, sells quality items made by self-help groups in the townships. There are many other stalls in the Red Shed, some interesting, some kitschy.

There is a small shop worth looking at in St George's Cathedral (Map 8). It has some guidebooks and crafts – and you know that the profits are going to people who need them.

African Image (Map 8), on the corner of Church and Burg Sts, has a very interesting range of new and old crafts and artefacts from South Africa and across the continent. Its prices are reasonable. For example, flowers made from aluminium cans cost R6 – you can pay R20 elsewhere. Nearby on Church St, Out of Africa, on the Church St Mall, is a very expensive but very good craft/antique shop. Pezulu (Map 8), 70 St George's Mall (near Hout St), is upstairs and can be difficult to spot, but it's worth making the effort.

A craft market is held on Sunday on Dock Rd (Map 4), just outside the Waterfront, with a more tourist-oriented art and craft market held in the Waterfront near the South African Maritime Museum (Map 9) on weekends.

Mnandi Textiles (Map 6), 90 Station St (near the corner of Lower Main Rd), Observatory, sells interesting printed cloth and some clothing made from it. You'll find cloth printed with everything from ANC election posters to animal patterns.

Bookshops
Exclusive Books (☎ 419 0905), upstairs in the Victoria Wharf complex (Map 9) at the Waterfront, has an excellent range; it's open to 11 pm on Saturday and from 11 am to 5 pm on Sunday.

The main mass-market bookshop/newsagent/stationer is CNA, which has many branches, including one on St George's Mall (Map 8) (in the Norwich Centre) and another at the Waterfront.

Several bookshops towards the mountain end of Long St sell mainly second-hand and rare books, with Clarke's Bookshop (☎ 23 5739), 211 Long St, specialising in books on Africana.

Ulrich Naumann's (Map 8) (☎ 23 7832), 17 Burg St, has a good range of German-language books, many of which are translations of South African books, including the coffee table variety.

For government publications, go to the Government Printers (Map 8), 90 Plein St. It's open on weekdays from 7.45 am to 12.30 pm and 1.15 to 3.15 pm.

24-Hour Shops
After hours it can be difficult to find vital bits and pieces like milk or cigarette papers. There are a few 7-11 shops, with the one on Main Rd in Sea Point (Map 3) (between Frere St and Rhine Rd) open 24 hours. Also, many petrol stations are open 24 hours and most stock basic necessities.

For a more traditional *kaffe* (corner store/food counter), also open after-hours, try the Cadiz Nosh Bar (Map 8) on the corner of Loop and Shortmarket Sts.

WHAT TO BUY
Antiques, Collectables & Old Books
South Africa's long isolation from the outside world means that there are troves of old goods for sale at very reasonable prices.

The Junk Shop (Map 8) on the corner of Long and Bloem Sts has some intriguing junk from many eras. In the same area there are several good second-hand and antiquarian bookshops, although the legendary Cranfords has closed. Not far away on Church St (between Long and Burg Sts) there is a pedestrian mall where a flea market is held on Thursday, Friday and Saturday (daily in summer). You'll find several antique shops here.

Out at Groot Constantia (Map 1) there's a market on weekends; it's next to the Tavern.

Wine
The wines produced in the Cape are of an extremely high standard and they are very cheap by international standards. Consider shipping a few cases home. You may have to pay duty, but as you can buy excellent wines for R30 or less, it's probably worthwhile. Several companies will freight wine for you, including Vaughan Johnson's Wine Shop (Map 9) (☎ 419 2121; fax 419 0040) at the Waterfront.

Note that the boom in international sales of South African wines will mean a shortage of Western Cape wines for at least a couple of years (until the new vines begin to bear), so prices will rise.

Crafts
Craftwork from the many different cultures of South Africa is available in Cape Town, but remember that none of the black cultures are indigenous to in this area. Traditional Zulu or Ndebele crafts, for example, have been brought here from other areas of the country and have hefty mark-ups. If you're going to travel around South Africa it's a good idea to look at the items in Cape Town's more upmarket craft shops to get an idea of quality and prices, then buy in the areas of the country where they were made. With luck you'll be buying from the people who made them. Not only is this likely to be much cheaper, but you'll be putting your money directly into the pockets of those who need it most.

As well as items associated with traditional cultures, there is a lot of craft generated for the tourist trade. There are some quality items among the dross. It's a matter of looking through the many informal stalls set up around the city. You'll find a clump of them on the seaside road to Hout Bay, just outside Bakoven.

If you're looking for gifts but don't want tacky tourist stuff, consider some township-produced crafts, which are the product of poverty plus ingenuity. Items such as boxes and simple toys made from recycled drink or oil cans are genuine artefacts from a vibrant culture (well, they were until recently – some

The Sound of Muzak

If you have a hire car and plan to do a lot of driving, your number one priority is to buy some good music for the cassette player, right? There's a problem with this, however. While there are places selling a fair range of mainstream popular music scattered throughout the city and suburbs, they sell mainly CDs. There are also plenty of shops selling tapes, but these are geared mainly to the non-white population. This is good if you want to listen to local and African music, but if you're planing to barrel across the Karoo for 12 or so hours, you might want silly holiday music. My yen was for Iggy Pop. Yes, Iggy was available on CD, but not on tape.

Why not? The reason probably comes back to economic apartheid, as do so many things in this sometimes infuriating country. Whites can afford CD players in their cars, non-whites can't, so music sold on cassettes is aimed at a non-white audience.

Jon Murray

semi-precious stones and gold and silver, and you can call in and see how it's done on a free guided tour.

Afrogem's large showroom offers many tempting gift ideas. Tours are available from 8.30 am to 4.30 pm on weekdays (to 3.30 pm on Friday). The showroom is open daily, except Sunday, from 8.30 am to 5 pm.

For an enormous range of beads, some in African designs, go to The Bead Shop (Map 8) on Long St, near the corner of Bloem St.

Traditional Medicine

Evelyn Kubukeli's sangoma shop at 190 Lower Main Rd has been recommended as the best place to pick up your traditional medicines.

Camping Gear

The excellent Camp & Climb chain (☎ 23 2175) has a branch at 6 Pepper St, near the corner of Long St. The Cape Union Mart chain has branches at the Waterfront (☎ 419 0019), the Cape Sun Gallery and on the corner of Spin and Corporation Sts (Map 8). If you're looking for an extensive range of gear, the big department stores (like OK Bazaars on Adderley St) are relatively inexpensive.

are now probably made for the trade) and are popular with the folks back home.

Jewellery

Afrogem (Map 8) (☎ 24 8048), Buitengracht St, produces jewellery and other items from

Excursions

Although Cape Town has enough attractions to keep you occupied for some time, you should see some of the surrounding area. This part of the Western Cape Province has spectacular and beautiful scenery, and interesting old towns, some tucked away in wine country first planted with vines more than three centuries ago.

If you want to see country more typical of the rest of South Africa you'll have to travel a little further afield, but you can get a glimpse of the Karoo on an easy two or three day trip, and it's well worthwhile. To find the famous African animals in their native habitat you'll need to travel quite a long way. Lonely Planet's *South Africa, Lesotho & Swaziland* has details.

See under Organised Tours in the Getting Around chapter for travel resources in the area. For details on the Cape Peninsula and False Bay between Strand and Cape Point, see the earlier Things to See & Do chapter.

THE WINELANDS

The wine-producing region around Stellenbosch, sometimes known as the Boland, is only one of the important wine-growing regions in South Africa, but it is the oldest and most beautiful.

The vineyards form a patchwork in the fertile valleys, overshadowed by dramatic mountains. The Franschhoek, Wemmershoek, Du Toits and Slanghoek ranges are all more than 1500m high, and they start close to sea level: the Franschhoek and Bainskloof passes that cross them are among the most spectacular in the country.

There are some pine plantations on the lower flanks, but the mountains are mostly cloaked in dense and shrubby mountain fynbos, including the ericoid (heath-like plants) and protea families (see the Cape Floral Kingdom boxed text in the Things to See & Do chapter).

Stellenbosch is the most interesting and lively town, Franschhoek has the most spectacular location and Paarl is a busy commercial centre with plenty to see. All three are historically important and attractive, and all three promote wine routes around the surrounding wineries. This region is the oldest European-settled region in the Cape, and at times there is an almost European atmosphere – in South African terms this means it is extremely well endowed with restaurants and interesting accommodation. It is worth considering a splurge on either a nice restaurant, guesthouse or both.

It is possible to see Stellenbosch and Paarl on day trips from Cape Town. Both are accessible by train, but Stellenbosch is the easier to get around if you don't have a car. If you really want to do justice to the region and spend time exploring the wine routes, you'll need wheels. Bicycle wheels will do.

Stellenbosch

Stellenbosch was established as a frontier town on the banks of the Eerste River by Governor Simon van der Stel in 1679. It's the second oldest town (after Cape Town) in South Africa, and one of the best preserved. The town is filled with architectural and historical gems (Cape Dutch, Georgian and Victorian), shaded by enormous oak trees.

The Afrikaans-language University of Stellenbosch, established in 1918, plays an important role in Afrikaner politics and culture. There are more than 12,000 students, which means there is actually quite a thriving nightlife (something of a rarity in South Africa).

Many people visit Stellenbosch on day tours from Cape Town but it's well worth staying at least one night.

Orientation The Stellenbosch train station is on the west side of town, a short walk from the town centre. The railway line effectively forms the western boundary of the town while the Eerste River forms the southern

continued on page 130

Stellenbosch Wine Region

False Bay

| 0 | 2.5 | 5 km |

Cape Wineries

The small community at Cape Town established by the Dutch East India Company soon began to expand into the surrounding regions that had been inhabited by the Khoisan. The fertile and beautiful valleys around Paarl and Stellenbosch were settled from the 1670s onwards.

Although Jan van Riebeeck, founder of the Cape Colony, had planted vines and made wine himself, it was not until the arrival of Governor Simon van der Stel in 1679 that winemaking seriously began. Van der Stel created Groot Constantia, the superb estate on the flanks of Table Mountain, and passed on his winemaking skills to the burghers settling around Stellenbosch. From 1688 to 1690, 200 Huguenots arrived in the country. They were granted land in the region, particularly around Franschhoek (French Corner), and although only a few had direct winemaking experience, they gave the infant industry fresh impetus.

For a long time Cape wines, other than those produced at Groot Constantia, were not in great demand and most grapes ended up in brandy. Today they are some of the best wines in the world and with South Africa rejoining the world economy winemakers are struggling to meet demand.

Jan van Riebeeck died in Batavia (now Jakarta), at the other end of the Dutch colonial empire, but his legacy is in the former Cape Colony. He planted the first vines here in 1655 and encouraged reluctant farmers to follow suit.

Wines

Currently South Africa is the world's eighth largest wine producing country. Most vineyards in the Western Cape, outside of Stellenbosch, Paarl and some coastal regions, are irrigated. Consequently yields are fairly high, at least by European standards. Slightly less than 4000 different wines are produced, with white wines outnumbering reds by about seven bottles to one.

The most common variety is chenin blanc, or *steen*, a white variety often served from 5L casks as 'Stein' at barbecues. In the last decade or so more fashionable varieties such as chardonnay and sauvignon blanc have been planted on a wide scale. Other widely planted whites include colombard, semillon, crouchen (known as Cape riesling) and various sweet muscats. Table whites, especially chardonnay, once tended to be heavily oaked and high in alcohol but lighter, more fruity whites are now in the ascendancy.

Older, more robust red varieties such as shiraz, cabernet sauvignon and the Cape's own pinotage (a cross between pinot noir and hermitage or shiraz which produces an almost overpowering wine) are being challenged by

The fine estate at Groot Constantia, in Cape Town's southern suburbs, is one of the oldest in South Africa. Legend has it that Napoleon would touch no wine other than Constantia's during his St Helena exile.

MIKE REED

lighter blends of cabernet sauvignon, merlot, shiraz and cabernet franc – making a style closer to Bordeaux wines. The reds attracting the highest prices are cabernet sauvignon and the Bordeaux-style blends.

Besides pinotage, a variety unique to South Africa and grown only in isolated plantings is pontac, which was probably imported from France. The Klein Constantia vineyard is pontac's biggest remaining stronghold. This red wine is perhaps more commendable for its deep colour than for its taste.

The inland wine region of Worcester is the national leader for fortified wines, including port, brandy and South Africa's own *hanepoot* (honey pot) dessert wine, made from the Mediterranean variety muscat of Alexandria to produce a strong, sweet and suitably high-alcohol tipple for the domestic market.

Apartheid-era sanctions and the power of the Kooperatieve Wijnbouwers Vereniging (KWV) to control minimum prices, production areas and quota limits didn't exactly encourage innovation. Since 1992 the KWV, which tended to favour grape-growers, has been relinquishing some of its influence and private winemakers have begun to thrive in the new environment. These more progressive winemakers have led South Africa's re-emergence onto the world export market, which in turn has helped Western Cape lead the country's economic growth. New wine-producing areas are being established away from the hotter inland areas, in particular in the cooler coastal areas east of Cape Town around Mossel Bay, Walker Bay and Elgin.

There are a few natural disadvantages that Cape winemakers must deal with. Cape soils tend to be heavily acidic, requiring a serious investment in lime and tartrate removal processes before bottling. Nevertheless, the mountains and valleys of the Cape region contain a wide range of soils – up to 50 in the Stellenbosch region alone. The intense African sun is somewhat alleviated in the Cape wine regions by the cold Benguela current flowing up the Atlantic coast and by the Cape Doctor summer winds, which can be powerful enough to damage the crop but help reduce humidity and fungal infestations.

While you're tasting the very fine wines, spare a thought for the coloured labourers who do most of the actual work in producing it. The infamous 'tot' system, whereby labourers' wages were partly paid in wine, still survives in some areas. Apart from the sheer economic injustice of this, the social and physical results were and are disastrous. For calculated cruelty there can't be many worse systems.

Stellenbosch Wine Region

The Stellenbosch Wine Route was the first to be established in South Africa and it's still the most popular. With nearly three dozen wineries offering sales and tastings there's a lot to see. The Stellenbosch Publicity Association has maps of the wine route or, for more specialised information, contact the wine route office (☎ (021) 886 4310; fax 886 4330). The following list is a very small sample of the wineries you can visit.

Boschendal

Boschendal is in the Franschhoek wine region, on the Pniel road (the R310 between Franschhoek and Stellenbosch), and is probably the most beautiful of all the Cape wineries – you *must* visit. Tucked in below some startling mountains, the Cape Dutch homestead (open daily from 11 am to 5 pm), winery buildings and vineyard are almost too beautiful to be real.

The estate is open daily but sales and tastings are not available on Saturday afternoon or Sunday.

There is an expensive but excellent restaurant with table d'hôte for R85. It's open daily for lunch; booking is essential (☎ 874 1031). For something lighter, but still excellent, go to *Le Café*, in one of the old buildings on the oak avenue. You can just have a coffee (or try the homemade lemonade) or something more substantial.

An even better alternative, if the weather is decent, is *Le Pique Nique*, where simple meals are served outside under umbrellas on the lawn from 1 November to 30 April. A basket including pâté, french bread and smoked-trout roulade is made up for you. Again, you must book ahead. It is not cheap at R42.50, but it is worth it. ■

Cape Dutch-style homestead on Boschendal's superb estate.

Blaauwklippen (☎ (021) 880 0133) is 4km south of Stellenbosch on the R44 to Somerset West. It's a beautiful 300-year-old estate with several fine Cape Dutch homesteads. Apart from recent vintages of white, red, sparkling and port, there's a farm shop selling chutney, jam, salami and pickles. Tastings and wine sales are available Monday to Friday from 9 am to 5 pm and Saturday until 1 pm. In December and January there are cellar tours on weekdays at 11 am and 3 pm, and at 11 am on Saturday. From 1 October to 31 April, from noon to 2 pm, a 'coachman's lunch' is sold.

Delaire (☎ (021) 885 1756) is on Helshoogte Pass and has good views of the surrounding mountain ranges. It's a smallish, friendly place, with sales and tastings daily, except Sunday, between 10 am and 5 pm.

Morgenhof (☎ (021) 889 5510) is 4km north of Stellenbosch on the R44 to Paarl. It's an old estate with fine architecture. Whites and reds are available for tasting and for sale on weekdays from 9 am to 4.30 pm, and from 10 am to 3 pm on weekends, from November to April. Picnic basket lunches are available from October to April from noon to 2 pm.

Hartenberg Estate (☎ (021) 882 2541) is about 10km north-west of Stellenbosch, off the road running from Koelenhof to Kuilsrivier. It was founded in 1692, and thanks to a micro-climate produces 16 cultivars and blended wines. It's open for tastings on weekdays from 9 am to 5 pm and until 3 pm on Saturday. From December to March it's also open on Sunday from 10.30 am to 3 pm. Lunch is available daily, except Sunday, from noon to 2 pm.

Uiterwyk Estate (☎ (021) 881 3711) is yet another old homestead (1781) and is open for tastings and sales on weekdays from 10 am to 4.30 pm (closing for lunch in the low season). There are cellar tours on Saturday at 11 am.

Paarl Wine Region

The information centre has a Wine Route brochure with a good map, showcasing a dozen or so of the area's wineries. Here is a small sample.

Kooperatieve Wijnbouwers Vereniging (KWV) Paarl is home to a unique phenomenon – the huge KWV wine cooperative (☎ (021) 807 3007). The KWV was formed in 1918 when farmers were struggling to deal with

Founded in 1918, the KWV brought some order to an industry which had been ravaged by pestilence (which forced many viticulturalists to try raising ostrich) and by peace (Cape wine prices virtually collapsed after the end of Franco-British hostilities in 1881). In recent years the giant regulatory body has lost some of its powers. KWV headquarters in Paarl is shown here.

problems of oversupply. Today, the KWV has statutory authority to completely regulate South Africa's grape production and prices.

It also purchases grapes and makes high quality wines, sherries and ports, which are mostly sold overseas (they attempt to avoid direct competition with their members within the country). Some KWV port and sherry is available inside South Africa because there is little direct competition; the wines, with the exception of those from Laborie, are only sold overseas. The fortified wines, in particular, are among the world's best.

On weekdays there are KWV tours and tastings (R10) in German at 10.15 am and in English at 11 am and 2.15 pm. On Wednesday there are also tours in French at 3 pm. On Saturday there are German tours at 10.15 am and English tours at 11 am. The knowledgeable tour leaders can give you suggestions for touring the winelands. The tours start in the KWV cellars on Kohler, not at La Concorde, the impressive head office on Main St. As well as the formal tours you can just have a tasting (R6), but only in December. The huge Cathedral Cellar is definitely worth seeing.

Laborie (☎ (021) 807 3390), Taillefer St, is the KWV's showcase vineyard, right in the centre of Paarl, just off the main road. In addition to selling wines, there is a restaurant in an old Cape Dutch homestead. The food is good but it's fairly pricey and they get a lot of tour groups – you should book. There is a long wine list but few are sold by the glass and fewer in small bottles. It's open daily for lunch and from Tuesday to Saturday for dinner. Tours of the winery are held during school holidays only, at 9.30 and 11.15 am and 2.15 and 3.30 pm.

Fairview (☎ (021) 863 2450) is a small winery and farm on the southwestern slopes of Paarl mountain. As well as good wines for sale there are sheep, goat and cow milk cheeses. It's open from 8 am to 5 pm on weekdays and until 1 pm on Saturday.

The wineries around Paarl are noted not only for the quality of their wines, but also for the quaint charm of their historic buildings.

GERHARD DREYER

SUSAN STORM

GERHARD DREYER

op: Many vineyards and estates in the Franschhoek (French Corner) region bear
ames which reflect their Huguenot origins.
Middle: Jonkershoek – the wine areas are resplendent with Cape Dutch-style estates.
ottom: Wellington's tranquil valleys offer a wonderful break from Cape Town's bustle.

GERHARD DREYER

GERHARD DREYER

Stellenbosch has plenty to explore and enjoy: take a stroll in the town's peaceful parklands (top) or among the autumn vines in one of the area's world-renowned wineries (bottom).

Landskroon Estate (☎ (021) 863 1039) is an old, pleasant estate with a nice terrace overlooking the vines where you can sit and contemplate the view. It's about 6km from town on the R44. It's open from 8 am to 5 pm on weekdays and from 8.30 am to 12.30 pm on Saturday. From November to the end of April they serve a 'vintner's platter' on weekdays, and there are some good cheeses for sale.

Nederburg Winery (☎ (021) 862 3104) is one of the biggest, best known and most acclaimed Cape wineries. It's a big, professional operation but they put an effort into welcoming visitors. Tastings and wine sales are available Monday to Friday from 8.30 am to 5 pm and on Saturday from 9 am to 1 pm. Tours in English, German, French and Spanish are available but you have to book in advance. The estate is about 7km from Paarl, off the road to Wellington.

Robertson Wine Region

As well as the famous Stellenbosch, Paarl and Franschhoek regions (which are more or less neighbours) there are several other wine regions within easy reach of Cape Town. The Robertson area of the Breede River Valley is worth a visit for its wine and scenery – and for the absence of tourist coaches. Staying the night in the nearby village of McGregor is a good way to end a day's tasting.

This area has long produced good red wines but now there are some fine whites as well, especially the colombard/chardonnay blend. There are many wineries in the area and the tourist office in Robertson will give you a complete list. Here is a small sample of some of the 20 or so wineries open for sales and tastings:

Robertson Winery (☎ (02351) 3059), in Robertson, is the region's oldest cellar, with a range of wines available. It's open weekdays from 8 am to 4.30 pm (closed for lunch between 12.30 and 1.30 pm) and on Saturday morning during school holidays.

McGregor Co-op Winery (☎ (02353) 741) is just outside McGregor and specialises in sweet muscatel and full-bodied whites. It's open from 8 am to 5 pm (closing for lunch between noon and 1 pm) on weekdays and on Saturday morning.

Van Loveren Wine Cellars (☎ (0234) 51505) produces a range of reds and whites and some heady fortified wines. Sales and tastings are available on weekdays from 8.30 am to 5 pm (it closes for lunch between 1 and 2 pm) and on Saturday morning.

Graham Beck Winery (☎ (02351) 61214) is a modern winery producing innovative wines. It's best known for its *méthode champenoise*. You can visit on weekdays from 10 am to 5 pm and on Saturday morning between October and May.

De Wetshof Estate (☎ (0234) 51853) produces some of the best chardonnay in the country. It's open for sales from 8.30 am to 4.30 pm on weekdays and on Saturday morning.

Jon Murray and Richard Plunkett

continued from page 122
boundary. Dorp St, which roughly parallels the river, is the old town's main street and is lined with numerous fine old buildings. The commercial centre now lies between Dorp St and the university to the east of the Braak. The Braak is the old town square.

Information The Stellenbosch Publicity Association (☎ 883 3584), 36 Market St (Mark in Afrikaans), is open Monday to Friday from 8 am to 5 pm, Saturday from 9.30 am to 5 pm and Sunday from 9.30 am to 4.30 pm. This must be one of the busiest tourist offices in the country. Staff are extremely helpful, especially when it comes to recommending B&Bs and providing information on nearby wineries. Pick up the excellent free brochure *Discover Stellenbosch on Foot*, with a walking-tour map and information on many of the historical buildings (also available in German) and *Stellenbosch & its Wine Route* which gives opening times and tasting information about the three dozen or so nearby wineries.

Guided walks leave from the Publicity Association three times a day. They cost R45 per person (minimum three people).

There's a Thomas Cook/Rennies foreign exchange office on Bird St, a block from Dorp St.

Ex Libris, on Andringa St, is a good bookshop with all the glossy coffee table books but also novels and a few Lonely Planet guides. There's also an interesting selection of old books on South Africa. There's a music shop next door with a good range of CDs and some inexpensive cassettes.

Walking Tour This walk around central Stellenbosch starts at the Publicity Association on Market St.

Walk a short way north-west on Market (Mark) St and you'll come to the Braak, the old town square. Several old buildings, including the VOC Kruithuis, an 18th century powder magazine, are on the Braak.

Cross the Braak and turn left (north) up Bird St, right onto Beyers St, left onto Andringa St and right onto Victoria St.

Follow Victoria St and you'll come to the University of Stellenbosch. This pretty campus is crammed full of buildings in Cape Dutch style, not surprising for the country's (and thus the world's) leading Afrikaans university.

After looking around the university, find your way back to Victoria St and head east until you come to Neethling St. Turn right down Neethling St and you'll soon come to the Botanical Gardens, on your right. Turn right into Van Riebeeck St and walk through a residential area (some of the fine old homes around here offer accommodation) to Ryneveld St, on the edge of the town centre. Turn left down Ryneveld St to visit the excellent Dorp (Village) Museum, which is a group of lovely old homes.

Follow Ryneveld St south to Kerk St and turn right, then turn left onto Andringa St and then right onto Dorp St for a walk down one of Stellenbosch's oldest and most impressive streets. There's a good collection of architectural styles behind the leafy oaks, with urban Cape Dutch predominating. You'll see Oom Samie se Winkel (Uncle Sam's Shop) on your right, with souvenirs ranging from very tacky to interesting, although you might have stopped for a good pub meal at De Acker just before Oom Samie's.

Further down Dorp St is the Stellenryck Wine Museum, and from here you can make your way back to the Publicity Association by backtracking along Dorp St to Market (Mark) St, where you turn left.

Village Museum The Village (Dorp) Museum is a group of carefully restored and period-furnished houses dating from 1709 to 1850 – eventually a house from the 1920s will be included. The odd stuffed cat adds a slightly macabre touch. The main entrance on Rynveld St leads into the oldest of the buildings, the Schreuderhuis. The whole block, bounded by Rynveld, Plein, Drostdy and Kerk Sts, is occupied by the museum and includes most of the buildings and some charming gardens. Grosvenor House is on the other side of Drostdy St. The museum is open from Monday to Saturday between

9.30 am and 5 pm, and on Sunday from 2 to 5 pm. Admission is R5.

Van der Bijlhuis This building dates from 1693, when it formed part of one of the area's original farms, and has in the past been a tannery. It is now the administrative centre for the Village Museum and three rooms are open to the public during office hours.

Braak The Braak (Town Square) is an open stretch of grass surrounded by important buildings. The **VOC Kruithuis** (Powder House) was built in 1777 to store the town's weapons and gunpowder, and now houses a small military museum. The **Burgerhuis** was built in 1797 and is a fine example of the Cape Dutch style; most of it is now occupied by the Historical Homes of South Africa, a company established to preserve important architecture. **St Mary's on the Braak Church** was completed in 1852.

Bergkelder This should be your first stop if you are interested in the area's wines. For R8 you get a slide show, a cellar tour and tastings of up to 12 wines. You get to pour your own, so take it easy or it might be your last stop for the day! The Bergkelder is a short walk from the train station; tours are held at 10 am, 10.30 am (in German) and 3 pm.

Simonsberg Cheese Factory Popular with hungry backpackers, the cheese factory (☎ 883 8640) has tastings and sells inexpensive cheese between 8.30 am and 4.30 pm. It's at 9 Stoffel Smit St.

Rembrandt van Rijn Art Gallery This small gallery on Dorp St displays 20th century South African works. The building which houses the gallery was built in 1783. It's open Monday to Friday from 9 am to 12.45 pm and 2 to 5 pm, Saturday from 10 am to 1 pm and 2 to 5 pm, and Sunday from 2.30 to 5.30 pm.

Stellenryck Wine Museum The small wine museum, also on Dorp St, has some old furniture and wine-making paraphernalia,

including interesting displays on growing cork oaks and making wine corks. The most impressive item is the massive wine press which you can see near the corner of Strand and Dorp Sts. It's open daily (afternoon only on Sunday).

Brandy Museum The international history of brandy and the role it has played in the Cape is traced through a collection of pictures and displays. The museum, in the Van Ryn Brandy Cellar (☎ 881 3875), is open daily.

Oom Samie se Winkel Uncle Sammy's Shop, 84 Dorp St, is a tourist trap but it's still worth visiting for the amazing range of goods – from high kitsch to genuine antiques and everything in between.

Activities There are 90 walks in the Stellenbosch area – see the Publicity Association for details. Jonkershoek is a small nature reserve in a timber plantation which offers walking and biking trails. Admission is R5 per car.

Ask the Publicity Association about permits and maps for the Vineyard Hiking Trails. The signposting isn't good but it is apparently being improved.

Amoi Horse Trails (☎ (082) 650 5794) offers tailor-made rides. For example, a three hour ride with a visit to a winery and a tasting costs R115 per person. There are no minimum numbers and they'll match you with a horse to suit your skill level.

The parachute club (☎ 58 8514) offers tandem jumps.

A food and wine festival is held in late October.

Places to Stay *Stumble Inn* (☎/fax (021) 887 4049, email stumble@iafrica.com), 14 Mark St, is a hostel in a nice old house with wooden floors and a good atmosphere. A pool is planned (it has been 'planned' for a few years now ...). The owners are travellers and are good sources of information. They arrange budget outings in the area, including to the beach at Strand and to a *shebeen* in Khayamandi, an enormous township between

PLACES TO STAY

2 Hillbilly's Haven
19 Bonne Esperance
20 Fynbos Villa
24 D'Ouwe Werf Hotel
25 Stellenbosch Hotel;
  Jan Cats Brasserie;
  Jan Cats Ladies Bar
33 De Goue Druif
38 Stumble Inn
42 Dorphus Hotel

PLACES TO EAT

7 Gallery Coffee Shop
9 Rustic Café
10 Legends Restaurant & Pub
11 The Terrace Bar &
  Restaurant
14 Bakoven
16 Café Nouveau
18 Decameron Italian
  Restaurant
26 Skippers
28 Ralph's
32 Avec Mari
45 De Volkskombuis

OTHER

1 Simonsberg Cheese
  Factory
3 Bergkelder
4 Minibus Taxis
5 Jacob's Ladder
6 Hospital
8 Sub-Mission
12 Dros
13 St Mary's on the
  Braak Church
15 Amex
17 Town Hall
21 Village (Dorp) Museum
22 Finlay's Wine Bar
23 Ex Libris Bookshop &
  Music Shop
27 Rennies Travel
29 Leotana Outdoors
30 Minibus Taxis to Strand
31 Thomas Cook
34 VOC Kruithuis
35 Burgerhuis
36 Stellenbosch Publicity
  Association
37 Van der Bijlhuis
39 De Acker
40 Oom Samie se
  Winkel
41 De Kelder
43 Rembrandt van Rijn
  Art Gallery
44 Stellenryck Wine Museum

Stellenbosch

Jan Marais Nature Reserve

Coetzenburg Sports Ground

To Jonkershoek Nature Reserve

To Franschoek

To Strand

To N1 & Paarl

To N1 & Cape Town

R304

To Cape Town via N1

To Strand, Hermanus & Cape Town via N2

To Cape Town via N2

0   250   500 m

Stellenbosch and Cape Town. Dorms are R25 and doubles are R70. They rent bikes (R40) and also offer a good, cheap winery tour (R45). Stumble Inn is popular, so it would pay to book ahead.

The other hostel is a more recent arrival but it also gets positive feedback. *Hillbilly's Haven* (☎ 887 8475), 24 Dennesig St, has dorms for R30 and doubles for R80. You can also camp.

The Publicity Association produces a booklet listing many B&B possibilities from around R60 per person (you'll have to press them to tell you about the very cheapest). If you have transport, ask them about self-catering cottages out of town, which can be great bargains.

De Goue Druif (☎ (021) 883 3555), on historic Dorp St (No 110), a rambling old house built in 1811, has very comfortable suites. Singles/doubles are from R260/390 with an excellent breakfast. It also has a simpler self-catering cottage and a very pleasant apartment in the block behind the house. This place is certainly recommended.

Stellenbosch Hotel (☎ (021) 887 3644), on the corner of Dorp and Andringa Sts, is a rather idiosyncratic country hotel, but it is also very comfortable. A section dating from 1743 houses the excellent Jan Cats Brasserie, a bar and dining room. The accommodation is in a modern section. Singles/doubles cost from R330/480.

Another very comfortable option is the nearby *D'Ouwe Werf Herberg* (☎ 887 4608; fax 887 4626), 30 Kerk St. Fully equipped rooms in this large Georgian guesthouse start at about R600 a double, with lower rates between May and September.

Outside Stellenbosch, *Nassau Guest Farm* (☎ (021) 881 3818) has well-equipped cottages for about R180 per person, and a collection of vintage cars. *Sanddrif Guest Farm* (☎ 881 3075), also out of town on Stellenbosch Kloof Rd, is a Cape Dutch-style house set among vineyards; B&B costs from R240/350. Dutch, German and French are spoken.

Places to Eat There are around 70 places

to eat and drink in Stellenbosch and several of the nearby vineyards have attached restaurants – see the Cape Wineries section in this chapter for more on the area's wineries.

Snacks & Cafés *Rustic Café*, off Bird St near Legends, stays open until 4 am. Another late night student hang-out is the *Gallery Coffee Shop* on Crozier St. It has a reputation for being super cool, but it's a relaxed and friendly place. The coffee is good, it's licensed, and there are cheap snacks. You can buy some amusing (if a little obscure) postcards by a local outfit called Bitterkomix. There are various places to eat in the *Studentesentrum* at the university, although most are franchise outlets and not especially cheap. Walk up Crozier St until it ends at the car park, and continue straight on. Look for signs to the Langenhoven – Studentesentrum.

Bakoven, at the entrance to the Bankcentrum, has pies and burgers. For takeaway seafood, *Skippers* is a high-quality fish and chippery on Dorp St near the corner of Louw St, with a few tables.

Café Nouveau, on the corner of Plein and Andringa Sts, is a small, plush-looking place for coffee, cakes and light meals, open daily from 7.30 am to 11.30 pm.

Restaurants *Legends Restaurant & Pub* on the corner of Du Toit and Bird Sts is good value and very popular with students. Lunches cost under R20.

For good food at reasonable prices try *Avec Mari*, 105 Dorp St. It seems to be a fairly formal restaurant but it is in fact friendly and relaxed, with a contemporary attitude to food and customers. It's open from Tuesday to Sunday for lunch and dinner (no dinner on Sunday). The menu is sort of Mediterranean with a nouvelle cuisine influence, which is a relief after the gargantuan servings you usually have to plough through. Main courses are around R30. If it's gargantuan portions you're after, try *Ralph's*, Andringa St. Main courses start around R30 and go much higher. This place is highly recommended.

EXCURSIONS

If you want the full name, *De Volkskombuis* (☎ 887 2121) is De Volkskombuis aan de Wagenweg naar de Kaap (The People's Kitchen on the Wagon Road to the Cape). It's on Strand Rd, just south of the river, and is one of the best places in the Cape to sample traditional cuisine – it's favoured by locals, not just tourists. The service is friendly and competent, a rare combination. Try the Cape country sampler (four traditional specialities) for R42. Booking is advisable. The restaurant is in an attractive Cape Dutch homestead designed by Sir Herbert Baker and the terrace looks across fields to Stellenbosch mountain.

Jan Cats Brasserie (☎ 887 3644) is in the Stellenbosch Hotel on the corner of Dorp and Andringa Sts. This colourful restaurant features straightforward dishes like pastas for R20, or Cape bobotie with sambal and yellow rice for R25. If the restaurant were named Jan's Cat rather than Jan Cats then presumably the statue of the Stellenbosch Hotel's cat, in front of the City Hall on Plein St, would be the animal in question.

Decameron Italian Restaurant, on Plein St, is classy and has authentic Italian food. Pasta costs around R20 and a full meal will set you back about R60, but it's worth it.

The Terrace Bar and Restaurant, on Alexander St next door to Dros, has pub food from R15 (see the Entertainment section).

Entertainment The students give Stellenbosch quite a lively nightlife. It's relatively safe to walk around at night, so it's worth checking a few options before you settle. Stumble Inn produces a handy pub crawl map for its guests.

On Alexander St, facing the Braak, is *Dros* – dark, panelled and a good place for a drink. There's sometimes live music.

Not far away, *Sub-Mission*, on the corner of Du Toit and Bird Sts (next to Legends), usually has a DJ and sometimes live music. When it's crowded it might be interesting but when it isn't the bar is pretty unappealing. Further along Bird St, *Jacob's Ladder* is a sizeable and relaxed upstairs bar with local 'alternative' bands on some nights.

De Kelder, 63 Dorp St, has a nice atmosphere and is popular with German backpackers. *De Acker*, on the corner of Dorp and Herte Sts, is a pub – a classic student drinking hole with cheap grub from R18. *Finlay's Wine Bar*, on Plein St is another rowdy, cheerful place.

Jan Cats Ladies Bar, upstairs in the Stellenbosch Hotel, is a very relaxed and cosy bar, ideal for a pre-dinner drink.

Getting There & Away Metro trains run the 46km between Cape Town and Stellenbosch; 1st/3rd class is R8.70/3.80 (no 2nd class) and the trip takes about one hour. For information, phone Stellenbosch train station (☎ 808 1111).

A minibus taxi to Strand (and thus the beach) can cost as little as R3.50. A minibus taxi to Paarl is about R6, but you'll probably have to change taxis en route. Buses to Cape Town are expensive and you can't book this short sector. Translux stops here on the run between Cape Town and Port Elizabeth, charging R20 or R40, depending whether you take a Mountain Route or a Garden Route bus. See the Getting There & Away chapter for more information.

You can get to Stellenbosch by car using either the N2 or the N1. The N2 runs past Khayelitsha township, so it's perhaps the more interesting route. From the N2 take the R310 turn-off, exit 33, for Stellenbosch.

Getting Around Budget Rent-a-Car (☎ 883 9103), 98 Dorp St, also rents bicycles. The countryside is mainly flat (unless you try to cross Franschhoek Pass) making it good cycling territory. Rikki's (☎ 887 2203) runs its tiny vans here, and R3 (sharing) will get you just about anywhere in town. Stellenbosch Motorcycles (☎ 883 9805), Latsky St, rents motorbikes.

Franschhoek
Franschhoek is really nothing more than a village, but it's tucked into arguably the most beautiful valley in the Cape. There is an interesting museum commemorating the Huguenots who settled in the region, and

**Paarl
Wine Region**

nearby are a number of good wineries and restaurants.

Orientation & Information The town straggles along the main road from Stellenbosch and Paarl. At the eastern end it reaches a T-intersection, with the Huguenot Memorial Museum directly in front. Turn left for the spectacular Franschhoek Pass.

The very helpful information centre (☎ 876 3603) is in a small building on the main street, next to Dominic's Pub. You can pick up a map of the area's scenic walks here. In season the centre is open from 9 am to 5 pm on weekdays, 10 am to 2 pm on Saturday and 10 am to 1 pm on Sunday.

Huguenot Memorial Museum The Cape's Huguenots were French Calvinists who fled France as a result of persecution in the 17th century. Some Huguenots went to Holland, and 200 found their way to South Africa. The names of some of the original settlers feature among the country's most famous Afrikaner dynasties: Malan, de Villiers, Malherbe, Roux, Barre, Thibault and Marais.

The museum was opened in 1976 to celebrate the Huguenot's history and to house the genealogical records of their descendants. There's an excellent collection of 17th and 18th century Cape Dutch furniture. The museum is open Monday to Friday from 9 am to 5 pm, from 9 am to 1 pm and 2 to 5 pm on Saturday, and from 2 to 5 pm on Sunday. Admission is R4.

Places to Stay The information centre will tell you about B&Bs and other accommodation in town and in the district. In town the cheapest B&Bs cost around R120 a double but prices drop if you stay out of town. *Chamoix Guest Cottages* (☎ (021) 876 3531) has self-catering cottages on a vineyard and charges about R50 per person. Other places also have whole cottages for about R120.

Hotel Huguenot (☎ (021) 876 2092), on Huguenot Rd, is in the centre of town. It's a rather garish old-style country hotel, but is reasonably comfortable. Each room has a private bathroom and the rate is around R120/200 a single/double.

La Cotte Inn (☎ (021) 876 2081), also on Huguenot Rd, is on the western outskirts of town. It has a certain idiosyncratic charm and charges a little less than Hotel Huguenot. Travellers report that the rates might be open to negotiation.

Auberge Bligny (☎ (021) 876 3767), 28 Van Wijk St, is one of the town's oldest houses and is now a guesthouse with six pleasant rooms. Singles/doubles cost from R145/165 with breakfast. No children are allowed. This place used to be called The Anchor. Readers recommend *Reeder Lodge*, a self-catering cottage near the information centre which charges R80 per person.

Le Quartier Francais (☎ (021) 876 2248), 16 Huguenot Rd, is the top place to stay in Franschhoek. It has very large guest rooms with fireplaces, huge beds and stylish decor set around a grassy courtyard. Dinner, bed and breakfast costs from R595/790. It's well worth a splurge.

Places to Eat There are quite a few places to eat, and the village is so small that it's easy to stroll around and see what appeals. *Dominic's Country Pub & Restaurant* is on the main street but has a pleasant, shady lawn where you can have coffee, pastries or meals. As well as the usual steaks (R27) there are light meals such as Cape Malay pickled fish (R15) or trout and salad (R20).

Further along, *Le Quartier Francais* (☎ (021) 876 2248) is a highly acclaimed restaurant, but it is not pompous or ridiculously expensive. For anyone who really likes their food it is highly recommended. It's on the main street of Franschhoek, but it opens out onto a cottage garden with views of the surrounding mountains. Entrées are around R20, main meals like roast rabbit or trout sausages range from R35 to R45, or you can spend more on dishes such as braised shank of springbok with waterblommetjies, couscous and spiced oranges. There are interesting desserts from R12. If the restaurant is beyond your budget there is also the bistro and deli, both open from noon to 5 pm for takeaways and lighter meals.

Getting There & Away It's possible, if you're fit, to cycle between Stellenbosch and Franschhoek. Otherwise, Borland Passenger Transport (☎ 872 2114) has infrequent buses between Paarl and Franschhoek.

Paarl

Paarl is a large commercial centre on the banks of the Berg River, surrounded by mountains and vineyards. There are actually vineyards and wineries within the sprawling town limits, including the huge Kooperatieve Wijnbouwers Vereniging (better known as the KWV), a cooperative that regulates and dominates the South African wine industry.

The town is less touristy than Stellenbosch in part because it's not as compact and as historically coherent, and is more difficult to get around on foot. There is still quite a lot to see, however, and the surrounding countryside and vineyards are beautiful. The Paarl Mountain Nature Reserve to the west of the town has some great walks.

Paarl also has some excellent Cape Dutch architecture, as well as significant monuments to Afrikaner culture. The surrounding valley was settled by Europeans in the 1680s and Paarl itself was established in 1720. It became a centre for wagon building. It is most famous, however, for its role in the development and recognition of Afrikaans as a separate language.

In 1953 Paarl gained the dubious distinction of being the first town in the country to use a new style of bus – one with separate doors for white and non-white passengers.

Orientation & Information Main St is 15km long and runs the town's entire length, paralleling the Berg River and the railway line. It is shaded by oaks and jacarandas, and lined with many historical buildings. The busy commercial centre is on Lady Grey St.

The Paarl Valley Publicity Association (☎ (021) 872 3829), 251 Main St, on the corner of Main and Auret, has an excellent supply of information on the whole region. Staff are particularly helpful in arranging accommodation in some of the numerous guesthouses that have sprung up around Paarl, and will make free bookings. The office is open from 9 am to 5 pm Monday to Friday, to 1 pm on Saturday and 10 am to 1 pm on Sunday.

Paarl Mountain Nature Reserve This popular reserve is dominated by three giant granite domes, which loom over the town on its west side. The domes apparently glisten like pearls if they are caught by the sun after a rainfall – this is why the town was named Paarl. The reserve has mountain fynbos and a particularly large number of proteas. There's a cultivated wild-flower garden in the middle of the reserve that makes a nice spot for a picnic, and there are numerous walks with excellent views over the valley.

Access is from the 11km-long Jan Phillips Drive, which skirts the eastern edge of the reserve; both the Afrikaans Language Monument and the reserve are signposted from Main St. The picnic ground is about 4km from Main St. A map showing walking trails is available from the Publicity Association.

Oude Pastorie Museum The old parsonage (1714) on Main St houses a collection of Cape Dutch antiques and relics of Huguenot and early Afrikaner culture. It's open weekdays from 9 am to 1 pm and 2 to 4 pm. Admission is free.

Afrikaans Language Museum The evolution of Afrikaans is chronicled in this museum, the former home of Gideon Malherbe, one-time meeting place for the Association of True Afrikaners and the birthplace of the first Afrikaans newspaper. The building has been painstakingly restored. It's open weekdays from 9 am to 1 pm and 2 to 5 pm. Admission is free. It's on Pastorie St, which is parallel to Main St.

Bhabhatane Handweaving Bhabhatane,

The Origin of Afrikaans

Afrikaans is based on Dutch, but in Africa, exposed to the diverse cultures of the Cape, it was transformed into an independent language. Grammatical forms were simplified and the vocabulary was influenced by German, French, Portuguese, Malay, English and indigenous African languages. Dutch remained the official language, however, and Afrikaans was given little formal recognition, especially after the takeover of the Cape by the English in 1806, when a deliberate policy of anglicisation was pursued.

The Afrikaners, however, deeply resented the colonial approach of the British and began to see their language as a central foundation of their own culture. In 1875 a teacher at Paarl Gymnasium High School, Arnoldus Pannevis, inspired a number of Paarl citizens to form the Genootskap van Regte Afrikaners (Association of True Afrikaners) which developed and formalised the grammar and vocabulary. Strangely, virtually all the founding members were descended from the Huguenots.

A small press was set up in Gideon Malherbe's Paarl house and the first issue of an Afrikaans newspaper, *Die Afrikaanse Patriot*, was published there, followed by many books. Malherbe's house is now the Afrikaan Language Museum, and a large monument has been erected to the east of the town. ■

1 Drommedaris St, is a church-based project producing a variety of handwoven goods.

Places to Stay The *Berg River Resort* (☎ (021) 863 1650) is about 5km from Paarl on the Franschhoek road (the R45), alongside the Berg River. It's an attractive municipal park with a swimming pool, canoes, trampolines and a café. There are five pricing seasons. Sites for two people cost R30, rising to R60; chalets cost from R130 for two people and from R240 in the peak season. The management is friendly and can collect you from the station.

Boschen Meer Leisure Resort (☎ (021) 863 1250) is a manicured and high-security resort, although prices aren't too high, with chalets from R70 per person. There are also sites.

Backpackers could consider the *Manyano*

Centre (☎ (021) 862 2537, 862 5074 AH) on Sanddrift St. It's an enormous accommodation complex used mainly by groups, although there's a fair chance that you'll be the only guest. Beds are R25 and you'll probably need a sleeping bag. If you're coming on a weekend, ring in advance. Huguenot train station is closer than the main Paarl station.

Queenslin Guest House (☎ (021) 863 1160), 2 Queen St, has a couple of rooms in a modern house overlooking the valley. You're guaranteed a hospitable welcome from the friendly family. Rates are around R110/170 a single/double. As usual, the publicity association is the place to get detailed information on the other B&Bs and farm cottages.

The Berghof (☎ (021) 871 1099) describes itself as not quite a guesthouse, not quite a hotel, but it is like a quality hotel with the service that is lacking in some mid-range places. You'll definitely need a vehicle to get there, as it's a long way up the side of the valley, with correspondingly excellent views down over the town. Rooms cost from R120/200 (more between December and April).

Cecil John Rhodes definitely had an eye for quality, so the fact that he once lived in the building that has become *Mooikelder Manor House* (☎ (021) 863 8491) points to its class. It's a beautifully restored Cape Dutch homestead, with a pool and terrace with great views, about 5km north of Paarl. Singles/doubles cost R235/390. *Mountain Shadows* (☎ 021) 862 3192) is another magnificent place to stay outside Paarl; it too is in a restored Cape Dutch mansion (a national monument built in 1823). There are only a small number of guests, a swimming pool and excellent food. The owners also arrange hunting, fishing and sightseeing tours. B&B rates start from around R200 per person, rising in the high season. On the slopes of Paarl Mountain is the five star *Grande Roche Hotel* (☎ (021) 863 2727), where rooms cost from R1200, with breakfast.

Places to Eat Several vineyards around Paarl have attached restaurants. They are probably

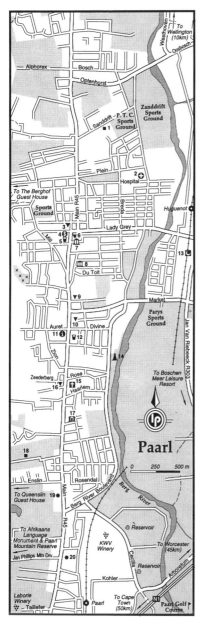

Paarl

the best places to eat if you're sightseeing. See the Cape Wineries boxed text earlier in this chapter for some Paarl area wineries.

Kontrehuis (☎ (02211) 22808), 193 Main St, is behind the Zomerlust guesthouse. It has very good-value meals – steaks from R25. Next door is *Lady Jayne's Pub & Restaurant*, in a Cape Dutch building. Off the courtyard behind Lady Jayne's, *Coffee Place* is a pleasant spot to escape the world.

Panarotti's Pizza, 263 Main St (on the north-east corner of Faure St), looks like the usual bland franchise. The food isn't bad, although genuine Italian it ain't. It's open from 10 am to midnight. *Jefferson's Family Restaurant* is a steakhouse in the same mould as Spur, Mike's Kitchen etc: predictable but reliable, with over-friendly service.

Pipers Tavern, on the corner of Main and Zeederberg Sts, has toasted sandwiches, fish and chips and other light dishes.

Getting There & Away Several interesting bus services come through Paarl although the stretch between Paarl and Cape Town is

---

PLACES TO STAY
1	Manyano Centre
18	Grande Roche Hotel

PLACES TO EAT
3	Jefferson's Family Restaurant
6	Nando's
9	Panarotti's Pizza
10	Kontrehuis; Coffee Place; Lady Jayne's Pub & Restaurant
16	Pipers Tavern

OTHER
2	General Hospital
4	First National Bank
5	Keg & Owl
7	Oude Pastorie Museum
8	Afrikaans Language Museum
11	Paarl Valley Publicity Association
12	Jailhouse Bar
13	Mosque
14	War Memorial
15	Huguenot Church
17	Klein Vredenburg Mansion
19	Schoongezicht Homestead
20	La Concorde, Head Office of KWV

much more expensive and inconvenient than the train. Paarl is a stop on the Translux services between Cape Town and Johannesburg (R310 from Paarl), Durban (R330), Port Elizabeth (Mountain Route, R140) and East London (R210, running via Graaf-Reinet, R165). Greyhound has similar routes and prices; Intercape's fares are somewhat cheaper.

There are a reasonable number of Metro trains between Cape Town and Paarl, at least a couple in the morning and a couple in the afternoon from Monday to Friday. They're a bit sparser on the weekends, but it's still a decent service. A 1st/3rd class ticket from Cape Town to Paarl costs R10/4.40, and the trip takes about 1¼ hours. You can travel by train from Paarl to Stellenbosch, but you must take a Cape Town-bound train and change at Muldersvlei.

If you are travelling by car, take the N1 from Cape Town.

BREEDE RIVER VALLEY

This region lies north-east of the Winelands on the western fringes of the Little Karoo. It's dominated by the Breede River Valley, but it's mountainous country that includes smaller valleys. The valley floors are intensively cultivated with orchards, vineyards and wheat.

European settlers displaced the indigenous Khoisan, and by the beginning of the 18th century had settled most of the valleys. The area did not really take off, however, until passes were pushed through the mountains in the 19th century.

The headwaters of the Breede River (sometimes called the Bree) are in the beautiful mountain-locked Ceres basin, escape via Michells Pass and flow south-east for 310km before meeting the Indian Ocean at Whitesands. Many tributaries join the Breede, and by the time it reaches Robertson it has been transformed from a rushing mountain stream into a substantial river.

Many travellers are likely to come through the region because it is bisected by the N2 between Cape Town and the north-east. Since the opening of the 4km Huguenot Toll Tunnel east of Paarl, towns like Robertson and Montagu are more quickly accessible from Cape Town (around a two hour drive), although if you do use the tunnel you'll miss the wonderful views from the old Du Toitskloof Pass.

Look out for the *Cape Fruit Routes* map in information centres. It covers the Breede

---

Spectacular Bainskloof

Bainskloof is one of the great mountain passes of South Africa and there just happens to be a superb caravan park halfway along. Andrew Bain developed the road and pass between 1848 and 1852. Other than having its surface tarred, the road has not been altered since, and it is now a national monument. It's a superb drive and it would be even better to bike.

The Western Cape authorities run the *Tweede Tol Caravan Park*, open only between October and May. It is a magical spot. There are swimming holes on the Witrivier and the camp site is surrounded by magnificent fynbos. Camping costs R30 for up to three people plus R5 per vehicle. The gates are open from 7.30 am to 4.15 pm.

There are several nearby walks, including the five hour **Bobbejaans River Walk** to a waterfall. This walk actually starts back at Eerste Tol and you need to buy a permit for a few rand from Hawequas Conservation Area office (☎ (021) 887 0111), 269 Main St, Paarl. This is also where you make bookings for the Tweede Tol Caravan Park, although they'll probably only be necessary in school holidays.

The **Pataskloof Trail** is a long day-walk that begins and ends at the Bakkies Farmstall & Tea Room on the road leading up to the pass from Wellington. You can make it an overnight walk by arranging to stay in a cave on the trail.

The R303 road runs from Wellington (only a few km from Paarl), across Bainskloof north to Ceres; the R43 branches south to Worcester. ■

River Valley, the Winelands and up to Montagu in the east.

Tulbagh

Tulbagh is one of the most complete examples of an 18th and 19th century village in South Africa. It can feel a little like Disneyland, particularly when you discover that many of the buildings were substantially rebuilt after earthquakes in 1969 and 1970, but it is a beautiful spot and the best buildings have been painstakingly restored. There is a whole street of Cape Dutch architecture. The town itself is overshadowed by the Witsenberg range.

Although most of Tulbagh's surviving buildings date from the first half of the 19th century, the Tulbagh Valley was first settled in 1699. The village began to take shape when a church was built in 1743. It was here, on the outer rim of the settled European areas, that early trekboer families brought their children to be baptised.

Orientation & Information The town's main street, Van der Stel St, is parallel to Church St, where every building has been declared a national monument.

A visitor's first port of call should be 4 Church St (☎ (0236) 30 1348), which is part of the Old Church Folk Museum. A photographic history of Church St is on display, and there is a general information counter.

Oude Kerk Volksmuseum (Old Church Folk Museum) This museum is made up of four buildings. Start at No 4 Church St, then visit the beautiful Oude Kerk itself (1743); follow this with No 14, which houses a collection of Victorian furniture and costumes; then go to No 22, which is a reconstructed 18th century townhouse.

The complex is open weekdays from 9 am to 5 pm and weekends from 10 am to 4 pm. Admission is R4.

Places to Stay *Kliprivier Park Resort* (☎ (0236) 30 0506), on the edge of town, is quite pleasant with reasonable modern chalets from R150 for two people on week-

ends, slightly less during the week. Caravan sites are available.

There are plenty of guesthouses and farmstays. *De Oude Herberg* (☎ (0236) 30 0260), 6 Church St, is a guesthouse in the old Tulbagh main street, surrounded by old buildings, and is built in traditional Cape architecture. It has been a guesthouse since 1885 (although not continuously) and B&B is available from R150 per person. It's a very friendly and very pleasant place (no smoking and no children under 12).

Die Oliene (☎ (0236) 30 1160) is a farm 6km out of town with good self-catering cottages for R150 or less. Ask at the information centre for other B&Bs and guesthouses (averaging around R80/170 a single/double) and farmstays (from R50 per person self-catering).

Places to Eat The *Paddagang Restaurant* (☎ (0236) 30 0242) is in a beautiful old homestead with a vine-shaded courtyard; it serves snacks and light meals, as well as some traditional Cape dishes such as waterblommetjie (R27) and local wines. The restaurant is open from 9 am to 5 pm for breakfast (R20 and very good), lunch and tea.

Die Oude Herberg restaurant is open during the day, with breakfast (R18), light lunches (R19 for smoked trout) and snacks. Dinner is also available but you must book by 4 pm – on a weekend it would pay to book well in advance. An excellent three course meal costs R38. Readers have recommended the restaurant at *Hotel Tulbagh* (☎ (0236) 30 0071), which is run separately from the hotel by a German chef.

Getting There & Away Most minibus taxis leave from the 'location' (non-white residential area), on the hill just outside town, but you might find one at Tulbagh Toyota (the Shell petrol station) on the main street. The fare to Cape Town's Belville train station is R15 and to Ceres it's R10.

If you are travelling by car, the most interesting route involves taking the N1 to Paarl, then driving to Wellington and crossing the spectacular Bainskloof Pass on the way to

Ceres. Alternatively, you could stay on the N1 all the way to Worcester and turn off there. Tulbagh is near the head of the valley, and if you drive north on the R44 you'll suddenly find yourself in very flat, very dry sheep country.

Getting Around You can hire bikes at 30 Church St (☎ (0236) 30 1448).

Worcester

Worcester is a fairly large town and not as interesting as some in this area, but it does have a couple of attractions. There are some impressive old buildings near Church Square (off High St), including the Worcester Publicity Association (☎ (0231) 71408), 75 Church St. It's open from 8 am to 4.30 pm on weekdays and from 8.30 am to 12.30 pm on Saturday.

Just off the town square, **Beck House** is a charming 1841 house furnished in late-Victorian style. The outbuildings, including a stable, bath house and herb garden, are particularly interesting. It's open weekdays from 9 am to 1 pm and 2 to 5 pm, Saturday from 8.30 am to 5 pm and Sunday from 2 pm to 5 pm.

The **Kleinplasie Farm Museum** (☎ (0231) 22225) is excellent. It takes you from a trekboer's hut to a complete functioning 18th century farm complex. It's really the Afrikaner equivalent of the black 'cultural villages' you'll find elsewhere in South Africa.

It's a 'live' museum in the sense there are people wandering around in period clothes and rolling tobacco, making soap, operating a smithy, milling wheat, spinning wool and so on. The place is fascinating and you can easily spend a couple of hours here.

At the museum shop you can buy single bottles of wine that are a whisker more expensive than direct from the winery next door, where you will often have to buy a case (holding a dozen). Prices are very reasonable, ranging from about R6 to R25. For a significantly more potent alcoholic experience, pick up a flask of *witblitz* (white lightning), a traditional Boer distilled spirit.

It's strong stuff but not bad. My favourite is the rooibos flavoured variety.

The museum is open from 9 am to 4.30 pm daily (from 10.30 am on Sunday). Admission is R8. It's best to visit in the morning when you can see activities like bread baking.

The museum is badly signposted, which is a bit strange considering how slick the rest of the operation is. Look for signs to the Kleinplasie Winery, which is next door to the museum.

The **Karoo National Botanic Garden** (☎ (0231) 70785) is an outstanding garden. It is about 1km north of the N1 and 2.5km from the centre of town. There are some 140 hectares of natural semi-desert vegetation (with both Karoo and fynbos elements) and 10 hectares of landscaped garden, where many of the plants have been labelled. If your interest has been piqued, this is an ideal opportunity to identify some of the Cape's extraordinary indigenous plants.

There is something to see at all times of the year; bulb plants flower in autumn, the aloe flowers in winter, and the annuals and vygies flower in spring. There's also a collection of weird stone plants and other succulents. The garden is open daily from 8 am to 4 pm and admission is R2.

The modern **KWV Cellar** and brandy distillery (☎ (0231) 70785) isn't as famous as the one in Paarl but it is the largest in the world under one roof. Tours (R7) are held at 9.30 and 11 am and 1.30 and 3.30 pm during the week, and on Saturday morning from December to April.

Places to Stay & Eat *Burger Caravan Park* (☎ (0231) 23461), De la Bat Rd, close to the N1, is fairly ordinary, but it would do at a pinch and it is next to the town's swimming pool. Tent sites cost R22. *Nekkies* (☎ (0231) 70945) is a better alternative. It's on the Breede River en route to Rawsonville, about 5km from the centre of town.

Cumberland Hotel (☎ (0231) 72641), 2 Stockenstroom St, is expensive but comfortable, with rooms for about R300. There are cheaper rooms but they are small and dark.

There are a number of small restaurants in the streets around the main shopping area. *St Gerans* on Church (Kerk) St is recommended – steaks start around R30.

Getting There & Away Translux and Greyhound services run between Worcester and Cape Town, but the fare is steep at R110. Most buses stop at the Worcester train station and you might find a less regular but much cheaper 'non-white' service there.

For train bookings phone ☎ (0231) 29 2202/3. The daily *Trans Karoo* between Cape Town and Jo'burg stops in Worcester. From Worcester to Cape Town 1st/2nd/3rd class tickets are R47/33/19. The *Southern Cross* between Cape Town and Port Elizabeth also stops here, on Friday evening heading east and early Monday morning heading west. The extremely circuitous *Trans Oranje* to Durban also stops here.

There are several rival minibus taxi companies in town and they use different stops. One company, WUTA Taxis, stops near the corner of Tulbagh and Barry Sts, near the entrance to the train station. A daily taxi to Cape Town (R20) leaves sometime after 6 am and there are less regular but probably daily taxis to Robertson (R13) and to Ashton (R15), the town at the bottom of the pass that runs up to Montagu. Other places to find taxis are near the corner of Grey and Durban Sts and around the OK Bazaar on High St. A useful service to Ceres (about R22) via Tulbagh leaves from the Shoprite supermarket.

If you are travelling by car, take the N1 from Cape Town. You have a choice of using the Huguenot Tunnel (toll R5.50) or the more scenic route over Du Toitskloof Pass. Although the pass is mentioned on many road signs, it isn't signposted at the intersection where you must turn off – take the R101, not the toll road.

Robertson

Robertson is an attractive, prosperous, rather complacent little town – one traveller reported an eerie sense of being in 'a wholesome US sitcom from the early 1960s'. Six thousand rose bushes, jacarandas and oaks line the streets, and the problems of South Africa seem a very long way away. It's now the centre for one of the largest wine-growing areas in the country and is also famous for horse studs.

The information centre (☎ (02351) 4437), on Church St, is open Monday to Friday from 9 am to 5.30 pm and on Saturday morning.

There is a laundromat open until 9 pm (earlier closing for service wash) at 62 Church St, two doors along from the information centre.

The **museum** at 50 Paul Kruger St (on the corner of Le Roux St, a few blocks north-east of the central church) has a notable collection of lace. It is open from 9 am to noon daily, except Sunday, and tea is served in the garden on the second and fourth Friday of the month.

There are a couple of overnight **hiking trails** which take you into the mountains above Robertson, offering great views. The information centre has details.

Places to Stay & Eat *Silverstrand Resort* (☎ (02351) 3321) is a large complex on the banks of the Breede River, off the R60 to Worcester. It gets pretty hectic during the high season and it's too far from town (3km) to be convenient for backpackers. Apart from that, it has a very attractive spot on the river. There are tent sites and chalets at average prices.

The *Grand Hotel* (☎ (02351) 3272), 68 Barry St, on the corner of White St, is a rare example of a hotel where the quality of the rooms is better than the quality of the foyer would suggest. It has been tastefully renovated and has a friendly and welcoming atmosphere. Some rooms have balconies. There are a couple of cheerful English-style pub bars downstairs. Single/double rooms go for R140/220 with breakfast, and there might still be a few cheaper rooms with shared bathrooms. The proprietors also arrange tours of the surrounding countryside. *Simone's Grill Room & Restaurant* has standard prices – kingklip and steaks around R35 – but the food is of a high standard. It has a good-value set-menu lunch for R25 and a popular Sunday carvery where you can eat as much as you like for R35.

The information centre can tell you about other options, including self-catering farm cottages which start at around R50 per person.

Getting There & Away Translux Mountain Route buses to Port Elizabeth (via Oudtshoorn and Knysna) stop at the train station. See the Getting There & Away chapter for more details. Fares from Robertson include Cape Town, R115; Oudtshoorn, R40; Knysna, R95; and Port Elizabeth, R140.

The cheaper Chilwans (☎ (021) 54 2506, 905 3910) runs to Cape Town and Oudtshoorn, and Munnik Coaches (☎ (021) 637 1850) runs to Cape Town and Montagu on weekends.

The weekly *Southern Cross* between Cape Town and Port Elizabeth stops here on Friday night heading east and early on Monday morning heading west.

Robertson Travel (☎ (02351) 61329), in the small Plaza shopping centre, is the agent for Budget hire cars. It closes for lunch between 12.30 and 2 pm (it's that sort of town).

Taxis running between Cape Town (R25) and Oudtshoorn (R75) stop at the Shell petrol station on the corner of Voortrekker and Barry Sts. These taxis also run through Montagu (R25). There are no daily services.

McGregor

McGregor feels as if it has been forgotten. It's one of the best preserved mid-19th century villages in the country, with numerous thatched cottages surrounded by orchards, vegetable gardens and vineyards. It has no through roads, and the only reason you'll go there is if you want a quiet, beautiful spot to get away from it all. If you want to get back to it all, there are about 30 wineries within half an hour's drive.

On the road between Robertson and McGregor is the **Vrolijkheid Nature Reserve** (☎ (02353) 621), with specially constructed

bird hides and about 150 species to see. There's an 18km circular walking trail.

The **Boesmanskloof Hiking Trail** begins at Die Galg, about 15km south of McGregor, and winds 14km through the fynbos-rich Riviersonderend Mountains to the small town of Greyton. For permits contact the Vrolijkheid Nature Reserve. Most people walk the trail there and back, stopping overnight in either McGregor or Greyton. You can't camp on the trail. Accommodation in Greyton includes the *Posthaus Guesthouse*, which is good, *Greyton Lodge* and *Greyton Hotel*. The start of the trail marks the end of a long-abandoned project to construct a pass across the Langeberg range.

You can rent bikes in the village – your guesthouse will help you organise it.

Places to Stay & Eat Guesthouses are the major industry in this village and more are opening all the time. In addition to the places listed in this section there are self-catering cottages on nearby farms. The information centre in the larger, nearby town of Robertson (☎ (02351) 4437) has a complete list.

Old Mill Lodge (☎ (02353) 841) is a beautiful old building surrounded by a clutch of modern cottages that have been tastefully and comfortably decorated. It's a beautiful spot, and if by chance you feel active there's a swimming pool and nearby fishing. The cottages have two bedrooms and en suite bathrooms. Dinner, bed and breakfast costs R205/370 a single/double. The food is excellent and you eat in the old mill house looking out across a vineyard – highly recommended. They also have cold lunches for R15, although you'll need to give at least an hour's notice.

The lovely *McGregor Country Cottages* (☎ (02353) 816) is a complex of seven cottages which surround an apricot orchard. Several cottages are national monuments. The cottages are fully equipped and cost around R160 a double or more – great value.

Green Gables (☎ (021) 761 5846 for bookings) is less spectacular but still pleasant and charges R155/250 a single/double with breakfast.

Getting There & Away McGregor is 21km from Robertson, a large, sedate town on the R60 between Worcester and Swellendam.

COAST ROAD TO HERMANUS
The coast drive from Gordon's Bay to Hermanus is stunning, almost as spectacular as Chapman's Peak Drive, and it carries much less traffic. The R44 skirts a magnificent stretch of coast facing False Bay and is dominated by 1000m-high fynbos-cloaked mountains. It passes a few tiny beaches, but getting to some involves scrambling down steep slopes.

Kogel Bay
Kogel Bay has good beach breaks (dangerous for swimmers) and an excellent caravan park right on the beach.

Kogel Bay Pleasure Resort (☎ (024) 56 1286) is a large, basic caravan park (with cheaper than average sites) but its position is hard to beat, although it is exposed to southwesterly winds.

Rooiels Bay
There isn't much to this hamlet but it is on an excellent little beach, with a lagoon for sedate swimming.

The Drummond Arms (☎ (02823) 28458) is a small, new building with friendly hosts, good-value pub lunches and some simple, inexpensive accommodation.

Betty's Bay
Betty's Bay is a small holiday village just east of Cape Hangklip. There are some interesting roads around the Cape itself and the surrounding area is renowned for the variety of fynbos it supports. The nearby **Harold Porter National Botanical Gardens** (☎ (02823) 9711) protects some of this fynbos, and is definitely worth visiting. There are paths for exploring the area and, at the entrance, a formal garden where you can picnic, as well as tearooms. The gardens are open from 8 am to 6 pm daily, and entry is R4.

There's a colony of jackass penguins at Stony Point.

Kleinmond
Kleinmond is not a particularly attractive town, but it is close to a wild and beautiful beach. Most people will only stop briefly on their way through to Hermanus, but there are a couple of places to stay. If the weather is good, you could be tempted. There are a couple of municipal caravan parks: *Palmiet Caravan Park* (☎ (02823) 4050) on the west side of town is right on the beach and is the more attractive. Sites cost from around R35.

HERMANUS
Hermanus is a popular seaside resort within easy day-tripping distance of Cape Town (122km). It was originally a fishing village and still retains vestiges of its heritage, including an interesting museum at the old harbour. It's becoming increasingly popular as a place to view whales.

Whales often come very close to shore and there are some excellent vantage points on the cliff paths that run from one end of Hermanus to the other. The best places are Castle Rock, Kraal Rock and Sievers Point. There's a telescope on the clifftop above the old harbour.

There are great beaches nearby, mostly west of the town centre. Rocky hills, reminiscent of the Scottish highlands, surround the town, and there are good walks and a nature reserve which protects the prolific fynbos. The pleasant town centre is well endowed with restaurants. Bear in mind that Hermanus gets very busy during the school holidays in December and January.

Orientation & Information
Hermanus is a large town with extensive suburbs of impressive holiday and retirement homes. The town centre, around the old harbour, is easy to navigate on foot. The new, working harbour is at the eastern end of town.

The Hermanus Publicity Office (☎ (0283) 22629), 105 Main Rd, has a worthwhile supply of information about the town and surrounding district, including walks and drives in the surrounding hills, and staff are helpful. It's open from 9 am to 4.30 pm on

EXCURSIONS

Where the Whales Are

Between June and November, southern right whales *(Eubalaena australis)* come to Walker Bay to calve. There can be 70 whales in the bay at once. This species was hunted to the verge of extinction (South Africa was a whaling nation until 1976), but its numbers are now recovering. Humpback whales *(Megaptera novae angliae)* are also sometimes seen.

It's only recently that the people of Hermanus told the outside world that the whales were regular visitors. They took them for granted. Now, however, the tourism potential has been recognised and just about every business in town has a whale logo.

There's also a whale crier, who walks around town blowing on a kelp horn and carrying a blackboard which shows where whales have recently been sighted.

The town holds a Whale Festival in the late September or early October.

Despite all this commercialism, boat viewing of whales is still banned (you can be jailed for up to six years if you approach or remain within 300m of the whales), so the mighty creatures have the bay to themselves.

Although Hermanus is the best known whale-watching site, whales can be seen all the way from Cape Town (False Bay) to Plettenberg Bay and beyond. ■

Humpback whales are less often seen these days, but southern right whales, so called because they were the 'right' whales to catch, are common in Walker Bay.

weekdays, and on weekends during the whale season and in December.

A craft market is held on Friday and Saturday at Lemms Corner, the north-east corner of Hoof and Harbour Sts.

The Surf Shop on Main (Hoof) Rd is open daily in summer and rents boards (surf and body) for R25 a day. It also rents diving gear. Cycle Scene, also on Main Rd, rents mountain bikes for R25 a day and tandems for R50. Lagoon Boat Hire (☎ (0283) 77 0925) at Prawn Flats, a lagoon 7km west of the town centre, off the road to Stanford and past the suburbs of big holiday houses, rents canoes (about R15 per hour) and a variety of other small craft.

Old Harbour

The old harbour clings to the cliffs in front of the town centre; there's a small museum and a display of old fishing boats. There's also an annexe to the museum in the old schoolhouse on the market square (Lemm's Corner). The museum is open daily, except Sunday, from 9 am to 1 pm and 2 to 5 pm. Entry is R3.

Places to Stay

Caravan Parks Unfortunately, the closest caravan parks to town (and they aren't very close) do not allow tents or vans. *Schulphoek Resort* does but it's quite a way from town. The turn-off is on the main road just east of

Hermanus, but then it's a long way to the resort down a lonely road to the end of a point. 'Resort' is an optimistic description – it's a basic camping area with few facilities and no onsite management. Contact the municipal offices for details.

Hostels The *Hermanus Travellers' Lodge* (☎ (0283) 22829) is on a farm out of town (they'll collect you) and charges R20 for camping, R25 for dorms and R60 for a double. Two guesthouses in town cater to backpackers. The *Kenjockity Guesthouse* (☎ (0283) 21772), 15 Church St, has a fairly

small backpackers' room where a bunk costs R30, more if you need bedding. A bit further from the sea, the *Zoete Inval* guesthouse (☎ (0283) 21242), 23 Main Rd, has dorm beds for R30. Rates in the guesthouse start at R80/120. Several travellers have written to recommend this place.

B&Bs, Guesthouses & Self-Catering In low season, self-catering cottages can be great value shared between a few people, and even in the high season you can find places for less than R250. The Publicity Office has listings; you can also book through the

PLACES TO STAY
1 Zoete Inval
3 Kenjockity Guesthouse
8 Windsor Hotel
11 Hermanus Esplanade
21 Marine Hotel

PLACES TO EAT
6 St Tropez; San Remo Spur
9 Ouzari Greek Trattoria
13 Burgundy Restaurant

17 Rossi's Pizzeria & Italian Restaurant
18 Something Special
19 Mallards
22 Hoy Ming
24 Bientang's Cave

OTHER
2 Hospital
4 Hermanus Accommodation Centre
5 Hermanus Publicity Office
7 Post Office
10 Surf Shop
12 Book Centre
14 Lemm's Corner
15 Village Square Shopping Centre
16 First National Bank
20 Cycle Scene
23 O'Hagan's
25 Museum

Hermanus

ATLANTIC OCEAN

Walker Bay

Castle Rock

Old Harbour

Blow Hole

0   200   400 m

Hermanus Accommodation Centre (☎ (0283) 70 0004), not far from the Publicity Office on Church St. Self-catering flats and houses on its books start at around R150 in the low season and from R300 in the high season. B&Bs range between R70 and R150 per person.

Of the several guesthouses, *Kenjockity Guesthouse* (☎ (0283) 21772), 15 Church St, has fair-sized rooms. While they are nothing special the guesthouse has a nice atmosphere and is a good size. Rooms start at about R95 per person, R125 with attached bathroom. You'll pay more in December.

Hermanus Esplanade (☎ (0283) 23610), on Marine Drive, has apartments overlooking the sea. Smaller apartments cost from R150 to R190 for two people. You probably won't find a vacancy in December.

Hotels *Windsor Hotel* (☎ (0283) 23727) is a large old place on Marine Drive which seems to make its living from coach tours. As well as the old section there's a new wing that has good (if small) rooms with full-length windows overlooking the sea, just across the road. At the right time of the year there's a good chance of seeing a whale without getting out of bed! Low-season rates (May to the end of October) are R167/244 for singles/doubles, with breakfast (R147/210 without sea views); high season doubles (only) cost R268 (R248 without sea views). From mid-December to early January the rates are higher.

Marine Hotel (☎ (0283) 21112; fax 21533) is a grand, old-style hotel which has been superbly renovated. It's comfortable and it's in a good spot. Singles/doubles cost from R213/302 (R346/370 sea-facing) up to R504/528, which is very good value.

Places to Eat
Hermanus seems on the brink of a boom in eating places, so it's likely that there will be more choice by the time you arrive.

There are a couple of interesting possibilities on High St, which runs parallel to Main (Hoof) Rd. *Rossi's Pizzeria & Italian Restaurant* (☎ (0283) 22848), 10 High St,

has a pleasant and relaxed atmosphere. It has a range of pasta dishes (from R15 to R23), pizzas (from R15) and steak or line fish (from R35). It's open nightly from 6.30 pm. *Something Special*, across the road from Rossi's, is a pleasant café serving snacks and reasonably priced meals.

St Tropez (☎ (0283) 23221), 28 Main Rd, has good-value pub lunches for under R15, although it is more expensive at night (closer to R20).

Burgundy Restaurant (☎ (0283) 22800), Marine Drive, is one of the most acclaimed and popular restaurants in the province. Prices are surprisingly reasonable, and booking is recommended. There's a garden area with sea views. Main courses are around R35 to R40 at lunch, more at dinner. At lunch there are also cheaper snacks such as the whale watchers' platter of cold meats, cheeses, salad and pâté for R19.50.

Right down on the water, between the museum and the Marine Hotel, *Bientang's Cave* (☎ (0283) 23454) really *is* a seaside cave, containing a good restaurant where you can eat a steak meal for under R20. Someone told me about a memorable meal here with a whale nuzzling the rocks a metre or so from their table.

Getting There & Away
The only bus service (apart from tours) between Cape Town and Hermanus is Chilwans Transport (☎ 905 3910) in Cape Town. Chilwans Transport has an evening service that runs from Cape Town to Gansbaai, passing through Hermanus, on Friday as well as on Saturday for about R20.

There aren't many minibus taxis. You might find one running to Bellville train station (Cape Town) for R20, but it won't leave daily. The taxi park, such as it is, is behind the publicity office.

CAPE AGULHAS
Cape Agulhas is the southernmost point of the African continent – latitude 34°, 49 minutes, 58.74 seconds. On a stormy day it really looks like the next stop is the South Pole, with green seas, squall clouds and

sheets of low, shattered rock. Otherwise, it isn't especially impressive. It has that air of anti-climax which attends the end of any great journey.

The lighthouse, built in 1848 and the second oldest in South Africa, has been restored and is open to the public Tuesday to Saturday from 9.30 am to 4.45 pm and Sunday from 10 am to 1.30 pm. There's a tearoom in the building.

There isn't much in the Cape Agulhas hamlet, but **Struisbaai**, about 6km east, is a little larger and has a *caravan park*. There's also a 14km-long beach here.

In the nearby village of **Waenhuiskrans** (also known as Arniston) further east, *Arniston Hotel* (☎ (02847) 59000) is a very classy getaway overlooking the wild waves of the south coast and surrounded by windswept dunes and whitewashed fisherfolk's cottages. Singles/doubles are R300/400, including breakfast, and a high-quality set dinner is R50. At the other end of the scale, the *Caravan Park* (☎ (02847) 59620) has basic four-bed bungalows with shared facilities and no bedding or crockery, for about R95. Sites are available at the caravan park, but they are a pricey R48.

WEST COAST & SWARTLAND

The region immediately to the north of Cape Town that straddles the N7 highway is often further divided into two contiguous regions – the West Coast and Swartland.

Around 60 million years ago, the coastal zone west of the N7 was a sandy, unproductive area of unstable dunes left behind when the sea retreated. The Swartland, which covers both sides of the N7 and stretches east to the foot of the mountains, is a rich agricultural area of rolling plains.

The barren western coastal strip has been transformed into productive country, thanks to the stabilisation of the dunes by the Australian Port Jackson wattle. The wattle now poses a major threat to the indigenous flora. See the Cape Floral Kingdom section in the Things to See & Do chapter.

Because of its relative barrenness and chilly waters, the coast has only recently

been discovered by Cape Town holiday makers. They were attracted by the distinctive, though somewhat bleak, landscape and the fact that it was relatively undeveloped. There are now several popular resorts, including Yzerfontein and Langebaan. There are also important fishing towns (Saldanha, St Helena Bay and Lambert's Bay), with fleets that exploit the rich fishing in the cold, nutrient-rich Benguela current. For reasons that are not understood, however, catches are down.

The Swartland was, it is now believed, named after the dark foliage of the distinctive *renosterbus* scrub that covered the plains. The fertile soil and the winter rainfall enable local farmers to produce more than 20% of South Africa's wheat, as well as high-quality wine.

Long before white settlement, the plains were occupied by the Khoikhoi Grigriqua tribe, while the mountains were the province of the San. Piketberg is named after the guards (pickets) who were stationed here in the 1670s to protect the Cape Town settlers from Khoisan attacks.

Except for the Cederberg Wilderness Area, this region need not have a high priority for short-term visitors.

Getting There & Away

Most public transport travels through this area from Cape Town north along the N7, either running all the way to Springbok and Namibia or leaving the N7 and running through Calvinia to Upington (where you can make connections to Jo'burg).

Intercape Mainliner's services between Cape Town and Upington and between Cape Town and Windhoek (Namibia) run past Citrusdal and Clanwilliam. Upington buses leave Cape Town at 7 pm on Sunday, Monday, Wednesday and Friday, arriving in Citrusdal (R80 from Cape Town) at 9.30 pm and Clanwilliam (R90) at 10.15 pm. The return bus leaves Clanwilliam at 3 am and Citrusdal (R135) at 3.45 am. Windhoek buses leave Cape Town at 2 pm on Sunday, Tuesday, Thursday and Friday, arriving in Citrusdal at 4.15 pm and Clanwilliam at

4.45 pm. The return bus comes through Clanwilliam at 8.30 am on Tuesday, Thursday, Saturday and Monday (45 minutes later at Citrusdal).

Getting to the coastal towns west of the N7 isn't easy if you don't have a car. You'll find information about the limited minibus taxi options under the relevant towns in this section.

West Coast National Park

The West Coast National Park is one of the few large reserves along South Africa's coastline. It covers some 18,000 hectares and runs north from Yzerfontein to just short of Langebaan, surrounding the clear, blue waters of the Langebaan Lagoon. Unfortunately, these waters might not be so clear in the future, as a steel mill is being built in Saldanha, on the north shore of the lagoon.

The park protects wetlands of international significance and important sea bird breeding colonies. In summer it plays host to enormous numbers of migratory wading birds. The most numerous species is the delicate-looking curlew sandpiper (which migrates north from the subantarctic in huge flocks), but flamingoes, Cape gannets, crowned cormorants, numerous gull species, and African black oystercatchers count among the hordes. The offshore islands are home to colonies of jackass penguins. See the Birdlife on the Cape section in the Facts about Cape Town chapter.

The park's vegetation is predominantly sandveld, which means it is made up of stunted bushes, sedges, and many flowering annuals and succulents; there's some coastal fynbos in the east. The park is famous for its wild flower display, usually between August and October. Several game species can be seen in the part of the park known as the Postberg section, including a variety of small antelope, wildebeest, bontebok and eland.

The rainy season is from May to August. The summer is dry with hot days, and occasional morning mists. The park is only about 120km north of Cape Town, so it could easily be visited on a day trip if you have a car.

Orientation & Information The park is made up of a peculiar mix of semi-independent zones, some of which are only leased by the national park authorities. The roads in the park are dirt and can be quite heavily corrugated. The park begins 7km south of Langebaan (it's clearly signposted). As the return trip between Langebaan and the northern end of the Postberg section is more than 80km, allow yourself plenty of time.

Places to Stay & Eat Outside the park in the adjoining town of Langebaan are three caravan parks owned and run by the local municipality. None allow tents, a rule intended to discourage rowdy parties of young Cape Towners. If you don't look like trouble, you might be able to persuade the manager to let you camp. *Old Caravan Park* (☎ (02287) 22115) has shady (but sandy) sites right next to the lagoon in the centre of town. *New Caravan Park*, on Suffren St, is very ordinary – a sort of large suburban block, surrounded by houses. *Seabreeze Caravan Park*, off the road into town and some way from the centre, has bungalows.

A traveller recommends *Oliphantscop Farm#Inn* (☎ (02287) 22326), across the road from the large Mykonos timeshare complex, for both mid-range accommodation and excellent food.

Die Strandloper (☎ (02287) 21278) is an open-air restaurant on the beach, specialising in seafood. It gets good reviews. You must book, and bring your own alcohol.

Getting There & Away

No public transport, not even a minibus taxi, runs to Langebaan. Saldanha is the nearest town with public transport to/from Cape Town.

Olifants River Valley

The scenery changes dramatically at the Piekenaarskloof Pass; travelling north on the N7 you suddenly find yourself overlooking the densely populated and intensively cultivated Olifants River Valley. The elephant herds that the explorer Jan Danckaert found there in 1660 have long gone.

Today, the river provides irrigation for acres of grape vines and orange trees, which are beautifully maintained by a huge coloured labour force. The white farmers' comfortable bungalows are surrounded by green and leafy gardens, masking them from the shanties where the coloureds live.

On the valley floor are some acclaimed wineries and co-ops (specialising in white wine), and you can find details on a wine route at tourist information centres. The eastern side is largely bounded by the spectacular Cederberg range, which is protected by the extensive Cederberg Wilderness Area.

Citrusdal and Clanwilliam, to the south and north of the wilderness area, are the two main towns.

As an alternative to the N7, there's a spectacular road (the R303) between Citrusdal and Ceres (to the south), a great drive through the Cederberg Wilderness Area from Citrusdal to Clanwilliam and another spectacular route (the R364) between Clanwilliam and Calvinia (to the north-east).

Cederberg Wilderness Area

The Cederberg is a rugged, mountainous area of valleys and peaks extending roughly north-south for 100km, between Citrusdal and Vanrhynsdorp. A good proportion is protected by the 71,000 hectare Cederberg Wilderness Area, which is administered by Cape Nature Conservation. The highest peaks are Sneeuberg (2028m) and Tafelberg (1932m), and the area is famous for its weathered sandstone formations, which sometimes take bizarre shapes. San paintings can be seen in some of the caves.

The area is also famous for its plant life, which is predominantly mountain fynbos. Once again, spring is the best time to see wild flowers. The vegetation varies with altitude, but includes the Clanwilliam cedar (which gives the region its name) and the rare snowball protea. The Clanwilliam cedar grows at altitudes of between 1000 and 1500m, but only survives in small numbers, and the snowball protea (now found only in isolated pockets) only grows above the snow line.

There are small populations of baboon, rhebok, klipspringer, grysbok and predators such as caracal, Cape fox, honey badger and rarely seen leopard.

Orientation The Cederberg offers excellent hiking and is divided into three hiking areas of around 24,000 hectares. Each area has a network of trails. However, this is a genuine wilderness area with a genuine wilderness ethos. You probably won't be given directions to the area's rock art; work out for yourself where the Khoisan were likely to have lived. The book *Some Views on Rock Paintings in the Cederberg* by Janette Deacon might help.

In the buffer zone of conserved land that sits between the wilderness area and the farmland, more intrusive activities such as mountain biking are allowed. Pick up a copy of the mountain biking trail map from the Citrusdal information centre.

Information The area receives around 900mm of rain annually, mainly in winter, and snow is possible from May to the end of September. There's no real season for walking: winter is tough but exhilarating; in summer water can be in short supply.

For information on the Cederberg Wilderness Area contact the office of the very knowledgeable and approachable Chief Nature Conservator at Citrusdal (see the following Citrusdal section). There's also an office at the Algeria Camping Ground (see the following Places to Stay entry).

A permit is required if you want to hike, and the number of visitors per hiking area is limited to 150. The maximum permitted size of a group is 12 and the minimum is two; three would be safer. Maps (R7) are available at Algeria and the Chief Nature Conservator's office in Citrusdal.

If you want to be sure of getting a permit you are advised to apply well in advance. Outside school holidays and weekends, however, there is a chance you will be able to get one on the spot, but you should phone before arriving to make sure. Permits must be booked through your friendly Chief

Nature Conservator, Cederberg, Private Bag XI, Citrusdal 7340, or phone ☎ (022) 921 2289 during office hours. Bookings open on 1 February for the March to June period, 1 June for July to October and 1 October for November to February. They cost R6 per person per day, plus the R3 admission charge.

The entrance to Algeria Camping Ground closes at 4.30 pm, except Friday when it closes at 9 pm. You won't be allowed in if you arrive late. Permits must be collected during office hours, so if you're arriving on Friday evening, you'll need to make arrangements.

We spent five days hiking in the Cederberg from Algeria. Great hiking, especially for the budget conscious. After you've paid for your permit the huts are free. The huts are *basic* (by New Zealand standards) but for zero rand, that's OK. Plenty of places to camp if the huts are full. We only saw two hikers in five days.

Kate Wall (NZ)

Places to Stay *Algeria Camping Ground* is in a beautiful spot alongside the Rondegat River, the headwaters of the Olifants River. The grounds are manicured and shaded by huge Australian blue gums and pine trees. It's a bit of a shame they didn't plant indigenous trees, but it's still an exceptional camp site. There are swimming holes and lovely spots to picnic beside the river. Camping costs about R30, rising in peak periods. Day visitors (not allowed during peak periods) are charged R3.

There's another excellent *camping ground* in the Kliphuis State Forest near the Pakhuis Pass on the R364, about 15km north-east of Clanwilliam. It's surrounded by rock walls, and cut by a fresh mountain stream. Facilities are fairly spartan but include water, toilets and showers. A camp site costs about R40. You'll need to book these camp sites in the same way you book hiking. There are basic huts for hikers in the wilderness area.

On the south-eastern side of the wilderness area *Kromrivier Tourist Park* (☎ (027) 482 2807) has tent sites for about R25 for two and doubles for R90; there's also

Sanddrif Cederberg Camping (☎ (027) 482 2825).

See the following Citrusdal and Clanwilliam sections for places to stay outside the Wilderness Area.

Getting There & Away The Cederberg range is about 200km north of Cape Town, accessible from Citrusdal, Clanwilliam and the N7.

There are several roads to Algeria (the main park entrance and camping ground), and they are all spectacular. It takes about 45 minutes to reach Algeria from Clanwilliam by car, much longer if you stop now and again. Algeria is not signposted from Clanwilliam, but you just follow the road above the dam to the south. It *is* signposted from the N7 and it's only 20 minutes from the main road; there's an amazing collection of plants along the side of the road, including protea.

There are some dusty but interesting backroads running south-east through Sederberg and on to Ceres. Sederberg is not much more than a big old farm, where you can buy fuel and stay in huts (about R80). There's a good walk from the farm up to the Wolfsberg Crack (a well known rock formation) which takes about two hours.

Public transport into Algeria is nonexistent, so you might want to go to Citrusdal and start walking from there. It should take about two days to walk from Citrusdal to Algeria, entering the Wilderness Area at Boskloof. The Chief Nature Conservator's office in Citrusdal has information on this route. Cederberg Lodge in Citrusdal will drive guests.

Citrusdal

Citrusdal is a small town which makes a good base for exploring the Cederberg, both the wilderness area and the surrounding mountains. The area is embracing the idea of ecotourism and mountain-biking and hiking trails are being developed. And, of course, there's the prime attraction of hiking in the Cederberg Wilderness Area. August and September is wildflower season, and the displays can be spectacular.

The very friendly information centre is housed in the Sandveldhuisie Country Shop & Tearoom (☎ (022) 921 3210) on Kerk St. The shop sells cakes, herbs and local art and craft. Not far away is the office of the Chief Nature Conservator for the Cederberg Wilderness Area (☎ (022) 921 2289).

If you're planning to hike in the Cederberg and don't have transport you can start walking from Citrusdal rather than go to the hassle (and it is a hassle) of finding transport to Algeria, the usual starting point.

A few km out of town, **Craig Royston** is a large old farm building housing a café, shop and small museum. There's nothing very unusual about this but two things make Craig Royston unique: it hasn't been renovated to within an inch of its life, and the old shop is where the farmworkers still buy their supplies. It's a welcome relief after all those squeaky-clean tourist ventures where the only non-whites you meet are pushing brooms. There are excellent light meals and you can sample (and buy) local wines. The proprietor is a local artist and she is a refreshing person to meet in rural South Africa. Craig Royston is open daily. From the road in from the highway, the turn-off is near The Baths turn-off; it's signposted but the signs are small. If you arrive in Citrusdal when the tourist office is closed, this is a good place to come for information.

Places to Stay Much of the accommodation is out of town. The exception is *Cederberg Lodge* (☎ (022) 921 2221), a reasonable small-town hotel. Rooms cost from R113/174 a single/double, more in summer and in August and September (flower season).

There are plenty of farmstays in the area, either B&Bs or cottages, and some places will collect you from the information centre. These are probably the best options, whatever your budget. You can get dinner, bed and breakfast for as little as R100 per person, or a self-catering cottage from about R120. These rates might be slightly negotiable, especially for backpackers.

The Baths (☎ (022) 921 3609) is a health spa about 16km from Citrusdal. It's a fairly simple place in a pretty wooded gorge and could be a good place to relax for a few days. Expect to pay around R25 for a camp site, from R20 per person for a room (minimum R80) and from R135 a double for a flat. Prices rise on weekends. They will pick you up from the bus stop on the highway.

Van Meerhoff Lodge (☎ (022) 921 2231) is a fancy new hotel near the top of the Piekenaarskloof Pass (on the R44), overlooking Citrusdal. There are luxury chalets (from R160/R280), two restaurants and a swimming pool.

Getting There & Away See Getting There & Away at the beginning of the West Coast & Swartland section for details of buses. Intercape stops at a petrol station on the highway outside town; Translux comes into town and stops at the Cederberg Lodge. Minibus Taxis stop at the Caltex petrol station and run to Cape Town and Clanwilliam.

If you're driving, there's an excellent scenic road (the R303) over Middelburg Pass into the Koue (Cold) Bokkeveld and a beautiful valley on the other side, which is only topped by the Gydo Pass and the view over the Ceres Valley. The back road into the wilderness area is also excellent.

Clanwilliam

Clanwilliam is a popular weekend resort. The attraction is the town itself (which has some nice examples of Cape Dutch architecture and a pleasant main street), the proximity to the Cederberg, and most importantly for locals, the Clanwilliam Dam which attracts noisy waterskiers. If you're in this part of the world, by all means use the Clanwilliam shops, then head to the mountains. There are some beautiful roads into the Cederberg and a great drive over the Pakhuis Pass to Calvinia.

Information The information centre (☎ (027) 482 2024) is in the old jail at the top end of the main street. It's open weekdays and Saturday morning, and daily during the flower season.

EXCURSIONS

Places to Stay & Eat If you have a tent or van, the best spot to stay near Clanwilliam is the Kliphuis State Forest about 30 minutes away, just before the Pakhuis Pass on the R364 – see under Places to Stay in the earlier Cederberg Wilderness Area section for more information.

Clanwilliam Dam Municipal Caravan Park & Chalets (☎ (027) 482 1933) overlooks the water-skiing action; it's on the other side of the dam from the N7. Travellers arriving here after weeks in Namibia are pleased to be able to pitch their tents on lush, grassy sites (R20). The chalets are very nice, but you would have to book ahead for the busy periods – school holidays and weekends. Rates start at around R120 for two people.

The information centre can put you in touch with B&Bs charging from R55 per person and there are farmstays in the area.

The comfortable and popular *Strassberger's Hotel Clanwilliam* (☎ (027) 482 1101) is a country pub which has been renovated to a high standard. It is good value at R120/210 (R170/310 in flower season), including breakfast. There's a pool. They also have an annexe in a delicensed pub nearby where rooms cost R85 per person, with breakfast. This isn't as nice as the hotel. *Faint du Barrys* (☎ (027) 482 1537), 13 Ougsburg Drive, is a pleasant guesthouse charging the same rates as the hotel. There is disabled access.

Strassberger's Hotel Clanwilliam has an à la carte restaurant, *Reinhold's*, in a building across the road, but the hotel dining room is cheaper and quite flash enough. A good set-menu dinner costs R45.

Getting There & Away For bus travel, see Getting There & Away at the beginning of the West Coast & Swartland section earlier in this chapter. All buses that go through Citrusdal also come through Clanwilliam. It's about 45 minutes between the two towns.

Minibus taxis running between Springbok and Cape Town also come through Clanwilliam. From Clanwilliam the fare to Cape Town is about R35. Heading to Cape Town

---

Rooibos Tea

Rooibos 'tea' is made from the leaves of species of the Aspalanthus plant, grown in the Cederberg region. Apparently it was the 'Malay' slaves who first discovered that the plant could be used to make a beverage, although it wasn't until this century that a Russian immigrant, Benjamin Ginsberg, introduced it to the wider community, and not until the 1930s that it began to be grown as a cash crop. Despite this, some brands feature trek wagons and other icons of old Afrikanerdom, and the packets make good souvenirs.

Rooibos, literally 'red bush', is a red-coloured tea with a distinctive aroma. It contains no caffeine and much less tannin than normal tea. This is probably its major health benefit, although other health claims have also been made for it. The tea does contain minute amounts of beneficial minerals such as iron, copper and magnesium, so drinking it might do you a little good. It's also a great thirst quencher, drunk straight or with lemon or milk.

You can visit the Rooibos Tea Natural Products works (☎ (027) 482 2155), near Clanwilliam, by arrangement. ■

---

minibus taxis pick up near the Clanwilliam Post Office at about 11 am.

FURTHER AFIELD

This section describes some of the places which could be included on an easy two or three day trip from Cape Town. It's just a small sample of this diverse area, and if you want the full story see the Western Cape and Northern Cape chapters of Lonely Planet's *South Africa, Lesotho & Swaziland*.

Matjiesfontein

Matjiesfontein (pronounced 'mikeys ...') is a small railway siding that has remained virtually unchanged for 100 years, its impressive buildings incongruous in the bleak Karoo landscape. People stop here on their way to or from Jo'burg – if not for a night, at least for a cup of coffee. It's about 224km east of Cape Town.

A night in the Lord Milner Hotel would be worth a stopover on the train trip between Jo'burg and Cape Town, although 24 hours in Matjiesfontein might be a bit long unless you have a good book. Alternatively, you could take the train here from Cape Town (arriving mid-afternoon), stay the night and catch the morning train back again next day. It's a 5½ hour trip.

The developer of the hotel and the other establishments was one Jimmy Logan, who once ran every railway refreshment room between the Cape and Bulawayo. Matjiesfontein was his home base, and the hotel and other accommodation, together with the dry climate, attracted wealthy people looking for a health resort.

As well as the attractive old buildings there's a museum (R2) in the train station that's worth a look.

Places to Stay The very impressive *Lord Milner Hotel* (☎ (023) 551 3011) is a period piece with rooms costing from R155/240 for a single/double, including breakfast (no children under 12). One of the grander rooms has twin baths! The same people also have accommodation in a nearby (everything in this village is 'nearby') renovated *old boarding house* with rooms at R125/190, including breakfast.

Getting There & Away The daily *Trans Karoo* train between Cape Town and Jo'burg stops here. Fares to Cape Town are R75/52/31 in 1st/2nd/3rd class. The *Blue Train* also stops here (see the boxed text between pages 32 and 33). If you are travelling by car take the N1.

Calvinia

Calvinia is just a small country town on the edge of the Karoo's vast emptiness, but it's an attractive place and worth a visit to give you some idea of what the rest of South Africa is like. The skies are huge and the air has an exhilarating clarity. This is no illusion, as Calvinia's 'starlight factor' is a very high 80%. A ridge of the Hantamsberg range dominates the town, which is itself over 1000m above sea level. As the church clock quietly tolls the hours it's easy to imagine that decades, if not centuries, have slipped away.

The First Merinos

In 1789 Charles V of Spain gave William IV of Holland six Escurial merinos. These were prized for the fine wool they produced and the Spanish carefully protected their monopoly. The merinos were sent to the Cape and placed in the care of a Mr RJ Gordon. They thrived and multiplied.

The Spanish got wind of this and demanded that their sheep be returned. Gordon obeyed the request to the letter, returning the original six sheep, but keeping their progeny. Most of the flock was later shipped to Australia. ■

Shear numbers: from six, South Africa now has more than 35 million sheep.

The surrounding countryside yields lovely spring wildflowers. It is a transitional zone with floral elements from the Namaqualand, the Karoo and the Cape areas.

Calvinia's economy is dependent on the surrounding merino sheep farms, and has been hard hit by the collapse of wool prices. Amazingly, 80% of sheep in the region are still shorn with hand clippers.

Information The friendly information office (☎ (0273) 41 1712; PO Box 28, Calvinia 8190) adjoins the museum. It has a range of suggestions for interesting accommodation and things to do, as well as a walking tour map of the town. Farmstays and B&Bs are thriving in the region, and the information office will help you to arrange something; bookings are advisable in the flower season. The office is open Monday to Friday from 8 am to 1 pm and 2 to 5 pm, and Saturday until noon.

Calvinia Museum For a small country town, this museum is of a surprisingly high standard, and is worth visiting. The main building was a synagogue – it's incongruous but not unusual to find disused Jewish buildings in tiny, remote towns in South Africa. The museum concentrates on white settlement, and there are some wonderful oddities, like a four legged ostrich chick (a fake used by a travelling shyster) and a room devoted to a local set of quadruplets. There's also a special section on the sheep industry. It has the same opening hours as the information office; admission is R1.

Places to Stay & Eat *Calvinia Caravan Park* (☎ (0273) 41 1011) is close to the centre of town, and is rather flat and ordinary but it may be the only option during Calvinia's Meat Festival in August. Sites are R25.

If you would rather find some basic self-catering accommodation, try *Calvinia Rest Rooms* (☎ (0273) 41 1513), which is behind the Total petrol station on Williston Rd. The rooms are pleasant enough at about R60 per person per night, and have kitchen facilities.

The best place to stay is in any one of the trio of restored historical buildings now run as guesthouses. *Die Tiushuis*, *Die Dorphuis* and *Bothasdal* are wonderful old places furnished with antiques. Depending on where you stay, rooms start at R70 per person or R110 with breakfast. Bookings (☎ (0273) 41 1606) can be made at Die Hantamhuis on Hoop St, the oldest building in town and now a café. This is where you'll have breakfast if you stay at one of the guesthouses. Breakfast is served from 7.30 to 9 am and is available to nonguests (but not on Sunday). It's highly recommended. If you order your meal a day in advance you can try *skilpadjie* or 'tortoise' (lamb's fry wrapped in caul). Other meals are also available.

Hantam Hotel (☎ (0273) 41 1512), Kerk St, is plain but comfortable, and it's as clean as a whistle. Rooms cost a reasonable R90 per person, plus R25 for breakfast. The hotel

has an à la carte steakhouse, the *Busibee*, where braaied lamb is a perennial feature of the menu.

Holden's Commercial Hotel (☎ (0273) 41 1020), Water St, is also of a high standard but ugly – a shame considering it was a beautiful old building before it was 'modernised'. There is talk of replacing its old verandah. The rooms are good and cost R80 per person; breakfast is another R25. Make sure you visit Cecil Traut in the bar.

The information office can suggest B&B possibilities. There are also a number of farmhouse B&Bs; most charge around R65 per person. Try *Vinknes Guesthouse* (☎ (0273) 41 2214), which is on a farm about 30km from Calvinia on the road to Nieuwoudtville. A number of farms have San cave paintings and excellent hiking possibilities.

Getting There & Away Intercape Mainliner runs buses to/from Cape Town (about six hours, R120) via Clanwilliam (2½ hours, R80). Book at the travel agency (☎ (0273) 44 1373), incongruously sited in the *slaghuis* (butcher shop); buses stop at the *trokkie sentrum* (truck centre), the Shell petrol station on the west (Vanrhynsdorp) side of town.

For minibus taxis try the trokkie sentrum. It's R75 to Cape Town but they don't run every day. If you have no luck here, try the Total petrol station on the east (Upington) side of town.

If you are travelling by car, take the N7 to Clanwilliam, then the R364 to Calvinia. Alternatively, continue along the N7 to

---

Cecil Traut's Tie Collection
The barman at the Calvinia Hotel is an engaging old character by the name of Cecil Traut. His claim to fame (and he has a modicum) is his collection of ties from around the country and the world. He has more than 500 ties which cover a wall of the bar, and he will be only too happy to show them to you. He has worked behind bars for a long time, and pours a good beer. ■

Vanrhynsdorp and take the R27. Either of these routes involve spectacular climbs and great views.

Swellendam

As well as being a very pretty town with a real sense of history, Swellendam offers those with transport a good base for exploring quite a range of country. The Breede River Valley and the coast are within easy reach, as is the Little Karoo. Swellendam is about midway between Cape Town and George, the first town on the Garden Route.

Swellendam is dotted with old oaks. To its south is beautiful rolling wheat country, but it backs up against a spectacular ridge of the 1600m Langeberg range. Author Breyton Breytenbach describes the town as 'lying in the crook of well-dressed, elderly mountains'. The distinctive square-topped outcrop is known locally as 12 O'Clock Rock because the sun is close to the rock at noon, making it impossible for anyone in town to see what is going on up there. I was told that this was a favourite place for diamond smugglers to do business, but it seems a long way to go. You can walk up and back in a day.

History Swellendam dates from 1746 and is the third oldest European town in South Africa. It was initially settled by independent farmers and traders from the Cape Peninsula who, by the 1740s, had drifted far beyond the control of the Dutch East India Company's (VOC) authorities at Stellenbosch.

As a result, Swellendam was established as the seat of a *landdrost*, an official representative of the colony's governor whose duties combined those of local administrator, tax collector and magistrate. The landdrost's *drostdy* included his office and courtroom as well as his living quarters. Swellendam's is the only 18th century drostdy to survive, and it is now the centrepiece for one of the best museum complexes in South Africa.

Information The Swellendam Tourist Office (☎ (0291) 42770), in the old mission or Oefeninghuis on Voortrek (the main street), is open Monday to Friday from 9 am to 5 pm

and Saturday to 12.30 pm. Note the twin clocks; one is permanently set at 12.15 pm. This was the time for the daily service and the illiterate townspeople only had to match the working clock with the painted one to know when their presence was required.

If you're at all interested in architecture or history, pick up a copy of the *Swellendam Treasures* brochure from the tourist office which details scores of interesting buildings in and around Swellendam; a good map is included.

For permits to walk in **Marloth Nature Reserve** in the Langeberg range, just 3km from town, contact the Nature Conservation Department (☎ (0291) 41410) during business hours. There are day, overnight and week-long hikes.

Drostdy Museum The Drostdy Museum is one of the finest museum complexes in the country. It features the beautiful drostdy itself, which dates from 1746. In addition to the drostdy, there is the old gaol, part of the original administrative buildings, the gaoler's cottage, a water mill and Mayville, another residence dating from 1853.

Some distance away, Morgenzon, 16 Van Oudtshoorn Rd, is an annexe of the museum. It was built in 1751 as a house for the landdrost's secretary.

The complex is open weekdays from 9 am to 4.15 pm, and weekends from 10 am to 3.45 pm; entry is R5.

Places to Stay *Swellendam Caravan Park* (☎ (0291) 42705) is in a lovely spot near the Morgenzon museum a 10 minute walk from town, tucked under the mountains and surrounded by leafy farms. Sites cost around R35 and there are chalets. It's a nice place but if you have transport consider staying at Bontebok National Park, 6km from town.

Swellendam Backpackers (☎ (0291) 42648) is at 5 Lichtenstein St. It's a pleasant enough place, charging R30 for a dorm bed and R25 for camping.

There are many excellent B&Bs and guesthouses in and around Swellendam, and they are the best accommodation options. The tourist office has a full list.

Roosje Van de Kaap (☎ (0291) 43001), 5 Drostdy St, is a friendly little guesthouse in a newly refurbished old house. It's surprising how well modern interior design complements Cape Dutch architecture. The four guestrooms overlook the small pool and cost around R90 per person. There's also a restaurant here. *Kadie Cottage* (☎ (0291) 43053), Voortrek St, is a large complex of old buildings with lawns running down to the river. There are self-catering units.

Moolmanshof (☎ (0291) 43258), at 217 Voortrek St, is a beautiful old home dating from 1798. The garden is superb and the house is furnished with period furniture. B&B rates are a very reasonable R90 per person per night. *The Old Mill* guesthouse (☎ (0291) 42790), 241 Voortrek St, is a cottage in a meadow behind the antiques/craft shop and café of the same name. It's a pleasant place. B&B costs about R90 per person or you can take the whole cottage and self-cater.

At *Swellengrebel Hotel* (☎ (0291) 41144), Voortrek St, the older rooms are fairly cramped (from R149/189) but newer double rooms (R220) are OK. *Carlton Hotel* (☎ (0291) 41120) is looking pretty tired and charges from R70/120 or R60/100 with shared bathroom.

Klippe Rivier Homestead (☎ (0291) 43341), fax 43337), a km or so south-west of town, just across the Keurbooms River, is an exceptional place to stay. Built on land granted in 1725, the Cape Georgian manor is a superb building and the standard of accommodation and catering is very high. There are six guest suites overlooking an oak-shaded lawn, from R260 per person.

Places to Eat *Mattsen's Steak House*, on Voortrek St near the tourist office, is popular. A big dinner costs about R50 and there are light meals and snacks.

Zanddrift Restaurant adjoins the museum and is in a building that dates from 1757. Unfortunately it's only open from 9 am to 5 pm. Breakfast is a must, with a huge platter

of omelette, ham, cheese, pâté, fruit and so on, all for R25. It's available all day. Other dishes depend on what's available that day.

The Old Mill, 241 Voortrek St, is a café open for lunch (and dinner for guests staying in the cottage). Light meals cost around R15. More substantial dishes include springbok steaks, guinea-fowl pies and other interesting specialities.

For an excellent night out, phone *Klippe River Homestead* (☎ (0291) 43341) to see if they have room at dinner for nonguests. A three course set menu costs R65.

Getting There & Away Intercape buses run to Cape Town (R65) and Port Elizabeth R120). Swellengrebel Hotel is the Intercape agent. Greyhound (☎ (0291) 42374) and Translux have similar services at higher prices. Some Translux buses also run to Oudtshoorn (R80). Milestone Tours (☎ (0291) 42137), 8 Cooper St, is the Translux agent.

The weekly *Southern Cross* train between Cape Town and Port Elizabeth stops here.

Minibus taxis stop at the Caltex petrol station on Voortrek St, opposite Swellengrebel Hotel. There's a daily service to Cape Town for R38.

If you are travelling by car, take either the N2 from Cape Town or the R60 from Worcester.

Bontebok National Park
Bontebok National Park (☎ (0291) 42735), 6km south of Swellendam, is a small chunk of land set aside to ensure the preservation of the bontebok. The bontebok is an unusually marked antelope that once roamed the region in large numbers. Unfortunately, it has been reduced to the verge of extinction.

As a national park, Bontebok doesn't offer much competition to Kruger and South Africa's other renowned parks, but as a nice place to relax it's hard to beat.

The park falls within the coastal fynbos area and is on the banks of the Breede River (swimming is possible). It boasts nearly 500 grasses and other plant species; in the late winter and early spring, the veld is covered with flowers. In addition to the bontebok there are rhebok, grysbok, duiker, red hartebeest and mountain zebra. Birdlife is abundant.

Admission is R11 per vehicle. There are six-berth 'chalavans' for R77 plus R12 per person (book through the National Parks Board in Cape Town) and pleasant camp sites for R35 for two people (book at the park).

Other Options

Several possible itineraries take in the preceding places (and most of the sights mentioned earlier in this chapter).

You could visit the **Winelands**, perhaps staying overnight (or longer), then continue up the N1 to **Matjiesfontein**. Rather than returning the same way, continue to the turn-off for **Prince Albert**, a very pretty village on the edge of the Karoo and under the lee of the **Swartberg mountains**. Hiking in this area is very popular.

The Prince Albert of Saxe-Coburg Lodge (☎ (04436) 267) is on the main street, across from the hotel, and charges from R60 per person, with breakfast. The owners are very experienced hikers and great sources of information. They also offer guided hikes.

On the south (Swartberg Pass) edge of town, Elaine Hurford's *Dennehof Karoo Guesthouse* (☎ (04436) 227) is in the town's oldest house (1835). As well as the usual accommodation, there's the self-catering Olyfhuis (Olive House) in its own little vineyard. Backpackers can stay here for R50. Elaine also arranges package tours including accommodation, meals and activities.

There are several other guesthouses in town (see the list on the museum's verandah) and it seems likely that more will open.

Swartberg Hotel (☎ (04436) 332), 77 Church St (the main street), is a nice old pub which is in the process of being renovated. Rates include breakfast and start at R160/ 250 a single/double. The dining room does excellent dinners and next door in the café,

good meals and snacks are served during the day.

From Prince Albert you can cross the spectacular Swartberg Pass to the more fertile **Little Karoo**, where the main town is **Oudtshoorn**, famous for its ostrich farms.

Places to stay in Oudtshoorn include the *NA Smit Caravan Park* (☎ (044) 272 4152), on Park Rd, with sites for R35/40 in the low/high season, rondavels from R75/100 for two and chalets. *Backpackers' Oasis* (☎ (044) 279 1163), 3 Church St, is a good hostel. *Bedstop Accommodation* (☎ (044) 272 4746), 69 Van der Riet St, is one of the cheaper B&Bs (from R60 per person). *Bisibee Guesthouse* (☎ (044) 272 4784), at 171 Church St, charges from R80/160 and is highly recommended. The *Queen's Hotel* (☎ (044) 272 2101), on Baron van Rheede, is an attractive old-style country hotel charging from R200/290, with breakfast. *Holiday Inn* (☎ (044) 272 2201), on the corner of Baron van Rheede and Van der Riet Sts, charges R270/520. Returning to Cape Town from Oudtshoorn, you can head south to the coast at **George** and drive a short section of the famous **Garden Route**. Alternatively, head west up the valley along the R62, through little towns such as **Barrydale**, then either travel south via **Tradouw Pass** to eventually join the N2 near **Swellendam**, or keep going up the valley to the pretty town of **Montagu**.

Places to stay in Montagu include the excellent *Mimosa Lodge* (☎ (0234) 42351; fax 42418), on Church St, from R250/450 a single/double for dinner, bed and breakfast. *De Bos* (☎ (0234) 42532) is a guest farm on the edge of town with camping (R15 per person), a backpackers' barn (R20), a bungalow (R25 per person) and an en suite double room for R80.

From Montagu you descend east to the Breede River Valley not far from **Robertson** and **McGregor**.

Glossary

ablutions block – a building containing a toilet, bath, shower and washing facilities (found mainly in caravan parks and game reserves)

advokate – equivalent of a barrister

ANC – African National Congress

animism – various definitions, but most useful seems to be: 'beliefs based on an existence of the human soul, and on spirits that inhabit or are represented by natural objects and phenomena, which have the power to influence human life for good or ill'

apartheid – literally 'the state of being apart'; a political system in which peoples are segregated according to ethnic background

AWB – Afrikaner Weerstandsbeweging (Afrikaner Resistance Movement). Extremist right-wing group active in pre-election South Africa, led by the recently jailed Eugene Terre-Blanche.

baai – bay

bakkie – utility, pick-up

bantustans – see *Homelands*

bazaar – market

bhundu – bush, wilderness

bilharzia – disease caused by blood flukes which are passed on by freshwater snails

biltong – dried and salted meat that can be made from just about anything from eland or ostrich to mutton or beef

black taxi – minibus taxi

bobotie – dish consisting of curried mincemeat with a topping of beaten egg baked to a crust, probably of Cape Malay origin

boerewors – spicy sausages, often sold by street vendors, and consumed at a *braai*, literally 'farmers sausage'

Bokkies – affectionate name for a national sports team, usually a rugby team; shortened from Springboks

bottle store – shop selling alcohol

braai – a barbecue featuring tons of grilled meat and beer ('and a small salad for the ladies'), a South African institution, particularly among whites

Broederbond – secret society only open to Protestant Afrikaner men, highly influential under National Party rule

buck – antelope

buppies – black yuppies

buy a donkey – 'thank you very much', 'many thanks', actually, it's *baie dankie*

cafe – (*kaffe* in Afrikaans) small-town shop selling odds and ends, plus generally unappetising fried food

camping ground – area where tents can be pitched and caravans parked

camp site – an individual pitch on a camping ground

cassper – armoured vehicle

coloureds – South Africans of 'mixed race'

comma – point, as in decimal point; numbers with decimals use commas, eg 2,5km not 2.5km; a space is used to separate thousands, eg 54,321.5 is written 54 321,50 in South Africa

dagga or **zol** – marijuana

dam – reservoir

difaqane – early 19th century migration by several South African tribes in the face of Zulu aggression; also called mfecane

donga – steep-sided gully created by soil erosion

dorp – small rural village

drankwinkel – literally 'drink shop'; South African off-licence

drift – river ford

drostdy – home (and office) of VOC magistrates, now the finest example of early Cape Dutch architecture

dumpy – smallest size of beer bottle

eh – (pronounced to rhyme with hay) all purpose ending to sentences, even very short ones such as 'Thanks, eh'

farm stall – small shop or shelter by a road, selling farm produce
Flying Squad – ready reaction force of armed police
forest – in this mainly unforested region, any large collection of trees, usually a pine or eucalypt plantation
fynbos – term for the vegetation of the area around Cape Town, literally means fine or delicate bush

Homelands – reserves for the black peoples of South Africa established under apartheid, reabsorbed into South Africa after 1994; also called bantustans
Hoofweg – Main Rd/St
howzit? – all purpose greeting

IFP – Inkatha Freedom Party; KwaZulu-Natal based political party, a longtime rival of the ANC
indaba – originally an assembly of Zulu chiefs; now applied to political meetings
inyanga – medicine man, herbalist
Izzit? – rhetorical question which most closely translates as 'Really?' and is used without regard to gender, person, or number of the subject. Therefore, it could mean 'Is it?', 'Is that so?', 'Did you?', 'Are you?', 'Is he?', 'Are they?', 'Is she?', 'Are we?', 'Amazing!' etc. Also 'How izzit?, for 'How are things?', 'How's it going?' etc.

jol – party, both verb and noun
just now – indeterminate future, but reasonably imminent (see *now*)

kaffe – see *cafe*
kaffir – black person (derogatory – do not use)
Karoo – semi-desert area covering most of the interior of the old Cape Province
kloof – ravine or gorge
kloofing – climbing, hiking, swimming etc in kloofs
knobkerry – traditional African weapon, a stick with a round knob at the end, used as a club or missile
koeksesters – small doughnuts dripping in honey – very gooey and figure-enhancing

kopje or koppie – little hill, usually flat-topped
KWV – Kooperatieve Wijnbouwers Vereniging – presently state-owned, the KWV has complete regulatory control over the local wine industry
kraal – Afrikaans version of the Portuguese 'curral', an enclosure for livestock or a fortified village

laager – a defensive circular formation of ox-carts, used by the voortrekkers for protection against attack
landdrost – magistrates, first established by the Dutch (see *drostdy*)
lapa – a circular building with low walls and a thatched roof, used for cooking, partying etc
larney – posh, smart, high quality (noun or adjective)
lekker – very good, enjoyable or tasty
Little Karoo – the more fertile Karoo area east of Cape Town
location – another word for township, more usually in rural areas

Madiba – a name by which Nelson Mandela is sometimes known
mampoer – home-distilled brandy made from peaches, prickly pear etc, often stronger than schnapps
mfecane – forced migration by several Southern African tribes in the face of Zulu aggression
mielie pap or **mealie meal** – maize porridge, a black African staple
muti – traditional medicine

Nationals – The National Party, usually known as 'the Nats'
now – soon, eg 'I'll serve you now' means in a little while; 'Just now' means 'I understand that you're impatient, and I'll be with you soon' or 'When I can get around to it'
now-now – immediately

oke – bloke, guy

PAC – Pan African Congress; Political party of some importance during the struggle for independence but now much diminished. It espoused 'Africanism' but the ANC's non-racialism has proved to be more popular.

plus-minus – meaning 'about', this scientific/mathematical term has entered common parlance, particularly among people who don't speak English as their first language, eg 'the bus will come in plus-minus 10 minutes', 'I've been here for plus-minus four years'

pronking – strange bouncing leaping by antelope, apparently just for fun

robot – traffic light

rondavel – a round hut with a conical roof, frequently seen in holiday resorts

rooibos – literally 'red bush' in Afrikaans; herbal tea which reputedly has therapeutic qualities

Russian – large, red sausage, fried but often served cold (and revolting)

SAB – South African Breweries, brewers of Black Label, Castle etc; loved and hated

samp – crushed maize used for porridge

SANDF – South African National Defence Force (formerly SADF)

sangoma – a traditional healer or herbalist

SASTS – South African Students' Travel Service

shame! – what a pity!

shebeen – drinking establishment in black townships, often illegal

sjambok – short whip, traditionally made from rhino hide

skilpadjie – literally 'tortoise', it's lamb's fry (don't ask what they fry) wrapped in caul

slaghuis – butcher shop

soutpiel – literally 'salt dick' – a man with one foot in South Africa and the other in Britain

Spar – a supermarket chain; it's becoming generic for any large supermarket

spruit – shallow river

squaredavel – see *rondavel* and work out the rest

stad – used on road signs to indicate the city centre

stadsaal – city hall

strand – beach

takkie – gym shoe

tickie box – public phone on private premises

township – black residential district, usually hidden on the outskirts of a white town

toyi toyi – jubilant dance often associated with political demonstrations

trokkie – lorry or semi

tsotsi – township hoodlum, gangster

uitlanders – 'foreigners'; name given by Afrikaners to the immigrants who poured into the Transvaal after the discovery of gold

Vaalies – slang name for whites from the former Transvaal Province

Van der Merwe – archetypal Boer country bumpkin and butt of English jokes

veld – open grassland (pronounced 'felt'); variations: lowveld, highveld, bushveld, sandveld

veldskoens – comfortable shoes made of soft leather (also called 'vellies')

Vienna – smaller version of *Russian*

vlei – any low open landscape, sometimes marshy (pronounced 'flay')

volkstaat – Homeland for whites, or rather Afrikaners. Conservative Afrikaner groups still agitate for their own volkstaat.

Voortrekkers – original Afrikaner settlers of the Orange Free State and Transvaal who migrated from the Cape Colony in the 1830s

... weg – literally 'way', but translated as 'street' or 'road' (eg Abelweg means Abel Rd)

witblitz – Afrikaner white lightning

yah well no fine – yes-no-maybe-perhaps

In African English, repetition for emphasis is common: something that burnt you would be 'hot hot'; fields after the rains are 'green green'; a crowded minibus with no more room is 'full full'; and so on.

Index

TEXT

Map references are in **bold**.

abseiling 92-3
accommodation, *see* places to stay
activities, *see* individual entries
African National Congress
    (ANC) 12-3, 22-3
Afrikaans, *see* language
Afrikaans Language Museum
    137
AIDS 48
air travel 55-7
    airline offices 55
    departure tax 55
    domestic flights 55-6
    international flights 56-7
    to/from the airport 61
airport 61
apartheid 11-2
aquarium 80
architecture 29-30
arts 25-6, *see also* books
Atlantic Coast 85-9
ATMs, *see* money

B&B organisations 96
baboons 91
Bainskloof 140
Bainskloof Pass 141
bands, *see* entertainment
Bantustans, *see* Homelands
bargaining, *see* money
Barrydale 159
bars & clubs, *see* entertainment
beaches 86, *see also* individual
    entries
Beck House 142
beer 104
Ben Schoeman Dock, *see*
    Docks, The
Bertram House Museum 72
Betty's Bay 145
bicycle travel 65-6, 93, *see also*
    mountain biking

Big Bay 86
bilharzia, *see* health
birdlife 18-21, 150, 159
    Birdlife on the Cape 18-21
Bloubergstrand 86
Blue Train *between pages* 32
    and 33
Bo-Kaap 25, 69, 71
    Bo-Kaap Museum 69, 71
Boat Bay 87
Boer War 11
Boers 10-1
bonteboks 158
Bontebok National Park 20,
    158-9
books 43-5
    culture 44-5
    history & politics 44
    literature 45
    personal accounts 45
    special interest 43-4
    travel guides 43
bookshops 119-20
Boschendal manor 29
Botanical Gardens
    (Stellenbosch) 130
Boulders Beach 90
Braak 131
Brandy Museum 131
Breede River Valley 140-5
Buffels Bay 91
Burgerhuis 131
bus travel 57-8
    domestic lines 57
    domestic routes 57-8
    within Cape Town 61
business environment 42-3, *see*
    also work
business hours 53

cableway 74-5
cafés, *see* places to eat
Calvinia 155-7
    Calvinia Museum 156

camping, *see* places to stay
camping gear, *see* shopping
Camps Bay 87-8
canoeing 93
Cape Agulhas 148-9
Cape Flats 22, 92-3, 116
Cape Minstrel Carnival 53
Cape Muslim Quarter, *see*
    Bo-Kaap
Cape Muslims 25
Cape of Good Hope Nature
    Reserve 19, 91-2, 94
car travel 59
    buying 63
    hazards 64
    rental 62-4
    road rules 64
cash, *see* money
Castle of Good Hope (The
    Castle) 70, 73
Cederberg Range 151
Cederberg Wilderness Area 94,
    151-2
Cemetery Beach 90
Ceres Valley 153
Chapman's Peak 89
Chapman's Peak Drive 88-9
children
    travel with 51
Church Square 71
cinemas, *see* entertainment
Circle of Karamats 25
Citrusdal 152-3
Clanwilliam 153-4
classical music, *see* entertainment
Clifton 87
climate 16-7
Clovelly 90
coast road to Hermanus 145
Company's Gardens (Botanical
    Gardens) 71
consulates, *see* embassies
costs, *see* money
craft shops, *see* shopping

Boxed Text

LONELY PLANET

Phrasebooks

Lonely Planet phrasebooks are packed with essential words and phrases to help travellers communicate with the locals. With colour tabs for quick reference, an extensive vocabulary and use of script, these handy pocket-sized language guides cover day-to-day travel situations.

- handy pocket-sized books
- easy to understand Pronunciation chapter
- clear & comprehensive Grammar chapter
- romanisation alongside script to allow ease of pronunciation
- script throughout so users can point to phrases for every situation
- full of cultural information and tips for the traveller

'... vital for a real DIY spirit and attitude in language learning'
                                                            – *Backpacker*

'the phrasebooks have good cultural backgrounders and offer solid advice for challenging situations in remote locations'
                                                   – *San Francisco Examiner*

Arabic (Egyptian) ● Arabic (Moroccan) ● Australian *(Australian English, Aboriginal and Torres Strait languages)* ● Baltic States *(Estonian, Latvian, Lithuanian)* ● Bengali ● Brazilian ● Burmese ● British *(English, dialects, Scottish Gaelic, Welsh)* ● Cantonese ● Central Asia *(Kazakh, Kyrgyz, Pashto, Tajik, Tashkorghani, Turkmen, Uyghur, Uzbek & others)* ● Central Europe *(Czech, German, Hungarian, Polish, Slovak, Slovene)* ● Costa Rica Spanish ● Eastern Europe *(Albanian, Bulgarian, Croatian, Czech, Hungarian, Macedonian, Polish, Romanian, Serbian, Slovak, Slovene)* ● East Timor *(Tetun, Portuguese)* ● Egyptian Arabic ● Ethiopian (Amharic) ● Europe *(Basque, Catalan, Dutch, French, German, Greek, Irish, Italian, Maltese, Portuguese, Scottish Gaelic, Spanish, Turkish, Welsh)* ● Farsi (Persian*)* ● Fijian ● French ● German ● Greek ● Hebrew ● Hill Tribes *(Lahu, Akha, Lisu, Mong, Mien & others)* ● Hindi/Urdu ● Indonesian ● Italian ● Japanese ● Korean ● Lao ● Latin American Spanish ● Malay ● Mandarin ● Mongolian ● Moroccan Arabic ● Nepali ● Papua New Guinea ● Pidgin ● Pilipino (Tagalog) ● Polish ● Portuguese ● Quechua ● Russian ● Scandinavian *(Danish, Faroese, Finnish, Icelandic, Norwegian, Swedish)* ● South-East Asia *(Burmese, Indonesian, Khmer, Lao, Malay, Tagalog Pilipino, Thai, Vietnamese)* ● South Pacific *(Fijian, Hawaiian, Kanak languages, Maori, Niuean, Rapanui, Rarotongan Maori, Samoan, Tahitian, Tongan & others)* ●   Spanish *(Castilian, also includes Catalan, Galician & Basque)* ● Sri Lanka ● Swahili ● Thai ● Tibetan ● Turkish ● Ukrainian ● USA *(US English, Vernacular, Native American, Hawaiian)* ● Vietnamese

Lonely Planet Journeys

J OURNEYS is a unique collection of travel writing – published by the company that understands travel better than anyone else. It is a series for anyone who has ever experienced – or dreamed of – the magical moment when they encountered a strange culture or saw a place for the first time. They are tales to read while you're planning a trip, while you're on the road or while you're in an armchair in front of a fire.

These outstanding titles explore our planet through the eyes of a diverse group of international writers. JOURNEYS books catch the spirit of a place, illuminate a culture, recount a crazy adventure or introduce a fascinating way of life. They always entertain, and always enrich the experience of travel.

MALI BLUES
Traveling to an African Beat
Lieve Joris (translated by Sam Garrett)
Drought, rebel uprisings, ethnic conflict: these are the predominant images of West Africa. But as Lieve Joris travels in Senegal, Mauritania and Mali, she meets survivors, fascinating individuals charting new ways of living between tradition and modernity. With her remarkable gift for drawing out people's stories, Joris brilliantly captures the rhythms of a world that refuses to give in.

THE GATES OF DAMASCUS
Lieve Joris (translated by Sam Garrett)
This best-selling book is a beautifully drawn portrait of day-to-day life in modern Syria. Through her intimate contact with local people, Lieve Joris draws us into the fascinating world that lies behind the gates of Damascus. Hala's husband is a political prisoner, jailed for his opposition to the Assad regime; through the author's friendship with Hala we see how Syrian politics impacts on the lives of ordinary people.

SONGS TO AN AFRICAN SUNSET
A Zimbabwean Story
Sekai Nzenza-Shand
Songs to an African Sunset braids vividly personal stories into an intimate picture of contemporary Zimbabwe. Returning to her family's village after many years in the west, Sekai Nzenza-Shand discovers a world where ancestor worship, polygamy and witchcraft still govern the rhythms of daily life – and where drought, deforestation and AIDS have wrought devastating changes. With insight and affection, she explores a culture torn between respect for the old ways and the irresistible pull of the new.

THE RAINBIRD
A Central African Journey
Jan Brokken (translated by Sam Garrett)
Following in the footsteps of famous Europeans such as Albert Schweitzer and HM Stanley, Jan Brokken journeyed to Gabon in central Africa. *The Rainbird* brilliantly chronicles the encounter between Africa and Europe as it was acted out on a side-street of history in a kaleidoscope of adventures and anecdotes. A compelling, immensely readable account of the author's own travels in one of the most remote and mysterious regions of Africa.

Lonely Planet Travel Atlases

L onely Planet has long been famous for the number and quality of its guidebook maps. Now we've gone one step further and produced a handy companion series: Lonely Planet travel atlases – maps of a country produced in book form.

Unlike other maps, which look good but lead travellers astray, our travel atlases have been researched on the road by Lonely Planet's experienced team of writers. All details are carefully checked to ensure the atlas corresponds with the equivalent Lonely Planet guidebook.

- full-colour throughout
- maps researched and checked by Lonely Planet authors
- place names correspond with Lonely Planet guidebooks
- no confusing spelling differences
- legend and travelling information in English, French, German, Japanese and Spanish
- size: 230 x 160 mm

Available now: Chile & Easter Island • Egypt • India & Bangladesh • Israel & the Palestinian Territories • Jordan, Syria & Lebanon • Kenya • Laos • Portugal • South Africa, Lesotho & Swaziland • Thailand • Turkey • Vietnam • Zimbabwe, Botswana & Namibia

Lonely Planet TV Series & Videos

L onely Planet travel guides have been brought to life on television screens around the world. Like our guides, the programs are based on the joy of independent travel and look honestly at some of the most exciting, picturesque and frustrating places in the world. Each show is presented by one of three travellers from Australia, England or the USA and combines an innovative mixture of video, Super-8 film, atmospheric soundscapes and original music.

Videos of each episode – containing additional footage not shown on television – are available from good book and video shops, but the availability of individual videos varies with regional screening schedules.

Video destinations include: Alaska • American Rockies • Argentina • Australia – The South-East • Baja California & the Copper Canyon • Brazil • Central Asia • Chile & Easter Island • Corsica, Sicily & Sardinia – The Mediterranean Islands • East Africa (Tanzania & Zanzibar) • Cuba • Ecuador & the Galapagos Islands • Ethiopia • Greenland & Iceland • Hungary & Romania • Indonesia • Israel & the Sinai Desert • Jamaica • Japan • La Ruta Maya • London • The Middle East (Syria, Jordan & Lebanon • Morocco • New York City • Northern Spain • North India • Outback Australia • Pacific Islands (Fiji, Solomon Islands & Vanuatu) • Pakistan • Peru • The Philippines • South Africa & Lesotho • South India • South West China • South West USA • Trekking in Uganda & Congo • Turkey • Vietnam • West Africa • Zimbabwe, Botswana & Namibia

The Lonely Planet TV series is produced by: Pilot Productions
The Old Studio
18 Middle Row
London W10 5AT, UK

FREE Lonely Planet Newsletters

We love hearing from you and think you'd like to hear from us.

Planet Talk

Our FREE quarterly printed newsletter is full of tips from travellers and anecdotes from Lonely Planet guidebook authors. Every issue is packed with up-to-date travel news and advice, and includes:

- a postcard from Lonely Planet co-founder Tony Wheeler
- a swag of mail from travellers
- a look at life on the road through the eyes of a Lonely Planet author
- topical health advice
- prizes for the best travel yarn
- news about forthcoming Lonely Planet events
- a complete list of Lonely Planet books and other titles

To join our mailing list, residents of the UK, Europe and Africa can email us at go@lonelyplanet.co.uk; residents of North and South America can email us at info@lonelyplanet.com; the rest of the world can email us at talk2us@lonelyplanet.com.au, or contact any Lonely Planet office.

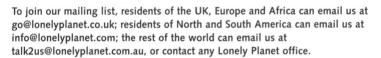

Comet

Our FREE monthly email newsletter brings you all the latest travel news, features, interviews, competitions, destination ideas, travellers' tips & tales, Q&As, raging debates and related links. Find out what's new on the Lonely Planet Web site and which books are about to hit the shelves.

Subscribe from your desktop: www.lonelyplanet.com/comet

LONELY PLANET

Guides by Region

Lonely Planet is known worldwide for publishing practical, reliable and no-nonsense travel information in our guides and on our Web site. The Lonely Planet list covers just about every accessible part of the world. Currently there are sixteen series: Travel guides, Shoestring guides, Condensed guides, Phrasebooks, Read This First, Healthy Travel, Walking guides, Cycling guides, Watching Wildlife guides, Pisces Diving & Snorkelling guides, City Maps, Road Atlases, Out to Eat, World Food, Journeys travel literature, Traveller's Advice titles and Illustrated pictorials.

AFRICA Africa on a shoestring • Cairo • Cairo Map • Cape Town • Cape Town Map • East Africa • Egypt • Egyptian Arabic phrasebook • Ethiopia, Eritrea & Djibouti • Ethiopian (Amharic) phrasebook • The Gambia & Senegal • Healthy Travel Africa • Kenya • Malawi • Morocco • Moroccan Arabic phrasebook • Mozambique • Read This First: Africa • South Africa, Lesotho & Swaziland • Southern Africa • Southern Africa Road Atlas • Swahili phrasebook • Tanzania, Zanzibar & Pemba • Trekking in East Africa • Tunisia • Watching Wildlife East Africa • Watching Wildlife Southern Africa • West Africa • World Food Morocco • Zimbabwe, Botswana & Namibia
Travel Literature: Mali Blues: Traveling to an African Beat • The Rainbird: A Central African Journey • Songs to an African Sunset: A Zimbabwean Story

AUSTRALIA & THE PACIFIC Aboriginal Australia & Torres Strait Islands • Auckland • Australia • Australian phrasebook • Australia Road Atlas • Bushwalking in Australia • Cycling Australia • Cycling New Zealand • Fiji • Fijian phrasebook • Healthy Travel Australia, NZ and the Pacific • Islands of Australia's Great Barrier Reef • Melbourne • Melbourne Map • Micronesia • New Caledonia • New South Wales & the ACT • New Zealand • Northern Territory • Outback Australia • Out to Eat – Melbourne • Out to Eat – Sydney • Papua New Guinea • Papua New Guinea Phrasebook • Pidgin phrasebook • Queensland • Rarotonga & the Cook Islands • Samoa • Solomon Islands • South Australia • South Pacific • South Pacific phrasebook • Sydney • Sydney Map • Sydney Condensed • Tahiti & French Polynesia • Tasmania • Tonga • Tramping in New Zealand • Vanuatu • Victoria • Walking in Australia • Watching Wildlife Australia • Western Australia
Travel Literature: Islands in the Clouds: Travels in the Highlands of New Guinea • Kiwi Tracks: A New Zealand Journey • Sean & David's Long Drive

CENTRAL AMERICA & THE CARIBBEAN Bahamas, Turks & Caicos • Baja California • Bermuda • Central America on a shoestring • Costa Rica • Costa Rica Spanish phrasebook • Cuba • Dominican Republic & Haiti • Eastern Caribbean • Guatemala • Guatemala, Belize & Yucatán: La Ruta Maya • Havana • Healthy Travel Central & South America • San Diego & Tijuana • Jamaica • Mexico • Mexico City • Panama • Puerto Rico • Read This First: Central & South America • World Food Mexico • World Food Caribbean • Yucatán
Travel Literature: Green Dreams: Travels in Central America

EUROPE Amsterdam • Amsterdam Map • Amsterdam Condensed • Andalucía • Austria • Baltic States phrasebook • Barcelona • Barcelona Map • Belgium & Luxembourg • Berlin • Berlin Map • Britain • British phrasebook • Brussels, Bruges & Antwerp • Brussels Map • Budapest • Budapest Map • Canary Islands • Central Europe • Central Europe phrasebook • Copenhagen • Corfu & the Ionians • Corsica • Crete • Crete Condensed • Croatia • Cycling Britain • Cycling France • Cyprus • Czech & Slovak Republics • Denmark • Dublin • Dublin Map • Eastern Europe • Eastern Europe phrasebook • Edinburgh • England • Estonia, Latvia & Lithuania • Europe on a shoestring • Europe Phrasebook • Finland • Florence • France • Frankfurt Condensed • French phrasebook • Georgia, Armenia & Azerbaijan • Germany • German phrasebook • Greece • Greek Islands • Greek phrasebook • Hungary • Iceland, Greenland & the Faroe Islands • Ireland • Istanbul • Italian phrasebook • Italy • Krakow • Lisbon • The Loire • London • London Map • London Condensed • Madrid • Malta • Mediterranean Europe • Milan, Turin & Genoa • Moscow • Mozambique • Munich • The Netherlands • Normandy • Norway • Out to Eat – London • Paris • Paris Map • Paris Condensed • Poland • Polish Phrasebook • Portugal • Portuguese phrasebook • Prague • Prague Map • Provence & the Côte d'Azur • Read This First: Europe • Rhodes & the Dodecanese • Romania & Moldova • Rome • Rome Condensed • Rome Map • Russia, Ukraine & Belarus • Russian phrasebook • Scandinavian & Baltic Europe • Scandinavian phrasebook • Scotland • Sicily • Slovenia • South-West France • Spain • Spanish phrasebook • St Petersburg • St Petersburg Map • Sweden • Switzerland • Trekking in Spain • Tuscany • Ukrainian phrasebook • Venice • Vienna • Walking in Britain • Walking in France • Walking in Ireland • Walking in Italy • Walking in Spain • Walking in Switzerland • Western Europe • World Food France • World Food Ireland • World Food Italy • World Food Spain
Travel Literature: A Small Place in Italy • After Yugoslavia • Love and War in the Apennines • On the Shores of the Mediterranean The Olive Grove: Travels in Greece • Round Ireland in Low Gear

LONELY PLANET

Mail Order

onely Planet products are distributed worldwide. They are also available by mail order from Lonely Planet, so if you have difficulty finding a title please write to us. North and South American residents should write to 150 Linden St, Oakland, CA 94607, USA; European and African residents should write to 10a Spring Place, London NW5 3BH, UK; and residents of other countries to Locked Bag 1, Footscray, Victoria 3011, Australia.

INDIAN SUBCONTINENT Bangladesh • Bengali phrasebook • Bhutan • Delhi • Goa • Healthy Travel Asia & India • Hindi & Urdu phrasebook • India • Indian Himalaya • Karakoram Highway • Kerala • Mumbai (Bombay) • Nepal • Nepali phrasebook • Pakistan • Rajasthan • Read This First: Asia & India • South India • Sri Lanka • Sri Lanka phrasebook • Tibet • Tibetan phrasebook • Trekking in the Indian Himalaya • Trekking in the Karakoram & Hindukush • Trekking in the Nepal Himalaya
Travel Literature: The Age of Kali: Indian Travels and Encounters • Hello Goodnight: A Life of Goa • In Rajasthan • A Season in Heaven: True Tales from the Road to Kathmandu • Shopping for Buddhas • A Short Walk in the Hindu Kush • Slowly Down the Ganges

ISLANDS OF THE INDIAN OCEAN Madagascar & Comoros • Maldives • Mauritius, Réunion & Seychelles
Travel Literature: Maverick in Madagascar

MIDDLE EAST & CENTRAL ASIA Bahrain, Kuwait & Qatar • Central Asia • Central Asia phrasebook • Dubai • Farsi (Persian) phrasebook • Hebrew phrasebook • Iran • Israel & the Palestinian Territories • Istanbul • Istanbul Map • Istanbul to Cairo on a shoestring • Istanbul to Kathmandu • Jerusalem • Jerusalem Map • Jordan • Lebanon • Middle East • Oman & the United Arab Emirates • Syria • Turkey • Turkish phrasebook • World Food Turkey • Yemen
Travel Literature: Black on Black: Iran Revisited • The Gates of Damascus • Kingdom of the Film Stars: Journey into Jordan

NORTH AMERICA Alaska • Boston • Boston Map • Boston Condensed • British Colombia • California & Nevada • California Condensed • Canada • Chicago • Chicago Map • Deep South • Florida • Great Lakes • Hawaii • Hiking in Alaska • Hiking in the USA • Honolulu • Las Vegas • Los Angeles • Los Angeles Map • Louisiana & The Deep South • Miami • Miami Map • Montreal • New England • New Orleans • New York City • New York City Map • New York City Condensed • New York, New Jersey & Pennsylvania • Oahu • Out to Eat – San Francisco • Pacific Northwest • Puerto Rico • Rocky Mountains • San Francisco • San Francisco Map • San Diego & Tijuana • Seattle • Southwest • Texas • Toronto • USA • USA phrasebook • Vancouver • Virginia & the Capital Region • Washington DC • Washington DC Map • World Food Deep South, USA • World Food New Orleans
Travel Literature: Caught Inside: A Surfer's Year on the California Coast • Drive Thru America

NORTH-EAST ASIA Beijing • Beijing Map • Cantonese phrasebook • China • Hiking in Japan • Hong Kong • Hong Kong Map • Hong Kong Condensed • Hong Kong, Macau & Guangzhou • Japan • Japanese phrasebook • Korea • Korean phrasebook • Kyoto • Mandarin phrasebook • Mongolia • Mongolian phrasebook • Seoul • Shanghai • South-West China • Taiwan • Tokyo • World Food – Hong Kong
Travel Literature: In Xanadu: A Quest • Lost Japan

SOUTH AMERICA Argentina, Uruguay & Paraguay • Bolivia • Brazil • Brazilian phrasebook • Buenos Aires • Chile & Easter Island • Colombia • Ecuador & the Galapagos Islands • Healthy Travel Central & South America • Latin American Spanish phrasebook • Peru • Quechua phrasebook • Read This First: Central & South America • Rio de Janeiro • Rio de Janeiro Map • Santiago • South America on a shoestring • Santiago • Trekking in the Patagonian Andes • Venezuela
Travel Literature: Full Circle: A South American Journey

SOUTH-EAST ASIA Bali & Lombok • Bangkok • Bangkok Map • Burmese phrasebook • Cambodia • East Timor Phrasebook • Hanoi • Healthy Travel Asia & India • Hill Tribes phrasebook • Ho Chi Minh City • Indonesia • Indonesian phrasebook • Indonesia's Eastern Islands • Jakarta • Java • Lao phrasebook • Laos • Malay phrasebook • Malaysia, Singapore & Brunei • Myanmar (Burma) • Philippines • Pilipino (Tagalog) phrasebook • Read This First: Asia & India • Singapore • Singapore Map • South-East Asia on a shoestring • South-East Asia phrasebook • Thailand • Thailand's Islands & Beaches • Thailand, Vietnam, Laos & Cambodia Road Atlas • Thai phrasebook • Vietnam • Vietnamese phrasebook • World Food Thailand • World Food Vietnam

ALSO AVAILABLE: Antarctica • The Arctic • The Blue Man: Tales of Travel, Love and Coffee • Brief Encounters: Stories of Love, Sex & Travel • Chasing Rickshaws • The Last Grain Race • Lonely Planet Unpacked • Not the Only Planet: Science Fiction Travel Stories • Lonely Planet On the Edge • Sacred India • Travel with Children • Travel Photography: A Guide to Taking Better Pictures

The Lonely Planet Story

onely Planet published its first book in 1973 in response to the numerous 'How did you do it?' questions Maureen and Tony Wheeler were asked after driving, bussing, hitching, sailing and railing their way from England to Australia.

Written at a kitchen table and hand collated, trimmed and stapled, *Across Asia on the Cheap* became an instant local bestseller, inspiring thoughts of another book.

Eighteen months in South-East Asia resulted in their second guide, *South-East Asia on a shoestring*, which they put together in a backstreet Chinese hotel in Singapore in 1975. The 'yellow bible', as it quickly became known to backpackers around the world, soon became *the* guide to the region. It has sold well over half a million copies and is now in its 9th edition, still retaining its familiar yellow cover.

Today there are over 350 titles, including travel guides, walking guides, language kits & phrasebooks, travel atlases, diving guides and travel literature. The company is the largest independent travel publisher in the world. Although Lonely Planet initially specialised in guides to Asia, today there are few corners of the globe that have not been covered.

The emphasis continues to be on travel for independent travellers. Tony and Maureen still travel for several months of each year and play an active part in the writing, updating and quality control of Lonely Planet's guides.

They have been joined by over 120 authors and 280 staff at our offices in Melbourne (Australia), Oakland (USA), London (UK) and Paris (France). Travellers themselves also make a valuable contribution to the guides through the feedback we receive in thousands of letters each year and on our web site.

The people at Lonely Planet strongly believe that travellers can make a positive contribution to the countries they visit, both through their appreciation of the countries' culture, wildlife and natural features, and through the money they spend. In addition, the company makes a direct contribution to the countries and regions it covers. Since 1986 a percentage of the income from each book has been donated to ventures such as famine relief in Africa; aid projects in India; agricultural projects in Central America; Greenpeace's efforts to halt French nuclear testing in the Pacific; and Amnesty International.

LONELY PLANET OFFICES

Australia
Locked Bag 1, Footscray, Victoria 3011
☎ 03 8379 8000 fax 03 8379 8111
email: talk2us@lonelyplanet.com.au

UK
10a Spring Place, London NW5 3BH
☎ 020 7428 4800 fax 020 7428 4828
email: go@lonelyplanet.co.uk

USA
150 Linden St, Oakland, CA 94607
☎ 510 893 8555 TOLL FREE: 800 275 8555
fax 510 893 8572
email: info@lonelyplanet.com

France
1 rue du Dahomey, 75011 Paris
☎ 01 55 25 33 00 fax 01 55 25 33 01
email: bip@lonelyplanet.fr
www.lonelyplanet.fr

World Wide Web: www.lonelyplanet.com *or* AOL keyword: lp
Lonely Planet Images: lpi@lonelyplanet.com.au

GERHARD DREYER

Top: Cape Town by night: beyond the city centre and the docks lies the stark contrast of exclusive suburbs and bleak townships.
Bottom: If you just need to stop and smell the fynbos, visit the gorgeous Kirstenbosch Botanic Gardens.

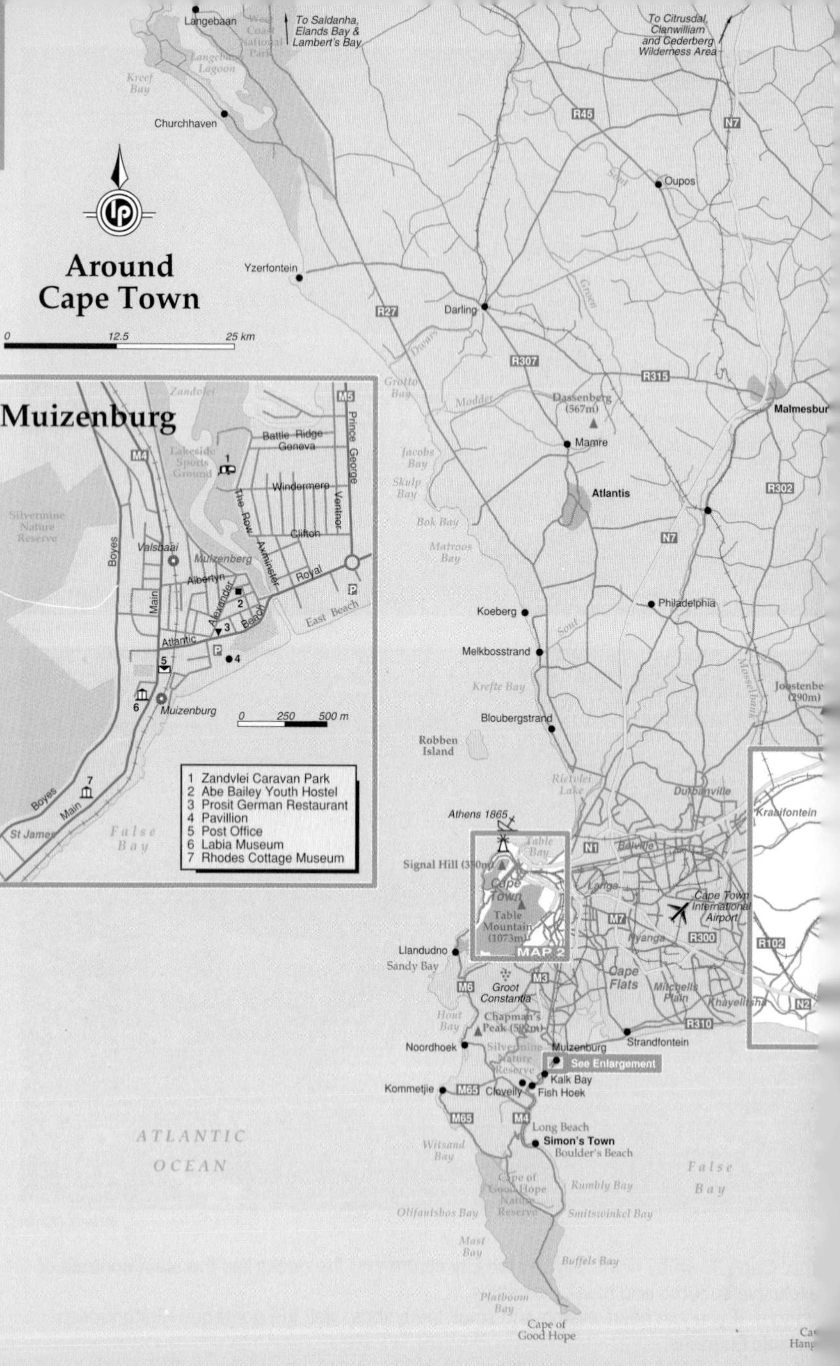

MAP 1

Around Cape Town

0   12.5   25 km

Muizenburg

0   250   500 m

1 Zandvlei Caravan Park
2 Abe Bailey Youth Hostel
3 Prosit German Restaurant
4 Pavillion
5 Post Office
6 Labia Museum
7 Rhodes Cottage Museum

Langebaan

To Saldanha,
Elands Bay &
Lambert's Bay

To Citrusdal,
Clanwilliam
and Cederberg
Wilderness Area

Kreef
Bay

Langebaan
Lagoon

West
Coast
National
Park

Churchhaven

Zandvlei

Lakeside
Sports
Ground

Silvermine
Nature
Reserve

Battle Ridge
Geneva

Windermere

Clifton

Valsbaai

Muizenberg

Albertyn

Atlantic

Muizenberg

St James

False
Bay

Boyes

Boyes

Main

Main

The Row

Atlantic

Prince George

Ventnor

Royal

East Beach

M4

M5

P

P

Yzerfontein

Darling

R27

R307

R45

R315

R302

N7

Oupos

Malmesbur

Dassenberg
(567m)

Mamre

Atlantis

Philadelphia

Joostenbe
(290m)

Koeberg

Melkbosstrand

Bloubergstrand

Robben
Island

Durbanville

Kraaifontein

R102

N1

R300

R310

N2

Grotto
Bay

Modder

Jacobs
Bay

Skulp
Bay

Bok Bay

Matroos
Bay

Krefte Bay

Rietvlei
Lake

Groen

Diep

Sout

Sout

Mosselbaai

Athens 1865

Signal Hill (350m)

Cape
Town

Table
Mountain
(1073m)

Llandudno

Sandy Bay

Groot
Constantia

Chapman's
Peak (592m)

Hout
Bay

Silvermine
Nature
Reserve

Noordhoek

Kommetjie

Clovelly

Muizenberg

See Enlargement

Kalk Bay

Fish Hoek

Strandfontein

Long Beach

Simon's Town

Boulder's Beach

ATLANTIC

OCEAN

Witsand
Bay

Cape of
Good Hope
Nature
Reserve

Olifantsbos Bay

Mast
Bay

Platboom
Bay

Cape of
Good Hope

Rumbly Bay

Smitswinkel Bay

Buffels Bay

False
Bay

Cape
Hang

Table
Bay

Table

Cape Town
International
Airport

Cape
Flats

Mitchells
Plain

Nyanga

Khayelitsa

MAP 2

M6

M3

M7

R300

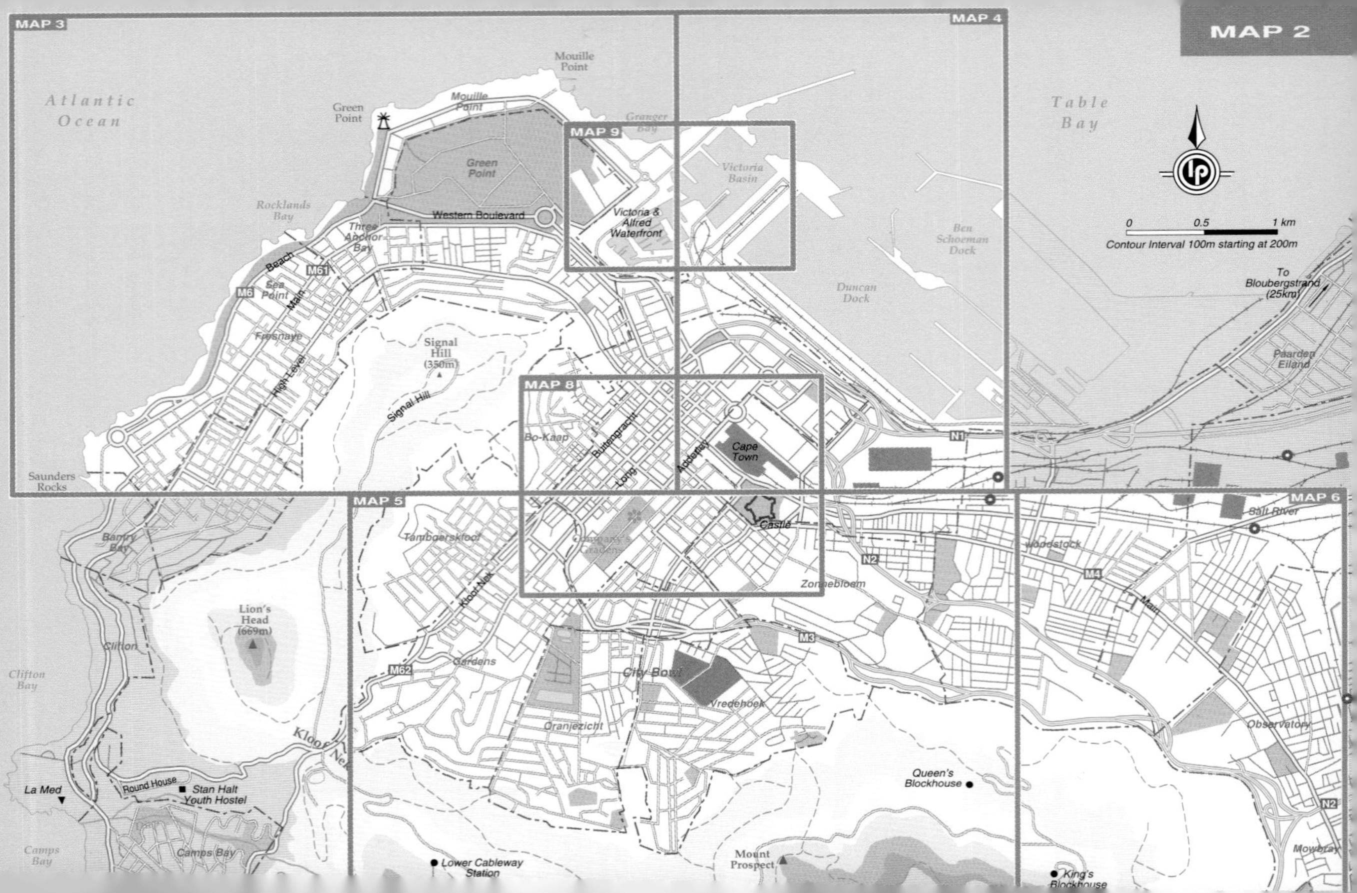

MAP 2

MAP 4

MAP 6

MAP 3

MAP 5

MAP 8

MAP 9

Atlantic
Ocean

Table
Bay

To
Bloubergstrand (25km)

Paarden
Eiland

0   0.5   1 km

Contour interval 100m starting at 200m

Saunders
Rocks

Mouille
Point

Green
Point

Rocklands
Bay

Three
Anchor
Bay

Signal
Hill
(350m)

Ben
Schoeman
Dock

Duncan
Dock

Victoria
Basin

Granger
Bay

Victoria &
Alfred
Waterfront

Green Point

Western Boulevard

Sea Point

Bantry
Bay

Clifton
Bay

Camps Bay

Lion's
Head
(669m)

La Med

Round House

Stan Hall
Youth Hostel

Kloof Nek

Cape Town

Foreshore

Castle

Bo-Kaap

Gardens

Tamboerskloof

Oranjezicht

Vredehoek

City Bowl

Zonnebloem

Woodstock

Salt River

Observatory

Maitland

Mowbray

King's
Blockhouse

Queen's
Blockhouse

Mostert Prospect

Lower Cableway
Station

N1

N2

M3

M62

M63

MAP 7

Rosebank

Rondebosch

Kenilworth

Southern Suburbs

Newlands

Claremont

Devil's Peak (1000m) ▲

Bishopscourt

Kirstenbosch National Botanical Garden

Van Riebeeck Hedge ●

M3

To Muizenberg

Klassenbosch

Hohenort

Constantia Heights

Bel Ombre

Aliphen

To Groot Constantia

Witteboomen

Maclear's Beacon (1086m) ▲

(1045m) ▲

Oranjekloof

(1077m) ▲

Waaikoppie (932m) ▲

Junction Peak (921m) ▲

Orion's Cave

Hely-Hutchinson Reservoir

Reserve Peak (847m) ▲

De Villiers Reservoir

Disa

Nursery Reservoir

Dommisse Hut ●

Victoria Reservoir

Klaasenskop (746m) ▲

Original

Upper Cableway Station ●

Table Mountain Café ▼

Table Mountain (1073m) ▲

Woodhead Reservoir

Scout M C Hut ●

C F M C Hut ●

Disa

Twelve Apostles

Kasteelspoort

Rontree

Bakoven

Locks

Bakoven Bay

The Bay Hotel ■
Dizzy Jazz ■
Blues ■

M6

To Llandudno & Hout Bay

Oudekraal

Groothop (652m) ▲

Hout Bay

MAP 3

PLACES TO STAY
1 The President
2 New Regency Hotel
3 Transatlantic Hostel
5 The Globe Trotter
8 St John's Lodge;
 The Wooden Shoe
9 Villa Rosa
10 Ashby Manor Guesthouse
19 Lion's Head Lodge
21 Olaf's Guest House
37 The Bunkhouse
38 Hip Hop Travellers Stop
39 One on Main
40 Victoria Junction Hotel
45 The Lodge

PLACES TO EAT
6 Joubert & Monti's Meat
 Boutique; New
 York Deli
11 Reise's Deli
13 Mr Chan's
17 Ari's Souvlaki
18 Steers; Ardi's and
 Other Eateries
22 Peasants
23 Dominos Bistro
28 San Marco
30 Nature's Best Health
 Food Store
31 Café Erté
33 L'Orient
34 Little Bombay
42 Noon Gun Café

OTHER
4 Spar Supermarket
7 Sea Point Pavilion Pool
12 Rennie's Travel
14 Saul's Saloon
15 Milton's Pool
16 Graaff's Pool
20 Laundromat
24 Post Office;
 Public Phones
25 Adelphi Centre
26 Rennies Travel
27 7-11
29 Elvis Snack & Dance
32 Ocean Divers International
35 Glengariff Pharmacy
36 Lighthouse; Museum
41 Noon Gun
43 Viewpoint
44 Café Manhattan
46 The Bronx
47 Angels
48 The Fireman's Arms

Atlantic
Ocean

Three Anchor
Bay

Rocklands
Bay

Saunders
Rocks

Bantry
Bay

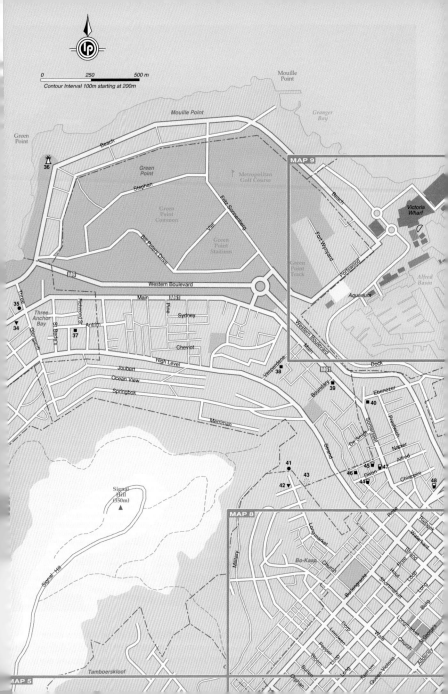

MAP 9

Victoria Wharf

Alfred Basin

Beach

Fort Wynyard

Portswood

Green Point Track

Aquarium

Western Boulevard

Main

Dock

MAP 8

Bo-Kaap

Church

Longmarket

Military

Boulengracht

Leeuwen

Dorp

Pepper

Bloem

Loop

Bree

Buitengracht

Shortmarket

Wale

Church

Longmarket

Loop

Long

Burg

Strand

Buitengracht

Plein

Keerom

Queen Victoria

St Georges

Adderley

Butler

Clifton

Military

Dixon

Waterkant

Napier

Prestwich

Mouille Point

Granger Bay

Green Point

Beach

Mouille Point

Green Point

Stephan

Metropolitan Golf Course

Green Point Common

Vrij

Fritz Sonnenberg

Green Point Stadium

36

Bill Peters Drive

M6

Western Boulevard

Main

M61

Three

Ocean View

35

34

Three Anchor Bay

Antrim

Richmond

Sydney

37

Cheviot

High Level

Joubert

Ocean View

Springbok

Merriman

Signal Hill (350m)

Signal Hill

Tamboerskloof

MAP 5

Vesperdene

38

Boundary

39

M61

Ebenezer

40

Somerset

De Smit

Prestwich

Napier

Alfred

Chiappini

41

43

42

46

45

44

Dixon

47

48

Strand

Rose

Longmarket

0   250   500 m

Contour Interval 100m starting at 200m

GERHARD DREYER

SUSAN STORM

Top: Table Mountain looms over the Victoria & Alfred Waterfront in the African dusk. Bottom: The Waterfront's reclaimed area is a gentrified melange of historic buildings, sailboats and trawlers, upmarket craft shops and fashionable cafés; it never closes early.

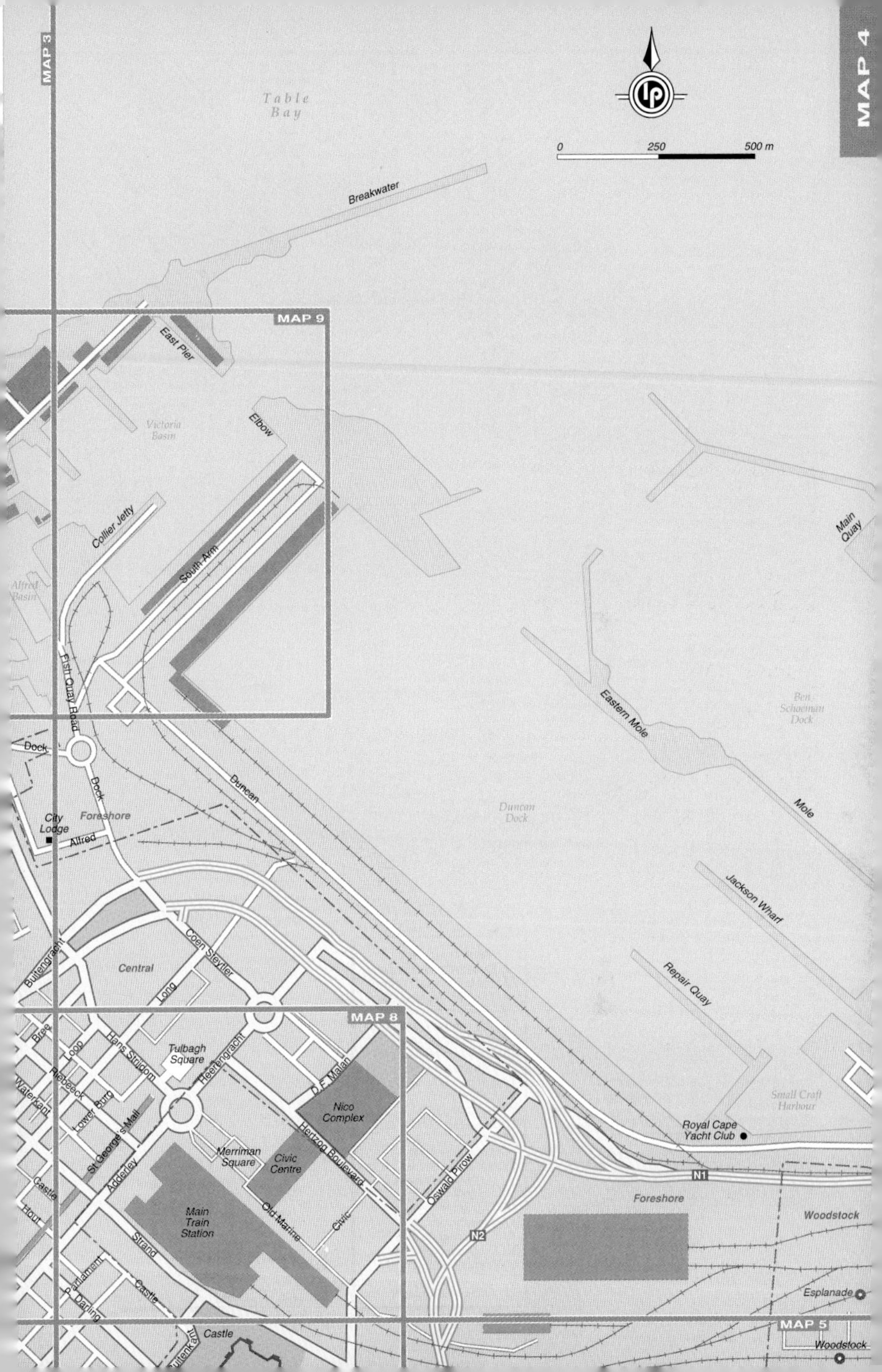

MAP 3
MAP 4

Table Bay

Breakwater

MAP 9

0   250   500 m

East Pier

Elbow

Victoria Basin

Collier Jetty

South Arm

Alfred Basin

Port Quay Road

Main Quay

Eastern Mole

Ben Schoeman Dock

Mole

Dock

Duncan

Duncan Dock

Jackson Wharf

City Lodge

Foreshore

Alfred

Central

Coen Steytler

Buitengracht

Long

Repair Quay

MAP 8

Tulbagh Square

Waterkant

Bree

Loop

Hans Strijdom

Heerengracht

D.F. Malan

Nico Complex

Long

Hout

Riebeek

Shortmarket

St George's Mall

Mostert

Burg

Adderley

Heerengracht

Civic

Merriman Square

Civic Centre

Old Marine

Oswald Pirow

Small Craft Harbour

Royal Cape Yacht Club ●

Castle

Hout

Strand

Main Train Station

Strand

Castle

Buitenkant

N1

N2

Foreshore

Woodstock

Plein

Darling

Castle

Buitenkant

Esplanade ○

Castle

MAP 5

Woodstock

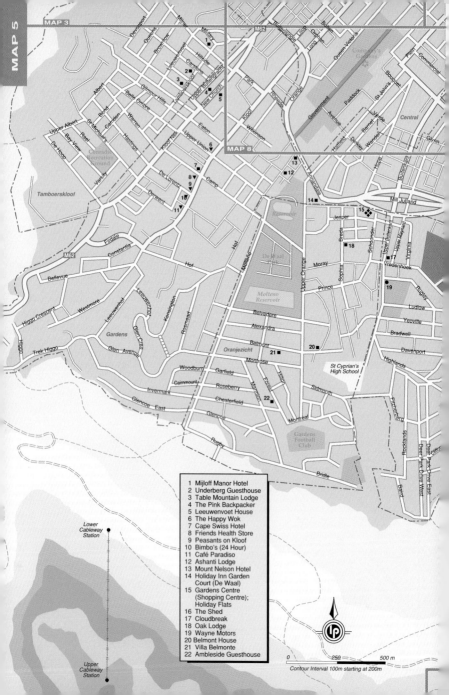

MAP 5

MAP 3

MAP 8

1 Mijloff Manor Hotel
2 Underberg Guesthouse
3 Table Mountain Lodge
4 The Pink Backpacker
5 Leeuwenvoet House
6 The Happy Wok
7 Cape Swiss Hotel
8 Friends Health Store
9 Peasants on Kloof
10 Bimbo's (24 Hour)
11 Café Paradiso
12 Ashanti Lodge
13 Mount Nelson Hotel
14 Holiday Inn Garden
   Court (De Waal)
15 Gardens Centre
   (Shopping Centre);
   Holiday Flats
16 The Shed
17 Cloudbreak
18 Oak Lodge
19 Wayne Motors
20 Belmont House
21 Villa Belmonte
22 Ambleside Guesthouse

Lower
Cableway
Station

Upper
Cableway
Station

0   250   500 m

Contour Interval 100m starting at 200m

SUSAN STORM

SUSAN STORM

SUSAN STORM

Top Left: A symbol of Cape Town: native and exotic flowers for sale on city streets.
Top Right: A young 'bottletop' dancer demonstrates the art of cultural resilience.
Bottom: The high-rise suburb of Sea Point is a hive of restaurants, nightspots and time-share apartments.

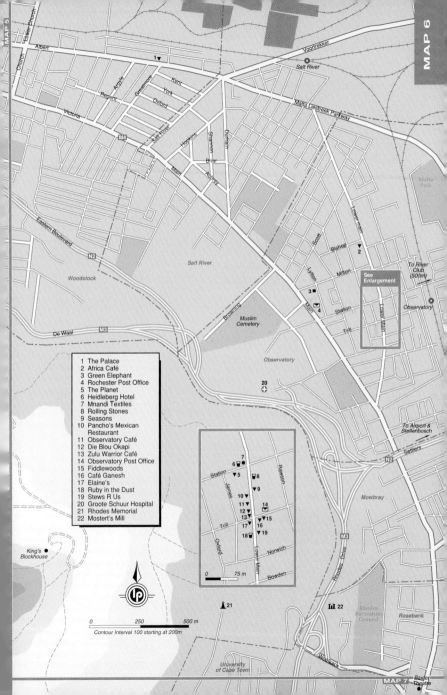

MAP 5

MAP 6

MAP 7

Voortrekker

Salt River

Albert

Church

Lower Church

Argyle

Regent

Greatmore

Kent

York

Oxford

Victoria

M4

Salt River

Hopkins

Shannon

Durham

Briar

Aldport

Main

Malta Liesbeek Parkway

Malta Park

Eastern Boulevard

N2

Woodstock

Salt River

Browning

Scott

Bishop

Lytton

Milton

See Enlargement

To River Club (500m)

3 ■

4

Station

Trill

Observatory

De Waal

M3

Muslim Cemetery

Observatory

20 ✛

To Airport & Stellenbosch

Settlers

N2

Mowbray

1 The Palace
2 Africa Café
3 Green Elephant
4 Rochester Post Office
5 The Planet
6 Heidleberg Hotel
7 Mnandi Textiles
8 Rolling Stones
9 Seasons
10 Pancho's Mexican
   Restaurant
11 Observatory Café
12 Die Blou Okapi
13 Zulu Warrior Café
14 Observatory Post Office
15 Fiddlewoods
16 Café Ganesh
17 Elaine's
18 Ruby in the Dust
19 Stews R Us
20 Groote Schuur Hospital
21 Rhodes Memorial
22 Mostert's Mill

Station

7
6 ●
▼ 5

James

8

Rawson

10 ▼
11 ▼

9

Trill

12 ▼
13 ▼
17 ▼

14
16
▼ 15

18 ▼

19

Oxford

Lower Main

Norwich

Bowden

0   75 m

M3

Rhodes Drive

Rosebank

King's Blockhouse

Rhodes Recreation Ground

🏕 21

♿ 22

0   250   500 m

Contour Interval 100 starting at 200m

University of Cape Town

Woolsack

MAP 7

Baxter Theatre

MAP 5

MAP 7

▲ (1045m)

Eastern
Table

Newlands
State
Forest

Maclear's
Beacon
(1086m)
▲

Cecilia
Plantation

Orchard Heights

Wilton

Ash

Poplar

M63

Newlands

Cherril Close

Rhodes Avenue

Fernwood
Parliamentary
Club

Cheryl

Bisset

Thistle

Boscari

Heath

Conifer

Moss

Aster

Holly

Church

Rose

Kirstenbosch
National
Botanical
Gardens

Aplian

St Athans

Salisbury

Kirstenbosch

Bishopscourt

Bishopscourt

0   250   500 m

Contour Interval 100m starting at 200m

To Van Riebeeck
Hedge (200m) &
Groot Constantia

MAP 6

Baxter
Theatre
Burg
University of
Cape Town
Upper Campus
Grotto
Lovers
Main
Beattie
Theatre
University of
Cape Town
WP Lawn
Tennis
Belmont Park
Church
Rondebosch
Rhodes Drive
Groote Schuur
Hare Krisna
Centre
Wilhelmina
Epworth
St Andrew's Road
The Grange
Princess Anne
Interchange
Princus Road
Rondebosch
Main
Rouwkoop
M4
Newlands
Reservoir
Union
Princess Anne
Mount Pleasant
Klipper
Albion
Mount
Dulwich
Ephram
Harrow
Westerford
Sports Field
M3
Rose
Alfred
Avenue
Dean
West
Besterbrau
Protea
Boundary
Sport
Newlands
Cricket
Rugby
Grounds
Forries
Pub
Cedar
Manson
Newlands
Anneberg
Montrose
Boundary
Letterstedt
Newlands
Camp Ground
Pinewood
Firdale
Maitland
Newlands
Hilton
Kildare
Cluny
Palmboom
Saint South
Cannon
Governor's
Van Reenen
Norfolk
Amherst
Broadway
Finsbury
Kildare
Bamsters
Pub
Main
Liesbeck
Kirkway
Midway
Heatherton
Lady Anne
Paterson
La Casa
Grande
Draper
Bernheck
Through
Orange
Ravensburg
Evangean
Paradise
Vineyard
Hotel
Vineyard
St Leger
Queen Victoria
Arum
Orchard
Daisy
Buckrorn
Colinton
Cavendish
Square
M4
Harman
Almond
Fernwood
Ripley
Protea
Main
Claremont
Brookside
Sports
Ground
Bishopscourt
Newlands
Ethel
Doris
Feldhousen
Hope
Upper Gorve
Claremont
Pearce
Spencer
Stanhope
First
Princess
Berta
Mountain
Carbrook
Brook
Ross Vale
Colenso
Robinson
Alma
Bowwood
Surrey
Maclear
Sylvia
Ethel
Claremont
Tennis
Bishopscourt
Itex
Shirley
Riviera
Letita
Herschel
Theatre
Arderne
Public
Gardens
Harfield
Dorham
Upper Sidmouth
To Muizenberg
via freeway
Edinburgh
M3
Josephine
Irene
Eyton
Linda
Harfield
Road

MAP 8

Schotsche
Kloof

501

Bo-Kaap

Riebeeck
Square

Greenmarket
Square

Company's
Gardens

See Enlargement

Tamboerskloof

Enlargement:
0   75 m

115
113
118   114
116
117
119
122   120
123   121
124

PLACES TO STAY
18 Tulbagh Protea Hotel
19 Diplomat Holiday Flats
20 Capetonian Protea
24 Formule 1 Hotel
33 Holiday Inn Garden Court (St George's Mall)
35 Cape Sun Hotel
38 Cape Town Inn
42 Metropole Hotel; Commonwealth Restaurant
65 Holiday Inn Garden Court (Greenmarket Square); Cycles
71 Tudor Hotel
87 Townhouse Hotel
91 Pleinpark Travel Lodge
108 Long St Backpackers
112 Travellers Inn
113 Hunter's Lodge
114 Lion's Den
118 Overseas Visitors' Club
124 Cat & Moose
127 Cape Gardens Lodge
135 Dunkley Inn
139 Mount Nelson Hotel
145 Albergo Backpackers
155 Zebra Crossing
156 The Backpack; Africa Travel Centre

PLACES TO EAT
3 Karima's Café
14 Spur Steakhouse
55 Wellington Dried Fruit
58 World of Coffee
61 Nino's
62 Cadiz Nosh Bar
63 Café Blue Moon
67 Off Moroko Café Africaine
77 Yellow Pepper
81 Mark's Coffee Shop
95 Gardens Restaurant
97 Jedz Pasta
98 Sooz Baguette Bar
99 Mr Pickwicks Deli
100 Backpacker Bob's
106 Mama Africa
115 Lola Café
116 Toledo's Tapas Bar
117 Cranford's Restaurant & Bar
119 Pasta Regalo
123 Serendipity
126 Kaapse Tafel Restaurant
134 Roxy's Coffee Bar
136 Maria's Greek Restaurant
137 Bistrot la Boheme
144 Sukothai
146 Mario's Coffee Shop
147 Café Bar Deli

148 Take Four Bistro
149 KD's Bar & Bistro
151 Rozenhof
152 The Blue Plate
157 Rustica

MUSEUMS
1 Bo-Kaap Museum
36 Koopmans de Wet House
41 Sendinnestig Museum
68 Townhouse Museum
84 Cultural History Museum
88 District Six Museum
128 South African Museum
129 National Gallery
130 Rust-en-Vreugd
138 Jewish Museum
140 Bertram House

ENTERTAINMENT
5 Shebeen on Bree
7 Hemingways; Martin Melck House
8 Crew Bar
9 Brunswick Hotel
10 Browne's Café du Vin
11 Café Comic Strip
12 The Rockin' Shamrock
15 Long Street Theatre
23 Nico Complex
53 District Six Café
64 The Purple Turtle
82 Manenberg's Jazz Cafe
85 Ploughman's Pub
89 The Fringe
101 Club Tropicana
105 Ricks
110 The Lounge
131 Kimberly Hotel
132 Perseverance Tavern
133 Stag's Head Hotel
141 Labia Cinema
143 Little Theatre
150 Firkin Brew Pub Company
153 The Whistle Stop

OTHER
2 Atlas Trading Company
4 Avis Car Rental
6 Lutheran Church
13 Imperial Car Rental
16 Southern Life Centre
17 BP Centre
21 Connection Internet C@fé
22 Broadway Centre
25 Civic Centre
26 Tourist Rendezvous
27 Jan & Maria van Riebeeck Statues

28 British Airways Travel Clinic
29 American Express
30 Thibault Square
31 Police Booth
32 Trustbank Centre; Air India
34 Namibia Trade & Tourism
37 Budget Car Rental
39 Surf Centre
40 National Parks Board Office
43 Ulrich Naumann's
44 Camera Care
45 Rennies Travel
46 Postnet
47 Gay es Cape
48 Woolworths
49 Golden Acre Centre; Air France
50 OK Bazaars
51 City Bus Terminal
52 Bus Information Kiosk
54 Town Hall
56 Pharmacy
57 Main Post Office
59 Stuttaford's Town Square
60 Pezulu
66 First National Bank (BOB)
69 African Image
70 Out of Africa
72 Namaqua House; Le Petit Paris
73 Audio Sound
74 Mike Hopkins Cycles
75 Tempest Car Rental
76 Cape Wine Cellar
78 Noor el Hamedia Mosque
79 South African Library
80 St George's Cathedral
83 Groote Kerk
86 Cape Union Mart
90 Department of Home Affairs
92 Government Printers
93 Houses of Parliament
94 De Tuynhuys
96 Cape Nature Conservation
102 Camp & Climb
103 Prolab
104 Alisa Car Rental
107 Select Books
109 The Bead Shop
111 The Junk Shop
120 Morris's Boerewors
121 ICafé
122 Peter the Haircutter
125 Long St Baths
142 Spar Supermarket
154 Le Cap Motorcycle Hire
158 Afrogem